GIFTS IN OPEN HANDS

Gifts in Open Hands

MORE RESOURCES FOR THE GLOBAL COMMUNITY

Maren C. Tirabassi
and
Kathy Wonson Eddy

THE PILGRIM PRESS
CLEVELAND

The Pilgrim Press, 700 Prospect Avenue, Cleveland, Ohio 44115-1100
thepilgrimpress.com
© 2011 by Maren C. Tirabassi and Kathy Wonson Eddy

Scripture quotations, unless otherwise noted, are from the New Revised Standard Version of the Bible, © 1989 by the Division of Christian Education of the National Council of Churches of Christ in the United States of America, and are used by permission. Changes have been made for inclusivity.

Printed in the United States of America on acid-free paper

15   14   13   12   11   5   4   3   2   1

Library of Congress Cataloging-in-Publication Data

Tirabassi, Maren C.
     Gifts in open hands : more resources for the global community / Maren C. Tirabassi and Kathy Wonson Eddy.
         p. cm.
     Includes bibliographical references and indexes.
     ISBN 978-0-8298-1839-0 (alk. paper)
   1. Liturgical adaptation.   2. Worship programs.   3. Church year. I. Eddy, Kathy Wonson, 1951–   II. Title.   III. Title: More resources for the global community.
BV178.T569 2011
264.0089—dc22   2011003130

Contents

PART FOUR

Our Hands Joined around the World: Resources for Justice and Peace

PART FIVE

Our Hands Offer: New and Old Treasures for the Householder of God

List of Illustrations

Preface

I heard a story about fifteen years ago about a Quaker nurse who went to work in a small town in Eastern Europe in the early 1920s. Her acts of kindness and service deeply touched a people recovering from the ravages of war and poverty. When she died, the peasants of the village asked that she be buried in the church cemetery, a request that was denied by officials because she was not of that faith. She was buried outside the cemetery fence. In grief and in fury that their beloved nurse was not allowed inside the cemetery, the peasants decided to take matters into their own hands. That night, with shovels and picks, they went back to the cemetery and moved the fence to include her!

We are all called to move the fences that separate people, to find creative ways to break down walls and barriers that isolate and divide. Maren and I believe that the luminous liturgical resources from all over the world gathered here in this book can continue the work of moving fences and uniting people. May you open your hands to receive these treasures. May we all discover, as we use these "gifts in open hands," God's very embrace encircling the whole earth and all its people.

—Kathy Wonson Eddy

It wasn't *easy!*

Kathy and I were surprised that technology made the gathering of worship resources not simpler but more complex than our experience almost eighteen years ago when we began working on *Gifts of Many Cultures: Worship Resources for the Global Community* and sent stamped letters to many correspondents around the world. Our strategy for this book was to e-mail the mission personnel of a number of denominations, but we discovered that people are likely to delete mail from unknown addresses. Even when they opened our e-mail they often forgot their intention to send in a contribution once our request slid down the inbox. We contacted denominational headquarters, seminaries, churches and conferences with international partners, and global interfaith and ecumenical organizations. These organizational modes of solicitation were unsuccessful. Nine months into the gathering process we were afraid that we would have to give up.

We prayed a lot.

And things changed. People found us. The first ones came from Aotearoa/New Zealand, Argentina, Canada, China, and a global Baptist peace conference. We began to make friends around the world. Those initial friends made others through personal conversations and contacts. We found new friends in Africa, then in Europe. Prayers started coming from fourth- and fifth-level contacts. We extended deadlines because many people don't work on a "deadline" model. The liturgies we waited for were beautiful, grace-filled, and varied. We celebrate the communities of faith from which they emerge and have learned many things about them.

We heard words of justice.

There are some unique aspects to *Gifts in Open Hands*. Many of these prayers focus on global justice and peace issues—such as concerns about refugees, the worldwide crisis about water, conflicts within and between nations. More material came to us in languages other than English. We offer translations but also invite people to read and pray the original words whether they "directly" understand them or must trust them to be Spirit-filled prayer. Finally, there is a wide age span in those who have shared prayers. Children and youth are well represented in their chapter and throughout other particular sections. Among the "adults" who have contributed include many who are twenty to twenty-five years of age and many who are older than seventy—some of whom have never before written out their prayers.

We were changed.

We were touched by the depth of thought, inspired by the beauty of poetry, taught about new landscapes, moved by stories of courage, and humbled by the generosity of these gifts. We try to keep our hands open. It isn't always *easy*. We invite you to open your hands.

—Maren C. Tirabassi

WORDS OF GRATITUDE

At the risk of sounding like an Academy Award recipient offering a laundry list of "thank you's," . . . thank you, thank you, thank you. *Gifts in Open Hands* is the collaboration of so many. One hundred and fifty-two writers, composers, and illustrators have contributed to this book. They have offered gifts of incredible insight that share God's grace with all of us. They "are" this book. We would not have found them without many facilitators—denominational executives, individual missionaries, faculty at seminaries, several simple travelers, a participant in a global Baptist peace event, leaders of mission trips, and even an editor from another publishing house who received my query for reprint rights for a single prayer and responded, "I know some wonderful writers across Canada; let me be in touch with them." These facilitators encouraged others to submit their work or literally gathered up writings and sent them in. We extend special thanks to Janice Arie, Frances A. Bogle, Eliki Bononga, David Bush, Christina Del Piero, Julie Graham, Florian Herrmann, Hanna Kristensen, Elizabeth Martinez, Kimberly McKerley, Debra Pallatto-Fontaine, Kenneth L. Sehested, Susan M. Valiquette, and Munib A. Younan. Then there were the translators. Google Translate is a tool; human translators are artists themselves. The wonderful people who translated for us are Molly Phinney Baskette, Katherine Chase, Sarah Fineberg-Lombardi, Katie Fiegenbaum, Ellen Fries, Fleur Houston, and Sr. Bernadette Ward, FMM.

Equally a part of this book are our congregations: Bethany United Church of Christ in Randolph, Vermont, and Union Congregational United Church of Christ in Madbury, New Hampshire. They gave us the time to work on this project and they heard many prayers, litanies, hymns, and parts of services in their Sunday worship. Bethany's administrator Phyllis Roberts provided invaluable computer assistance.

Halfway between Braintree, Vermont, where Kathy lives, and Portsmouth, New Hampshire, where Maren lives, is Hopkinton, New Hampshire. For the last year and a half First Congregational Church UCC of Hopkinton has offered us work space, coffee, and friendship, thanks to the hospitality of pastor Gordon Crouch and administrator Margaret Serzans.

Bob Eddy and Don Tirabassi have been patient and helpful—they have read and listened, laughed and wept over these wonderful prayers. We have had the joy to work again with Kim Martin Sadler, an editor who has inspired us in the moments when this process seemed long and difficult, assisted us with all the details, and shared her vision of faith resources for the church. Kristin Firth had an amazing grasp of details in working with these many distinctive writing styles, and Rick Porter has made a tapestry of design from an incredibly diverse collection of texts and illustrations. Scott Ressman's musical settings were the invaluable final piece of the puzzle.

There are many styles of worship for the contemporary church, and much that happens is never written down. It is of the moment and of the heart. We are so grateful for these more concrete prayers, descriptions, art, music, and poetry of young and old and for our ability to share them, believing that they literally unfence continents and communities of faith. We are most grateful that it is the Holy Spirit who prays within and through the body of Christ in all ways, times, and places.

USING THESE RESOURCES

Permission to copy these worship resources is freely given for church bulletins, newsletters, congregational and educational use, and even personal blogs, as long as there is appropriate acknowledgement. There is no need to contact copyright holders, either The Pilgrim Press or those listed in the source notes who have retained their rights.

We have tried to include full services whenever possible to share their beauty and eloquence. Occasional adaptations with integrity by abridging, altering to express or include a local community concern, or gently rewriting to change the season of the year or include a particular local concern honor the original intention of these authors, so that their work may continue to live and breathe. For example, Richard Bott from British Columbia, Canada, has an Epiphany call to worship that includes the name of his town of Maple Ridge. That might change to reflect your town. Barbara Peddie offers a prayer for a Methodist annual meeting in Aotearoa/New Zealand. Another denomination or other geographical details may be inserted. Archbishop Malkhaz Songulashvili from Georgia contributes a wedding ceremony. The custom of a couple walking around the communion table after their vows or even the placing of crowns on their heads may enhance a wedding ceremony in another community while other prayers in that particular service might sound artificial. These are *gifts* to be opened and enjoyed.

It may be that small pieces from a number of different countries may effectively create a full worship service. A World Communion service might have a call to worship from Canada, an invocation from Korea, a confession from South Africa, an assurance of grace from China, a prayer of dedication from Turkey, an invitation to communion from Germany, a prayer of thanksgiving after communion from Mexico, and a benediction from Aotearoa. The four-week Advent candle lighting liturgy may include an Advent poem by Savithri Devanesen of India, Allen Myrick's "O Come Emmanuel to Africa," "Adviento de paz" from Argentina, and the prayer of the Magi from Indonesia. On the Sunday after Christmas four readers might offer the message. One might read "No One Knows My Name," the story of the woman who turned Gabriel down, written by Isobel de Gruchy of South Africa. Two more might read "The Innkeeper's Wife" and the "Traveler on the Road to Bethlehem," written by Rosalie May Sugrue of Aotearoa/New Zealand. The fourth could read a character sketch written by a member of your congregation. These are *gifts* that invite your creativity.

Use of global liturgy by clergy and lay worship preparers on a weekly basis, in addition to World Communion Sunday and Pentecost, broadens Sunday worship throughout the year. There are resources here for all the liturgical and natural seasons of the year and for special occasions such as Access Sunday and Earth Day. Other uses include outreach fairs, mission suppers, retreats, youth groups, outdoor ministry, university programming, educational forums, and, of course, ecumenical, interfaith, multicultural, and communitywide services. Many of these resources include not only an English translation but the original text. These *gifts* are flexible.

Reprinting these resources in other forms, such as in a book, a curriculum, or a workshop for which a fee is charged, requires the additional permission of the copyright holders listed in the source notes or The Pilgrim Press. This is intentional—you may discover wonderful new resources. The website of the artist He Qi is an example of a place to which we would love to direct you. Honoring copyrights and checking with copyright holders is a courtesy that respects their work. They will be pleased to have their liturgy used in new and exciting ways. We have attempted to give you clear, current, and accurate information in the source notes. The Pilgrim Press is the source for all the resources not specifically listed. These are *gifts* to be honored and remembered.

A SPECIAL WORD ABOUT INCLUSIVE LANGUAGE

It is our belief that the words and images used in the worship of God should be welcoming of all people and that verbal, visual, and musical expressions that cause pain, even if that pain is unintentional, should be avoided in faith communities. An example would be the use of "black" or "blind" as a description of sin. This might reflect unintentional repetition of early source material or resistance to the hard work that is hospitality. We have tried to avoid re-printing those kinds of metaphors in this book and ask forgiveness for any failures in this regard.

Gender inclusive language in particular has been a concern throughout the preparation of *Gifts in Open Hands*, as it was with its predecessor, *Gifts of Many Cultures: Worship Resources for the Global Community*. We have tried to balance the justice concerns of inclusion with those of cultural integrity. As editors we have worked with several contributors to adapt language. We have chosen to remove male nouns or pronouns for God's children. Many languages contain both masculine and feminine imagery and names for God. We have not altered these. Some of the distinct pieces use multiple metaphors, and in other cases we have used page placement to create an artistic contrast. We have, however, chosen to retain such male metaphors as "Father" and "King" for those authors for whom that usage is consistent with and significant for cultural tradition.

We have, therefore, included many pieces of liturgy that may not be fully usable in all the congregations reading this book. We feel strongly that if we insist that the "gifts" given to us conform to our current linguistic guidelines, we would not truly have "open hands." We have chosen to accept liturgy of wide artistic diversity and profound theological integrity. We invite those who read and share them with others to be grateful for their beauty and to be flexible in using them to enhance the worship of God's children. That may entail a discussion with a congregation, a footnote in a worship bulletin, a shorter portion of a longer work used, or a shift of language with a note indicating that the original writing was adapted.

Part One

Our Hands are Open
Resources for Community Worship

SAVOR
HERE.
REFRESHING
GRACE.

—Norman J. Goreham
Aotearoa/New Zealand

1 ✿ GATHERING WORDS

Rini Templeton

Maker of all things wise and wonderful—
elephants and egrets, pineapples and pelicans,
striding camels, waddling ducks
and hedgehogs that curl into prickly balls—
You fill our world with miracles and mysteries and humour.
Fill us now with the wonder and delight
that are our ongoing worship.
God, oh God,
may our delight be the acceptable worship in which you
    can delight.
Amen

—Beverley L. Osborn, Aotearoa/New Zealand

CALL TO WORSHIP (*Written for Easter 3, Year B*)

ONE: Who are we, gathering in this place?

ALL: Disciples of the Christ.

ONE: Why are we here?

ALL: To journey on the Way.

ONE: Where does this Way take us?

ALL: To the knowledge—
    in our heads *and* in our hearts—
        that death is not victorious.
    That God: Creator, Christ, and Spirit,
        is in all, is with all, is of all!

ONE: And how do we follow this Way?

ALL: By loving God.
　　By loving our neighbour.
　　By loving ourselves.
ONE: This is our purpose.
ALL: This is our Way.
　　Thanks be to God!

—Richard Bott, Canada

CALL TO WORSHIP

We come
Just as we are
To worship . . .
We come to this time
　　　to give—
　　and to receive
　　　　　In Jesus' name
A blank canvas stands before us
　　Outlined perhaps by expectations of familiar hymns and songs
　　　Or patterns from the history of our church
Upon this canvas, Lord,
　　We are about to put the colours,
　　　　　　the textures,
　　　　　　　　the shapes of our service to you
Here we propose to sketch an outline: to work out our plans
　　from data projector,
　　　from organ,
　　　　from voice and printed page
Here and now we invite you to create the image of your truth:
Something to carry us through coming days
　　Something to speak to past damage
　　　Something to build on frailties,
　　　　　shortcomings, sins even:
That your Breath, your Spirit, your Wind may take what we all offer now
And bring into creation
　　a painting of Love,
　　　　Truth
　　　　　and Grace for your kingdom.

—Alan K. Webster, Aotearoa, New Zealand

CALL TO WORSHIP FROM AFRICA (Psalm 104)

Praise be to God, who is very great!
You are clothed in honor and majesty.

Praise be to God, who set the earth on its foundations.

You raised the mountains of Africa
and spread out the valleys below.

You fill them with zebra and elephant, impala and giraffe.
You make the rivers flow, full of fish, hippo, and crocodile.

You provide rain for the crops, sun's rays that they may grow,
grain and fruit in abundance.

Your children dwell in village and town;
they walk the dusty roads and till their fields,
they toil in factory and mine.

They seek justice and hunger for peace
and long for equity among the nations.

O God, how many are your works,
in wisdom you have made them all!
Praise be to God!

—Allen Myrick, USA, Zimbabwe

Knocking at the Door   He Qi

OPEN DOORS

[1]When the doors are tightly shut,
can the peace of God be shared?
There the church may gather, but
how its witness is impaired!

[2]With the doors flung open wide,
all its energy and strength
flow to those around, outside,
held no longer at arms' length.

[3]Welcome to this holy place!
Come with others or alone.
Savour, here refreshing grace,
here where peace from God is known.

[4]Peace to all who enter here!
Peace be with each passerby!
Peace dispelling anxious fear,
peace from God, who hears each sigh!

[5]May this building be a place
where the peace of God is found!
Welcome, then, to sacred space!
Welcome, then, to hallowed ground!

(Meter: 7.7.7.7. Suggested tune: "Lauds." Dedicated to North Lowestoft United Reformed Church, Suffolk, England, in celebration of its "Open Doors" policy)

—Norman J. Goreham, Aotearoa/New Zealand

DISTURBING COMFORTER

O God, who comes as the disturbing comforter,
shattering the rigid preconceptions of our minds and hearts,
give us the grace to welcome your coming,

to trust beyond where we can see,
to have hope in the midst of chaos,
to learn from our mistakes,
to accept your forgiveness
and to walk steadfastly in the way of Gospel gladness.

—William Livingstone (Bill) Wallace, Aotearoa/New Zealand

CALL TO WORSHIP *(Written for the Sixth Sunday after Epiphany, Year B)*

ONE: Hey, Creator!

ALL: Hey, Creator!
What do you want this world to look like?
How do you want us to live?
Who do you want us to be?

ONE: Hey, Christ!

ALL: Hey, Christ!
What can we do to help?
What can *I* do to help?

How can I show my love—
>	to you,
>	to myself,
>	to everyone and everything
>		around me?

ONE: Hey, Holy Spirit!

ALL: Hey, Holy Spirit!
Open our eyes.
Open our hearts.
Open our lives—
>	so that we might share hope
>	with the world!
Amen!

—Richard Bott, Canada

CALL TO WORSHIP

We gather from our different experiences of the week just gone:
For some of us, it has been just like any other . . . just another set of days of the calendar, with little to mark it off from any other time . . . routine, hum-drum, ordinary.
For some of us, there has been momentous news: an irruption of change that we rejoice in . . . a new job, a new grandchild, a new diagnosis, a new appointment with someone who can help.
For some of us, the irruption has been a storm cloud brewing . . . a threat of change that we dread and fear, that carries with it all kinds of unknowns.
And here we gather,
>	in our differences
>		yet united in expectation of communion,
>			in our facing the same way,
>				in our singing the same songs,
>					in our reception of the same words.
In the great and glorious event that is worship
>	we come together in our differences to be brought from our week behind that we may go into the week ahead in hope
>			in faith
>			in love
experiencing grace in all our dealings with the God whom we serve and love.

—Alan K. Webster, Aotearoa/NewZealand

MAY THIS BUILDING
BE A PLACE

WHERE THE PEACE
OF GOD IS FOUND!

WELCOME THEN
TO SACRED SPACE

WELCOME THEN
TO HALLOWED GROUND!

—Norman J. Goreham
Aotearoa/New Zealand

OPENING PRAYER

En el comienzo de nuestra jornada,
nos reunimos como tu pueblo, Señor,
buscando vida para nuestra vida.
Gracias por recibirnos en tu casa
y por abrirnos las puertas de tu amor.
Tu Palabra nos nutre,
los abrazos de nuestros hermanos nos renuevan,
tu Espíritu nos anima
y celebramos ¡*Fiesta!*
Porque abunda tu gracia
y tu mirada nos acaricia.
Cantamos, aplaudimos, sonreímos
y abrimos el alma al encuentro
de tu presencia solidaria y generosa.
Somos un pueblo feliz
que quiere servirte con alegría.
En tiempos de confusión y de tantas dudas,
en momentos de egoísmos y de ambiciones,
queremos caminar tus caminos de justicia,
escuchar tus palabras que liberan,
aprender de tus juicios serenos,
extender, como la tuya, nuestra mano abierta . . .
Que este encuentro renueve en nosotros
la capacidad de seguirte y de amarte,
cada día, allí donde tú nos llames.

At the beginning of our journey,
we gather as your people, Lord,
looking for life for our life.
Thanks for having us in your home
and for opening the doors of your love.
Your Word nourishes us,
hugs of our brothers and sisters renew us,
Your Spirit encourages us
to celebrate—*Fiesta!*
For your grace abounds
and your eyes caress us.
We sing, clap, smile

and open the soul to find
your presence and generous solidarity.
We are a happy people
and we want to serve you with joy.
In times of confusion and so many doubts,
in moments of selfishness and ambition,
we desire to walk your ways of justice,
hear your words of release,
learn from your lawsuits serene
extend, like yours, our open hand . . .
May this meeting renew in us
the ability to follow you and love you,
every day, wherever you call us.

—Gerardo Oberman, Argentina

PRAYER OF APPROACH (*Written for the third Sunday after Pentecost, Year B*)

ALL: Bring us back to the beginning, God.
    Help us to hear in the scriptures
    the stories that open our eyes;
        to who Jesus was;
            to who Christ is;
                to who we are.
    Bring us back to the beginning, God—
    so that we might journey his Way.
    In Christ's name and in your love,
        we ask these things. Amen.

—Richard Bott, Canada

❈

You asked for my hands
that you might use them for your purpose.
I gave them for a moment, then withdrew them,
for the work was hard.
You asked for my mouth
to speak out against injustice.
I gave you a whisper that I might not be accused.

You asked for my eyes
to see the pain of poverty.
I closed them, for I did not want to see.

You asked for my life
that you might work through me.
I gave a small part that I might not get too involved.

Lord, forgive my calculated efforts to serve you,
only when it is convenient for me to do so,
only in those places where it is safe to do so,
and only with those who make it easy to do so.

Father, forgive me,
renew me
send me out
as a usable instrument
that I might take seriously
the meaning of your cross.

—Joe Seremane, South Africa

Senhor, ajude nos nas tentações da vida, ganancia, desejos demais por riquezas matérias, e inveja de quem tem mais.

Senhor, ajude nos na tentação de pensar mais em nós mesmos e menos nos outros

Senhor, ajude nos na tentação de esquecer os problemas na comunidade e no mundo no qual fazemos parte.

Senhor, ajude nos na tentação de procurar apenas nossa satisfação imediata, sem pensar nas conseqüências.

Senhor, ajude nos na tentação de não nos comprometemos com nossos deveres na família, na comunidade e no mundo, querendo nos isolarmos na nossa vida individual.

Senhor, ajude nos na tentação de não entendermos que seu amor e gratuito e é para todas as criaturas.

Senhor, ajude nos na tentação de não entendermos que Você criou tudo que existe, e colocou-nos para tomar conta e viver em harmonia com a natureza.

Senhor, ajude nos na tentação de agir com violência nos nossas ações com os outros para resolver problemas.

Senhor, ajude nos na tentação de não perdoar, não procurar a reconciliação.

Senhor, ajude nos na nossa revolta com a violência, a corrupção, o desinteresse dos governadores na justiça e igualdade e dê para nos a paciência necessária para que possamos trabalhar, cada um para a paz, e justiça que só amor do Senhor faz acontecer, mas primeiramente no coração de cada um.

Lord, help us in the temptations of life, of too much desire for material riches, and envy of those who have more.

Lord, help us in the temptation of thinking more of ourselves, and less of others.

Lord, help us in the temptation of forgetting the problems in the community and in the world of which we are a part.

Lord, help us in the temptation of seeking merely our immediate satisfaction, without considering the consequences.

Lord, help us in the temptation of not committing to obligations to our family, our community, and our world, and wanting to isolate ourselves in our individual lives.

Lord, help us in the temptation of not understanding that your love and gratitude is for all of your creatures.

Lord, help us in the temptation of not understanding that You created all that exists, and asked us to care for and live in harmony with nature.

Lord, help us in the temptation to turn to violence to resolve our problems with others.

Lord, help us with the temptation to not forgive, not seek reconciliation.

Lord, help us in our anger with violence, corruption, and the lack of interest of our leaders in justice and equality. Give us the patience that is necessary for each of us to work for the peace and justice that only love of you, Lord, can achieve, but that first must reside in each of our hearts.

—Barbara M. De Souza, Brazil

Sündenbekenntnis:

Eine: Gott unser Schöpfer,
du hast uns alles geschenkt;
was wir sind und haben.
Befreie uns von Selbstgerechtigkeit
und befähige uns zu teilen
was wir sind,
was wir wissen,
was wir haben;
untereinander in diesem Gottesdienst
und mit der von dir geliebten Welt.
In Christi Namen, der dieses Teilen möglich macht.
Herr, erbarme dich.

Alle: Herr, erbarme dich / Christe, erbarme dich /
Herr, erbarm dich über uns.

Gnadenzuspruch:

Eine: In Christus liegt unsere Hoffnung an jedem neuen Tag.
Steht auf und lebt als befreite Menschen Gottes
Lobsinget Gott, erhebet seinen Namen.

Alle: Ehre sei Gott in der Höhe und auf Erden Fried, den Menschen ein Wohlgefallen.

Confession of Sins:

One: O God, our creator,
who gave us all
that we are and have,
Release us from self-centeredness

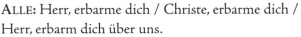

to be able to share
what we are,
what we know,
what we have
with one another in this worship
and in the world, which you love.
In the name of Christ, who makes sharing possible.

ALL: Lord, have mercy. Christ, have mercy. Lord, have mercy.

Assurance of Grace:

ONE: In Christ our hope is new every day
and there is no condemnation.
Rise up and live as free people of God.

ALL: Glory to God in the highest and on earth peace,
good will to all.

—Detlev Knoche, Germany

PRAYER FOR THE BEGINNING OF WORSHIP

This week we have heard whispers of your grace
    And we have not always listened . . .
Those whispers have come from unlikely places . . .
    and our ears were stopped because of our heart walls
Those whispers have challenged us in ways we prefer not to think about
Those whispers call us to places that look too different,
                                        too risky,
                                            too unsafe.
For our selective deafness we ask your forgiveness, Lord
But this last week we have also heard and noticed songs of grace that have stayed with us
In the unexpected warmth of a friend
In the reminders of family
In the unlooked-for kindness of strangers
In random beauty . . . heard, seen, tasted, smelled, felt
Known in the deep places
And for those songs we are grateful
We choose this morning to be carriers of goodness and grace. Amen

—Alan K. Webster Aotearoa/NewZealand

PRAYER OF CONFESSION AND PEACE

ONE: Dearest Friend, gentle Spirit, breath of life, source of our being, from the peacefulness of silence, the silence that preceded Creation, your Word entered the void and said, "Let there be light." This afternoon we sit mindful that we are kin and covenanted to that Word and to your light. We are grateful to you, source of our being.

Yet even as we are bold to come before you with our prayers of petition for peace, we are mindful of our shortcomings. And so . . . first things first. You are slow to anger and quick to forgive but let us not take advantage or your gracefulness and mercy; rather let us freely confess our sins.

We have failed to do those things that you would have us do, and we have done things that you would not have us do. Dearest Friend, gives us a moment as we collect our thoughts and offer up to you our sins in this moment of silence.

Lord in your mercy,

ALL: Hear our prayer.

ONE: Loving Spirit, you call us into fellowship with you and with one another. We lift up to you our broken relationships, broken relationships amongst family, amongst friends, amongst acquaintances with whom we harbour a hard heart. Be patient with us as we pause and focus on specific broken relationships where our hearts need softening in order to mend the relationship, that our hearts might be healed in us from our sin. Again, in this silence we offer up to you our trespasses and transgressions.

Lord in your mercy,

ALL: Hear our prayer.

ALL: Loving Spirit, your son, our brother, Jesus Christ, taught us that you are loving and generous with your mercy. We bask in your light, assured of your forgiveness and love. With that done, we pray for peace.

—Theodore Gobledale *(written for Order of St. Luke, Dandenong, Victoria, Australia)*

PRAYER OF CONFESSION

O God, forgive us for the times when we bemoan our sinfulness.

Forgive us for the times that the confessing of our litany of sins has left us satisfied that we have kept our side of the pact between us—we confess and you forgive. There is more to it than that. Help us to understand that the times we recognise we have fallen short of the standards of love and patience and honesty are opportunities for growing or lessening the growth of your spirit within us. Teach us to recognise that we can

NEVER fall out of your loving. Help us to find ways to heal where we have hurt, build where we have damaged, begin again and again and again in love.

Assurance of Pardon

Oh God, you accept us as we are and love us still. It is through your loving that we have the desire and the strength of confidence to let your spirit grow in us.

—Beverley L. Osborn, Aotearoa/New Zealand

HEAR THE WORD OF GRACE (Isaiah 2:4, Micah 4:3)

[1]Hear the courteous word of grace,
all you people in this place:
"Let your inner conflicts cease:
God forgives you. Be at peace."

[2]And the turmoil all around,
where mistrust and hate abound?
If forgiveness there should flow,
peace would flourish, hope would grow;

[3]enemy transformed to friend
then would work for wars to end;
nations, in contrition, would
join to seek the common good.

[4]Therefore, when disputes arise,
may we hold before our eyes
visions of a better way,
where the Prince of Peace holds sway.

[5]God's own Spirit turn our hearts
to more gentle, peaceful arts,
to the reconciling word,
to the ploughshare, not the sword.

[6]All you people in this place,
hear again the word of grace:
"Take this gift of glad release:
God forgives you. Live in peace."

(Meter 7.7.7.7. "God forgives you. Be at peace" is one form taken by the Absolution in the liturgy. The Absolution is sometimes known as "the word of grace.")

—Norman J. Goreham, Aotearoa/New Zealand

Forgiveness is forgetting bad things. Remember good things. Forgiveness is love.

—Wu Yang (Evelyn), China

God of our minds,
God of our hearts,
God of our bodies and our souls:
    we offer you all that we are,
    and all that we aren't.
We offer you our fears and confusions,
    our hopes and our dreams.
We offer these,
    knowing that they will be changed,
    knowing that we will be transformed,
        by your Love.
In Christ's name we ask it—amen.

—Richard Bott, Canada

This story happened on a self-study course in my high school. I studied hard in the quiet classroom. Suddenly, my friend who sat at the same table began to talk with a boy. I said to her: don't speak! Just study! She said sorry and stopped. After a little time, they began to talk again. And they talked happily and loudly. I was very angry. So I lifted my hand and knocked the table ferociously. Her face became red. After class, she said sorry again. But I said nothing to her. In the evening, she brought a flower to my bedroom. She said: please forgive me and receive my love and flower . . . . Then she held me in her arms.

—Shen Ben (Judy), China

3   Prayers of Praise and Thanksgiving

ONE: God of our Islands where the Long Clouds lie,
here we are, Lord, in this remote place below the curve of the earth. We thank you for the different races who have gathered here, some guided by the stars your fingers put in place. Lord, we thank you for the blessings you have bestowed upon our place, the Bay of Plenty.

ALL: We thank you, Lord.

ONE: Thank you for the long white beaches, for the hushing of the breakers as they drop onto the sand, rippling from one end to the other. Thank you for the tang of salt air, the gulls and molly hawks circling, the pheasants in the dune grasses, and the flocks of small birds flying over our homes to the flat pasture lands.

ALL: We thank you, Lord.

ONE: Thank you for the fruitfulness of the land, for farms and market gardens, for orchards and the kiwifruit crop, for the stillness of our bush.

We thank you for the fish and seafood in bay waters, for the Kaimai ranges that shelter us from many winter storms.

ALL: We thank you, Lord.

ONE: We pray that we will remember your provision for our lives, that you supply all our needs.

ALL: Lord, hear our prayer. Amen.

—Barbara Murray, Aotearoa/New Zealand

PRAYER FOR THE CREATOR

One dark night you whispered in Beethoven's ear and an "Ode to Joy" was born.
On a windswept hill you painted the autumn sky and Tom Thompson recorded
    with an artist's eye the beauty there.

In the depths of the sea you place rainbows.
In the heights of the heavens, oceans of stars too plentiful to count.
In the perfect mathematical language of the universe Bach wrote your songs,
     so simple and yet too complex to fathom.
With the pure voice of angels Ella Fitzgerald sang of love and loneliness
     and the longing of the human spirit.
These gifts so abundantly given, so abundantly shared, come from One source,
     One inspiration, one longing to be one with you.
We are your ode to joy.
You remind us with every sunset, every moon rise, every gentle rain, every thunder clap,
     every evensong, we are yours and you are ours.

When our hearts turn to stone the sun still rises and the moon still sets and rain still falls.
When our hearts turn to stone flowers still bloom and food still grows and we are fed.
When our hearts turn to stone babies are born and life goes on, past grief and sorrow.

When our hearts have turned to stone we busy ourselves with empty busyness,
     just in case you STOP.

But you have promised
And we trust in the promise.
Soften our hearts, we pray, to see and hear you.
Let us never STOP being yours and you ours—One.

—Pat Rodgers, Canada

When I step on my way with the gospel
When I stretch my hand for sowing with tears
Oh! Lord, I am looking forward to
The heavenly sound shaking the earth,
     The eternal hymn waking the universe

When I follow you with the eternal hope
When I sing with praise out of my chest
Oh! Lord, I am looking forward to
The lands sowed by your own hand
     The souls saved in your grace.

I do not want to be fruitless
I do not waste your grace

I want even the smallest reward in the heavenly banquets.
Oh! Lord, help me to sow in humility.

Help me to be faithful in trial.
Give me strength in patience.
Oh! To fight for the gospel is my work.

To sacrifice my life for the holy mission—
Oh! Lord, please purify me as your golden wares.

—Li Liya, China *(pastor in rural China who wrote this prayer
in thanksgiving for God's love)*

God of brilliant sunsets and shining rainbows,
God of golden daffodils and glowing autumn leaves,
God of all the blues of sunlit seas,
God of all the shades of green in bush and field, in rivers and oceans and lakes, in rough
stones on a beach and polished jewels in a showcase,
God of people, brown and amber, pink and ebony,
artistic and athletic, practical and visionary, compassionate and laughter-bringing,
God who colours us a world of variety,
We thank you that you have made each of us unique, that you call us to contribute our
special colours to the life around us.
We come to you in thanksgiving and worship. Amen

—Beverley L. Osborn, Aotearoa/New Zealand

Lord Jesus! Praise be to you that I have experienced you in my life. You have chosen me
since within my mother's womb, chosen me to be your worker. My entire life, I only pray
that I may live within you. I have another hope, and that is to be used by you forever, used
for your will. Lord! I pray that you mold your instrument for your purposes and according
to your will. My Father! I offer my flesh and spirit to you; act according to your will. I
pray that you make use of this small instrument and pray that you resurrect Chinese
churches in these years. China belongs to the Lord forever. I pray in the name of our Lord
Jesus Christ! Amen!

—Mary Shen, China *(student at Yan Jing Seminary in Beijing)*

4 ❀   PRAYERS OF PETITION AND INTERCESSION

PRAYER FOR WISDOM

Lord, we pray,
"Give us grace to accept with serenity the things that cannot be changed,
courage to change the things that should be changed,
and the wisdom to know the difference."
I also pray,
Give me compassion to help when help is needed,
kindness to stand back when help is not wanted,
and the wisdom to know the difference.
Give me openness to share something of my journey if helpful,
humility to keep quiet if I'm only boasting,
and the wisdom to know the difference.
Give me gentleness to ask concerned questions,
reticence to probe intrudingly,
and the wisdom to know the difference.
Give me willingness to organize and advise freely,
patience to not interfere,
and the wisdom to know the difference.
Give me courage to be honest in my response if that is called for,
Sensitivity to refrain from honesty if that would be more compassionate,
and the wisdom to know the difference.
Through Jesus Christ our Lord, Amen

—Isobel de Gruchy, South Africa

✣

God of kindliness,
we pray for your Church
here and in every land:
for the Church asleep,
that it might awake;
for the persecuted Church,
that it remain glad and certain of your cause;
for the confessing Church,
that it may be nothing for itself alone
but live alone for your fame.
We pray for all rulers and authorities
in the whole world;
for those that are good,
that you preserve them;
for those that are evil,
that you change their hearts
or put an end to their power
according to your pleasure;
for all, that you prove to them
that you are the one whose servants they are
and must remain.
We pray that all tyranny and disorder be resisted
and all suppressed nations and peoples
be helped to their rights. Amen

—Reformierte Liturgie, Wappertal, Germany

WE WANT TO MOVE
INTO THE FUTURE
IN HOPE AND FAITH
CARRYING CHRIST'S
LIGHT

WHEREVER
WE GO.

—Barbara A. Peddie
Aotearoa/New Zealand

PRAYER OF PETITION AND BLESSINGS IN SHONA

Tinomubonga Baba Mwari kubudikidza ndi Mambo wedu Jesu Christ mupi weupenyu hwedu. Tinonamatira maoko nepfungwa dzevatungamiriri vedu kuti imwimwi muzvikomborere. Komborerai hurumende yemubatanidzwa kuti ikwanise kuona vanhu kwete kudziona. Izvi zvinoitika kwega kuti kwega kuti imwimwi musiki wezviro zveshe mwatonga moyo yavo. Komborerai ivhu redukuti rikwanise kubereka mbesa kuti tikohwe mwaka yese. Femerai mweya wenyu wakachena kuti tiite mwaka usina udyi uye une mvura yakakwana. Titukireiwo mweya yehondo nezvirwere munyeka mwedu. Vandudzai zvicherwa zvedu kuti zverege kuva zveropa asi zvinoriritira vanhu vasvo.

Our Father and Creator, we want to thank you for giving us our Saviour Jesus Christ. We are praying for our leadership to be concerned leadership to its people. Bless their hands, minds, and ambitions so that progress might be witnessed through the Unity Government in place. Transform their minds so that they see people rather than self. Breathe your Holy Spirit into our crop-growing season so that our season might be a blessed one. Move away political violence and minds of war. Form our eyes so that we can see progress. Turn our minerals from blood minerals into national blessing minerals for all. All this can be possible if you indwell them. It is our trust and hope that you will bless our nation.

—Fungayi Mutsumbei, Zimbabwe

PRAYER OF HEAVY HEARTS

Our hearts are heavy today, Lord.
Our hearts are heavy today, Lord, because there is too much poverty in the world.
    We are saddened, Lord, by the degrading life that millions, if not billions,
    of people live, by the way in which poverty steals their humanity.
Our hearts are heavy today, Lord, because there is too much corruption in the world.
    We are saddened, Lord, by the greed that dwells in the hearts of too many
    powerful people, by the way in which corruption steals their humanity.
Our hearts are heavy today, Lord, because our human family has lost its spiritual
    direction. We covet and work for the material things of life that do not really
    matter while at the same time neglecting and disregarding the spiritual things of
    life that really do matter. In this process, our lives have become shallow, without
    depth and meaning. We thrash around wondering where we have gone wrong
    without turning toward you for the nutritious spiritual food that you offer us.
Today, Lord, we come before you to seek your guidance, your wisdom, your love, for we
    know that without turning to you we will continue to have poverty, corruption, and
    empty lives. "We offer all these prayers to you, Lord, in your Son's name. Amen."

—Bruce Van Voorhis, Kowloon Union Church, Hong Kong

COLLECTS

For a service honoring teachers and mentors

Wise God, you are our teacher and our guide. You have given us faithful leaders and mentors to show us your paths, and you have called us to serve you and your people. We pray for all those who have been called to teaching, mentoring, and spiritual leadership—ministers, rabbis, imams, and others. Grant that they and we may be servants who follow the guidance of your Spirit and work to gather people into your reign of love. In the name of Jesus Christ, our Teacher, Amen.

For the forgotten

Holy God, your Spirit moves among us and dwells within us. You have promised that you will never forget us or leave us alone. Grant that we may remember those whom we have forgotten—the elderly, orphans, the mentally ill, those who are abused, those whose lives are torn apart by violence and war—may they be filled with your presence and know that they are not alone. And may you convict us to be your love and presence in their lives. Amen.

—Manda Adams, USA

LITANY: A PRAYER FOR THE WORLD

ONE: Let joy throughout the world be from God,

ALL: People will have happiness.

ONE: Let peace throughout the world be from God,

ALL: People will be love.

ONE: Let patience throughout the world be from God,

ALL: People will pardon others.

ONE: Let justice throughout the world be from God,

ALL: People will have less hate for others.

ONE: Let kindness throughout the world be from God,

ALL: People will respect others.

ONE: Let hope throughout the world be from God,

ALL: People will have confidence within themselves.

ONE: O Lord, give us strength to believe in you,

ALL: O Lord, your name is always praised. Amen.

—Fu (Lily), China

PRAYER FOR ECUMENISM FOR TWO VOICES AND CONGREGATION

ALL: God, you have created the light clear and pure,
and still you have broken it up into the colours of the rainbow.
Each in the horizon of their own experiences;
the power
to see you
that we might share our experiences with one another;
thereby discovering more and more

of you in all your truth and beauty.
Let us all bring to one another our experiences
of truth and salvation,
of repentance and renewal,
so that the whole inheritance be preserved
and be within the reach of all who call you Father,
through him, in whom your fullness is to be found,
your only Son, Jesus Christ, our Lord.

ONE: Let us pray to God, our Father,
for the gift of unity—
which inspires us and motivates us:
The following prayers may be added (selectively):

TWO: Sometimes we are in danger
of resigning ourselves to the offence of division.

ONE: Lord, shake us out of our sleep,
and awaken anew our enthusiasm
so that through our growing unity with you
and with one another
the world may come to faith.

Diane Wendorf

TWO: Sometimes we are too focused on our own tradition
and become narrow-minded, even fanatical
in relation to others.

ONE: Lord, free us from false pride
and careless or arrogant opinions,
so that we might behave towards one another
with self-assurance and tolerance.

TWO: We are thankful that we know better
our brothers and sisters in other communities
and in their appearance learn to respect them.

ONE: Lord, help us to accept one another as we are,
so that we might learn to live with one another
according to your will.

TWO: We must recognise and declare honestly
that many things still cut us off from one another
and hinder the full community we long for.

ONE: Lord, give us courage
to overcome divisions
so that we might celebrate
the gifts of grace in other people.
Give us readiness to share the various traditions
in a spirit of fraternity.
Give us a hunger for your Word and your bread,
so that we might soon find a seat together
at the communal meal of unity and love.

TWO: Much is already achieved; much still lies before us
on the way to reconciliation
for unity and peace,
a peace, which shall be accorded to all people.

ONE: Lord, let us harvest in thanksgiving the good fruits
of our ecumenical work
and let us grow in faith, hope, and love,
so that we come nearer you and one another.

TWO: The world rightly expects of Christians
service to the poor and commitment to peace in justice.

ONE: Lord, lend your aid to our efforts,
so that our witness to Christ
and our service to the world
might be convincing and effective.

—Adapted from Agenda I, edited by Church Office of the Evangelical Church of Kurhesses-
Waldeck, Kassel, 1996, Germany

PRAYER FOR A DENOMINATIONAL MEETING

Lord of creation:
We, who have gathered together in this place, represent many cultures;
some of us have called this land of Aotearoa "'home'" for many generations;
some of us trace our roots back to the other side of the world;
some of us carry the memory of island beaches and the sound of the sea;
but all of us are called to reflect your image.
We are the people called Methodist,
and within that family are many branches and many traditions;
we sing our faith in different languages and pray using different words,

but we all rejoice in your gift of grace
and do our best to follow your call to love and service.
As the rivers in our eastern plains flow down from the mountains,
    dividing and re-joining,
    surging in flood, or disappearing beneath the stony surface,
    but all moving towards the same sea,
so we, your people, move on different courses and at different speeds
towards the goal of building your commonwealth of love and peace in this place.

O God, lover of the world,
we pray for our wounded world torn apart by warring and greedy factions.
    May we be makers and menders.
We pray for our country, Aotearoa New Zealand
    May we, who live in this fortunate place,
    work to bring about your vision of justice and integrity.
We pray for our church facing the challenges of this rapidly changing time.
    May we use our shared vision and differing strengths
    to empower each other in mission.
We pray for ourselves.
    Strengthen us to answer your call,
    to offer our different gifts and skills in your service.
    Nothing is impossible.
Whatever confronts us, we are the people who have inherited
    courage and freedom, vision and responsibility.
We will move into the future in hope and faith
carrying Christ's light wherever we go. Amen.

—Barbara A. Peddie, Aotearoa/New Zealand

Inclusive God
Sometimes people miss out
They feel like the good things in life are passing them by
and they don't have the energy to fight through the crowd or the initiative to climb a tree
We hold in our hearts those who are disillusioned or despairing
Those who find life too hard and have given up
We think particularly of those who are contemplating suicide
May we support the despairing and be trees for them to climb that they might see you

Hospitable God
Sometimes people feel unwelcome
They feel uncomfortable, unwanted and out of place
in our homes, our churches, our cities, our country
We hold in our hearts those who feel they are the wrong colour, the wrong race,
    the wrong size or have the wrong education or the wrong values
We think particularly of those who encounter racism
May we open our hearts to those who feel unwanted and be refuges for them
    to experience your love
Forgiving God
Sometimes people are dishonest
They cheat, lie, or steal to satisfy their greed, to give meaning to their life,
    or simply to survive
We hold in our hearts those who have succumbed to the temptation to be dishonest
    and those who are contemplating dishonesty
We think particularly of those who are addicted to gambling and must steal
    to feed their addiction
May we be compassionate to the dishonest and show them your forgiveness

—Penny Guy, Aotearoa/New Zealand

Lord, we pray for your church
to all the ends of the earth.
Fill it with the spirit of service, simplicity, and fidelity.
We pray for all
who suffer on grounds of poverty
and for those who are lonely in their wealth.
We pray for those who are ill,
because they have nothing to eat
and for those who are ill
because they have too much to eat.
We pray for all who take life lightly
and for those who weep because of the misery of others.
We pray for those who are self-confident
and for those who are mocked and excluded.
Give to each one of us

a simple, loyal heart,
that can sympathise.
We pray in the silence.

—Adapted from Testi Liturgi, Italy

Dear Christ Jesus, I experience more and more about your love and richness. I love you and want to be your appreciated and faithful servant. Please guide me and keep my feet on your way. Please hold my hands and lead me to the day when I meet you face to face. Your mercy and care will help me to live in you. And also protect the church in my homeland so she may be holy and have vivid testimony for your living name. In Jesus name I pray.

—JiaoYu E, China

PRAYERS OF THE PEOPLE

ALL: Lord, be our compass, our signpost, our pathway
Guide us when we stumble on our way

ONE: We pray for the world
For the people of our planet
From different backgrounds, ethnicities, and cultures
With different religions, beliefs, and practices
We pray for the nations of the world
For wise government that works for everyone, free from corruption and bribery,
For policies to look after their people
For freedom of speech, an end to persecution and political imprisonment
ALL: Lord, be our compass, our signpost, our pathway
Guide us when we stumble on our way

ONE: We pray for the environment—a constant and ever important part of our lives
A fragile balance where we have just one chance to make things right
We pray for an end to the catastrophic processes of mining and deforestation,
     which have reduced nations to barren wastelands, for sustainable use of the earth's
     resources—fish, wood, water—and an end to resource exploitation
ALL: Lord, be our compass, our signpost, our pathway
Guide us when we stumble on our way

ONE: We pray for our own country, Aotearoa
For our beautiful rivers, lakes, coastline, high mountains, deep valleys, lush forests,
     rolling grassy plains, for our extraordinary wildlife

For the places that we call home, and the places where we find to clear our heads
Alone except for the elements
We pray for the protection of these amazing features that make our nation such a
    special place to live, from the pressures of our modern-day lifestyle—we pray
    especially for those who dedicate their time and efforts to make this a reality.
ALL: Lord, be our compass, our signpost, our pathway
Guide us when we stumble on our way

ONE: We pray for the people of our nation
Those who have grown up here, and those who are later arrivals, from every walk
    of life from around the world
We pray for the hope that we can continue to welcome people to Aotearoa with open
    minds and open hearts, regardless of background—we pray that the government
    will realise the incredible contribution that these people make to our diverse society
We pray for jobs—and for the people who keep our country running
    For teachers, doctors, supermarket cashiers, bankers, fast food workers, bus drivers,
    caregivers, lawyers, lifeguards, and journalists—and we pray for equal opportunities
    for all—for those whose jobs are constantly in the news, and those who never get a
    mention yet tirelessly work for the benefit of others
And, at this point, we pray for those who have lost their jobs and their livelihoods, and
    the challenges they are facing because of this
We pray too for those who carry out volunteer work in our community—our lives
    would be much poorer without the selfless dedication of these people to their causes
ALL: Lord, be our compass, our signpost, our pathway
Guide us when we stumble on our way

ONE: And finally, Lord, we pray for ourselves
Our children, our parents, brothers, sisters, grandparents, aunts, and uncles.
Our families and whanau*
Our companions and our enemies, neighbours and friends
Our households and our homes, and the many places that we call home:
Flats, apartments, state houses, quarter-acre sections, bungalows, and cottages
We pray for our varied and interesting lifestyles, and all the different paths
    that we have chosen to take in life
Lord, help us in whatever we do, and guide us in our decisions
ALL: Lord, be our compass, our signpost, our pathway
Guide us when we stumble on our way. Amen

*whanau—a Maori word for extended family

—Hugh Laurenson, Aotearoa/NewZealand

PRAYER OF THANKSGIVING AND INTERCESSION

Gracious God,
you have created the peoples of the earth,
and you have chosen your people from all nations.
We thank you
that you have also spoken to us
and included us in your plan
to overcome separation,
to reconcile enmity,
to integrate entrenched boundaries.
God, your desire is that we should be one with one another,
and so we thank you
for the fellowship of the Protestant churches in Europe.
We pray, consolidate our unity
and strengthen our confidence
in the wideness of your compassion.
We pray for all churches that are still self-reliant.
Let them also find feasible ways
to be led together in reconciled diversity—
as a sign of hope for our very discordant world.
God, you know, that in our Europe
there is still much hostility, old and new, between nations
and groups of people.
Protect us from despairing of our responsibility
to pray and to work for a peaceful co-existence.
Grant those in positions of responsibility
in politics and economics
wisdom and humanity,
that they may serve peace and increase righteousness.
Make all who work in education be skillful
to convey the worth of every single life
and to practise the proper measure of reserve and openness.
Strengthen all who are there for the sick and despairing:
preserve them in their sensitivity to others' pain.
God of compassion,
sustain the happiness of lovers,
protect the carefree nature of children,
and keep us in all security with you. Amen.

—Sylvia Bukowski, Germany

Loving God
We may like to see ourselves as masters of your world but in private we are often fearful.
People may be fearful of large things such as:
Global warming
Nuclear war
Epidemics

Or their fears may be more personal.
The young may fear:
Losing the approval of their peers
Not succeeding in what they attempt
Making the wrong decision

Older people may fear:
The loss of someone close
Infirmity
A loss of independence

We recognise that people in some countries may have other fears:
Famine
Torture
Death

It is said that perfect love casts out fear. May this love flow through us and be felt by all who are fearful, giving them courage to face whatever eventuates. Amen

—Penny Guy, Aotearoa/New Zealand

PRAYERS OF THE PEOPLE FOR BIBLE SUNDAY

Our God, you have created the rich diversity within this world,
diversity of colour, shape, and form in land and in plant life,
diversity in water life, in animals, birds, and people.
We thank you for all this and today we thank you especially for the rich diversity
within the words of languages in which people communicate and build
communities of understanding.
Thank you that you are *the Word* of life and that you understand and can
communicate in the innermost thoughts of each person in whatever language
those thoughts are formed.

We give you thanks too for the Bible Society workers who seek to translate the Bible and make it available for ever increasing numbers of people in different language groups around the world. We pray for your continuing blessing on those who give and those who receive, that people and whole communities may come to know that you truly are the Word of Life.

We think too of people working for you around the world in difficult and dangerous situations to share your message in word and in action. We think of the people of Zimbabwe and the difficulties they face. We think of aid workers continuing in disaster areas long after the news headlines and TV coverage are past. We pray for them and for the people and situations they work among. May they know that you are with them however dark and impossible their situation seems. And may the outcomes be better than anyone but you had ever hoped or dreamed.

You know, our God, the people and the concerns that are in our personal thoughts and deep in our hearts. In a minute of silence we bring them to you . . .

Thank you, our God, that you hear our prayers. In the breadth of your love, you are with those we have prayed for and with us in the working out of all these situations.

We bring these prayers in the name of our Lord Jesus Christ. Amen

—Elaine E. Bolitho, Aotearoa/New Zealand

Dear Jesus, I thank you for your salvation. You are my savior. You love everyone in this world. Before I was born, you had known me. You sacrificed yourself on the cross for us. You give us a new life. You are the only son of Almighty God. Now we can be in the presence of God through you.

I thank you for giving us the Holy Spirit, who is our teacher, comforter, and counselor. The Holy Spirit teaches us to know you more. I also believe the Holy Spirit gives us wisdom to understand the Bible.

Now I pray to you for anyone who believes in you in this world. Please help them to follow you closely and pray much to you from their hearts. Please lead them walking in your path and serving you with their hands and minds.

Dear Jesus, I pray to you for those who don't know you in this world. Please choose them and give them wisdom to know you. Please help them believe you are the only savior. I pray in the name of Jesus.

—Stephen Yu, China

Eternal God, our guide, our strength, and our Sustainer,

We thank you for the opportunities of Sundays—for these regular roadside stops on this trip of a lifetime, where we can service our hearts and minds with a simple communion feast, fine-tune our attitudes, check the travel-guide and map of our journey in your scriptures, and share our experiences with our fellow travelers. Remind us, God, that this time is not a pit-stop in a frantic high-speed race, but an opportunity to connect with you, our designer, our trip organizer, our tour guide on this journey of life.

We thank you for the company of the seasoned travelers on this journey—those vintage and veteran Christians whose life-trips have been long and wide-ranging, whose experiences are inspirational, and whose advice is so much valued. We thank you for the company of the L-plate* and P-plate* travelers in this family of believers, whose trip with you is just beginning—who are enthusiastic, optimistic, taking one day at a time, and taking in the wonders and sights of their trip without rigid plans or preconceptions—just with faith. We especially thank you for those on this road through life, with little children in tow, for Jesus himself valued the children highest of all, and so must we, for they are the precious future of your kingdom on Earth.

God, you know only too well that some of us are not good travelers.

We can lose our way.

We can become sidetracked.

We can be fooled by some awful, "tacky" attractions along the way, and we can take bad advice without thinking of the consequences.

We sometimes miss the signs that matter, and we are often too stubborn to ask for help when we are so obviously lost. We forget that your roadside service is available day and night.

Lord God, when we sometimes think we know the road ahead, we are forgetting that this lifetime trip can be dangerous, or puzzling, or frustrating. It can be shrouded in the fog of sadness, or battered by the storms of relationships turned sour.

Forgive us our burst of road-rage towards fellow travelers. Sometimes we think that we alone are the perfect ones on our journey—the only ones with a complete understanding of the rules and the skills necessary to reach the destination. Help us instead to be considerate, kind, and courteous. Teach us humility.

Forgive us our U-turns—those times when we get discouraged and tired and are tempted to turn back. And protect us from people who are traveling the wrong way. Forgive us those moments when we are stuck in life's roundabouts, going in circles and getting nowhere. Keep us patient and calm in the traffic jams of our journey, we pray.

And Lord, teach us compassion! Encourage us not to be in such a hurry that we can't pull over and help fellow travelers who have broken down or who have run out of fuel.

Don't let us speed past those on limited resources—the hitchhikers or backpackers
on Faith Road. Don't allow us to miss an opportunity to give them a lift on their
life journey.

And remind us, Lord, to take time out to appreciate the scenery—the sights and
sounds, the beautiful scents and aromas of this magnificent world through which
we are travelling. Inspire us to turn out of the fast lane, off the freeways and tollways,
and to appreciate the lovely places and people on the quieter, meandering roads that
still lead to life's destination. Lead us beside the still waters—the placid lakes and
the gentle streams.

God, help us to feel your Spirit when the life road gets rough, and especially when it
descends suddenly into the deep shadowy valleys of despair, depression, or death.
And when the view from the mountaintops of life is so beautiful that it makes our
hearts sing or takes our breath away, we want to recognize that you are the source
of this creation, the beginning and the end of our journey, the God of grace,
compassion, and love.

So guide us still, great Jehovah, through the coming week of this trip of a lifetime.
We want your Spirit to be our constant travel companion, directing our paths.

We pray in the name of Jesus, who paid in advance—and in full!—the cost of our
journey, and who waits for us with you at journey's end. Amen

*L-plate = learner drivers, ages sixteen to eighteen, displaying an "L" plate on their vehicles to warn
other drivers. *P-plate = provisional drivers, ages nineteen to twenty-one, displaying a "P" plate on
their vehicles to warn other drivers.

—D. S. Allen, Boronia Church of Christ, Boronia, Australia

THE FLOOR
OF MY HEART
HAS BEEN
TILED
WITH
SADNESS

—Lina Andronoviene
Lithuania

ZIMBABWEAN PRAYER OF OUR SAVIOUR (LORD'S PRAYER)

Shona is the first language of about 80 percent of Zimbabweans, Ndebele is the first language of the other 20 percent. Both are spoken in the United Church of Christ in Zimbabwe (UCCZ). The Ndau dialect of Shona is the primary dialect spoken in the UCCZ.

Ndau dialect of Shona	Ndebele	English
Baba vedu vari mudenga, ngariremeredzwe zina renyu. Umambo hwenyu ngahuuye. Kuda kwenyu ngakuitwe munyika kudai ngomudenga. Tipei nange iri zuva kudya kwedu kunotamika nyamashi. Tirekererei ndaa dzedu kudai tisu takarekerera avo vane ndaa kwetiri. Usatipinza mukuedzwa, asi tinunure kuno uwo wakashata: Ngokuti ngehwenyu umambo, nesimba neuthende, hunoti mbera nekare, Amen.	Baba wethu osezulwini, kalidunyiswe ibizo lakho, umbuso wakho kawuze, intando yakho kayenziwe, emhlabeni njengasezulwini. Siphe lamhla ukudhla kwethu kwensuku ngensuku Usithethelele izono zethu, njengalokhu lathi sibathethelela abasonayo Ungasingenisi ekulingweni, kodwa usikhulule ebubini. Ngoba umbuso ungowakho, lamandla, lobukhosi, kuze kube nini lanini. Amen	Our Father, who art in heaven, hallowed be thy name. Thy kingdom come. Thy will be done on earth as it is in heaven. Give us this day our daily bread. And forgive us our debts, as we forgive our debtors. And lead us not into temptation, but deliver us from evil. For thine is the kingdom, and the power, and the glory, for ever. Amen.

—Kim McKerley, contributor

5 ❀ AFFIRMATIONS OF FAITH

WE AFFIRM,
AS CO-CREATORS
IN YOUR CREATIVE
WORK, THAT
A LASTING PEACE
AND REAL JUSTICE

ARE POSSIBLE ONLY
IF EVERY PERSON
ASSUMES PERSONAL
RESPONSIBILITY THAT,
IN YOUR ETERNAL
LOVE,
YOU GAVE US.

—Gerardo Oberman
Argentina

We gather as people of the Way
Leaving paths that have brought us this far
To find new directions,
discover new stories,
daring to explore horizons and truth.

On the Way, life meets us, hungry for justice,
for bread and for peace;
It calls us to see,
To hear and to act,
Finding new words and the courage to speak.

In our meeting together comes strength
To serve; the least and the little,
the unseen, the neglected,
the lost and rejected,
And love overcoming fear of the cost.

We come celebrating the Way that we travel,
The community created,
The joy of experience,
The love we walk,
And the peace, that never lets us rest.

For the way that stretches in front of us,
We say thank you.
For the way that lies behind us,
We say thank you.
For the Way that we will become,
We hope with thankful hearts. Amen.

—Erice Fairbrother, Aotearoa/New Zealand

A PROPOSAL FOR A SERVICE FOR CHURCHES, AGENCIES, AND INSTITUTIONS IN LATIN AMERICA, BASED ON THE CREED OF HUMAN RIGHTS

We believe in you, God of Life, who created us free
and equal in dignity and rights.
We affirm that these rights, which given us in your grace,
are valid for every person without distinction of race, color,
sex, language, religion, political opinion, national or social origin,
property, birth or other status.
We believe we have the right to life
and to live that life in full freedom,
in an atmosphere of security and respect,
because everyone is equal
before the law of this world,
equal in our thoughts and actions.
We affirm that no person should be held in slavery
nor to any form of bondage or oppression.
We believe in you, Mother Creator, and that no one
should be subjected to torture
or cruel, inhuman or degrading treatment.
We affirm that we cannot be arbitrarily arrested
or detained or prosecuted or banished without a cause.
We believe we have the right to speak our truth
and be heard with respect and fairness.
We affirm that it is a sin to violate the privacy of others
in order to attack their honor or reputation.
We believe that you, O God, who combines all the names,
give us the right to a name,
to a nationality, to freedom to raise a family

and to build a space where they can live.
We affirm that like all men and women, great and small,
we have a right to our thoughts and opinions,
we have a right to meet and to profess our faith,
to educate without economic barriers,
to grow and develop with equal opportunities,
to work and to participate in political life,
to receive free health care,
to enjoy decent, fair, and adequate pay,
to enjoy an old age free from want,
to rest our body and spirit,
to create, to propose, to share,
without conditions of any kind.
We believe we have the right to play, sing and laugh,
because you, Infinite Wisdom, have created us to be happy.
We affirm that it is a sin to hoard what we have,
and live isolated from solidarity with others,
because when some have too much,
others are deprived of their right
to clothing, housing, health care and daily bread . . .
We believe that tolerance and understanding,
in political and religious issues,
in spite of ethnic, social, economic differences
are the basis for blessed coexistence
and the path to a society
with room for all.
We affirm, as co-creators in your creative work
that a lasting peace and real justice
are possible only
if every person in every place on this Earth,
assumes as his or her personal obligation
protecting each of these rights
that, in your eternal love, you gave us.

(Afirmación of faith based on the Universal Declaration of Human Rights adopted and proclaimed by General Assembly resolution 217 A (III) of December 10, 1948. Formulation liturgical)

—Gerardo Oberman, Argentina

MY CREED—MY BEATITUDE

I believe in the precious nature of each individual.
Peace to the people who respect their challenging and exciting
neighbours.
I believe in Justice for all people.
Peace to the people who support the right for people to be
accepted for who they are.
I believe in the acceptance of women and men of whatever
sexual orientation and persuasion.
Peace to the people who speak out against persecution, bullying,
verbal and physical abuse of individuals and groups of people.
I believe in an Inclusive Church.
Peace to the people who, with their love and desire for the wholeness
of humankind, create communities and churches where we are
enabled to worship in the spirit of diversity, honesty, and love.

—Geoffrey Duncan, England

I believe, Lord,
that everything good in the world
comes from you.
I believe in your great love for all people,
I believe that, because you preached love,
freedom, and justice,
you were humiliated,
tortured, and killed.

I believe that you continue
to suffer in our people . . .
I believe that you call me
to defend your cause,
but I also believe that you accompany me
in the task of transforming this world
into a different one
where there is no suffering or weeping;
a world where there is a gigantic table
set with free food where everyone is welcome.

I believe that you accompany us
in waiting for the dawning of a new day.
I believe that you will give us strength
so that death does not find us
without having done enough,
and that you will rise
in those who have died seeking a different world.

—A peasant woman, El Salvador

Rini Templeton

CREDO MIO/MY CREED

Esteemed sisters and brothers, I offer this creed fashioned by me after sixty-five years of Baptist life in Cuba. I think it arises from the fully lived experiences of these complex years of our human history. May our God bless you in every moment. An embrace. (*Deacon Samuel Francisco Rodriguez Cabrera, of the First Baptist Church of Matanzas, Cuba, and coordinator of the community work of the Kairos Center*)

Creo en el dios que por encima de todo, respeta hasta las últimas consecuencias, el libre albedrío;

creo en el dios que no puede evitar los tsunamis, los huracanes, los volcanes, los terremotos, que azotan preferentemente las zonas más pobladas del planeta, y más empobrecidas, donde mueren millones de personas y otras pierden lo poco que tienen; *y acciones de amor surgen a favor de los damnificados;*

creo en el dios que no puede evitar que unos tengan más que otros, tanto, que unos mueren de hambre y enfermedades curables mientras otros gastan en dietas por

pura estética personal, tratamientos médicos por hipocondría o moda de asistir a
lujosos centros médicos;
y acciones de amor surgen a favor de los injusticia dos;
creo en el dios que no puede evitar guerras, donde mueren los que no tienen nada que
ver con ellas, que no les deben nada a quien los mata primero;
y acciones de amor surgen a favor de los que mueren y sus familiares;
creo en el dios que no pudo evitar la muerte del Nazareno, ni de Gandhi, ni de King,
ni de Martí, ni Lennon, ni de los poetas, ni de las monjas, ni sacerdotes, obispos,
pastores, de todos los que denuncian la injusticia y se ponen del lado de los débiles;
y acciones de amor surgen de esas sangres derramadas;
creo en el dios que no puede evitar que millones de niños nazcan para morir de hambre,
y madres también, y padres;
y acciones de amor surgen para que cada vez sean menos los que mueran;
creo en el dios que no puede evitar que millones de mujeres, hombres, niñas y niños
no puedan o no sepan hacer otra cosa para subsistir, que vender sus cuerpos como
objetos de placer para el otro o la otra, que seres humanos tengan que vender
órganos de sus cuerpos para al menos medio vivir y los compradores tienen con
qué hacerlo, para seguir injusticiando a los primeros;
y acciones de amor surgen para cuidarles, para dignificarlos;
creo en el dios que no puede evitar que por color de la piel, o lugar de nacimiento,
o práctica de religión, o cualquier otra diferencia, unos sean mejores que otros con
todo lo que esto implica;
y acciones de amor surgen con la intención de unirnos;
creo en el dios que no puede evitar la envidia, el odio, la mentira, el egoísmo; y acciones
de amor surgen y hacen una canción que termina diciendo "seamos un tilín mejores
y mucho menos egoístas";
creo en el dios que sabe que solo cuando el ser humano, en uso de su libre albedrío
quiere, desaparece todo lo imposible para dios . . . , porque sin dios, el ser humano
nunca será capaz de amar. Pero aún así, ese dios en quien creo, que es el amor, es
capaz de violar su respeto al libre albedrío, en favor de la paz y la justicia universal.

I believe in the god who above all respects, even to the ultimate consequences, Free Will.
I believe in the god who cannot prevent tsunamis, hurricanes, volcanoes and earth-
quakes, which always seem most likely to afflict the most populous zones on the
planet, and the poorest, where millions die and others lose what little they have;
and that acts of love pour forth on behalf of the damned.
I believe in the god who cannot change that some have more than others, so much so
that some die of hunger and of curable illnesses while others spend on diets based

purely on pleasure and personal taste, or on medical treatments for hypochondria, or on visits to luxurious medical centers;

and that acts of love pour forth on behalf of those suffering from injustice.

I believe in the god who cannot stop wars in which people die who have no stake and who owe no debt to those who kill them first;

and that acts of love pour forth on behalf of those who die and their families.

I believe in the god who could not stop the death of the Nazerene, nor of Gandhi, King, Marti, or Lennon, nor of the poets, the monks, priests, bishops, or pastors, not of any of those who denounce injustice and place themselves on the side of the weak;

and that acts of love pour forth from that spilt blood.

I believe in the god who cannot save the millions of children who are born to die of hunger, and mothers as well, and fathers;

and that acts of love pour forth so that every time there will be fewer who die.

I believe in the god who cannot stop that millions of women, men, boys, and girls cannot, or don't know how to do anything else to survive but to sell their bodies as objects of pleasure for someone else; that human beings have to sell their organs in order to at least half live, and that the buyers of such things have the ability to do so, and can continue to perpetuate an injustice on those who sell;

and that acts of love pour forth to care for them, and to give them dignity.

I believe in the god who cannot stop that, by the color of their skin, or place of birth, or religious practice, or any other difference, some are seen as being better than others;

and that acts of love pour forth to unite us in spite of our differences.

I believe in the god who cannot stop envy, hatred, lies, and selfishness;

and that acts of love pour forth and create a song that ends, saying, "we are a trifle better and much less selfish." *

I believe in the god who knows that only when human beings desire, through the use of our own free will, will all that is impossible become possible . . . because without god, the human being will never be capable of loving.

But even so, that god in whom I believe, who is love, is capable of violating god's own respect for free will, in favor of universal peace and justice.

Es de una canción del cantautor cubano Silvio Rodríguez, que se titula "Cita con ángeles" (It's a song by Cuban singer Silvio Rodriguez, entitled "City with Angels")

—Samuel Francisco Rodriguez Cobrera, Cuba

A SELECTION FROM "THE POSITIVE DIARY" ("IL POSITIVIARO")

(A collection of phrases to live happy each day)

This small diary of positivity will serve to those who have not yet lit the light. With the light everything shines and all is more alive and radiant and you can also see the brightness and beauty of everything, and of any living being. Staying in the dark is not needed. It makes us grow old before others, and before our time.

Stay positive and happy in every moment of your life, and for every moment I mean here and now. Doing so will increase your awareness and will make you awake, active, and involved. "To everyone who wants to be happy and touch the power of Positivity . . . and to YOU, my Universe."

Love

Love is like a medicine. When you are lost, you have to take it! Love is the nourishment of the soul. Love purifies the air of our hearts. You can't see the Love, you can only live it and you will feel it inside. Love is as a wizard . . . . It can transform your life. You can't teach love, it is already within us . . . you only turn it on.

I am grateful. I thank you. I love you. Forgive me if I was wrong. Give me the positive power. (Io) Sono grato. Ti ringrazio. Ti amo. Perdonami se ho sbagliato. Dammi l'energia positiva.

Gratitude

Showing gratitude, for what we are and for all that we have, makes us feel better but, above all, it helps to attract toward us the miracles of life. . . . Gratitude is a way to tell the universe that we also are into it. . . . In gratitude of each day is hidden the miracle that can change your life. It is only with gratitude that we discover we have something more.

I am grateful. I thank you. I love you. Forgive me if I was wrong. Give me the positive power. (Io) Sono grato. Ti ringrazio. Ti amo. Perdonami se ho sbagliato. Dammi l'energia positiva.

Joy

Through joy we express feeling and emotion with which we overcome the enemy of sadness. Joy hasn't color, nor taste and neither smell but the noise that it clatters in our hearts is greater than any war. The joy of a sincere child is similar to the uncontaminated water of a river: even if the sand makes peat in the color, we can just wait a little and its purity will return afloat. Anyone who feeds on joy will be fat of happiness and will not have need of any diet for the soul. If you want to make someone happy . . . just be happy; if you want to make someone envious, show that you are happy with all your joy. The joy of living is like a light in the dark that you have inside, and with that light, you discover that you are a piece of paradise called life. Without you the Universe will not be complete.

I am grateful. I thank you, I love you. Forgive me if I was wrong. Give me the positive power. (Io) Sono grato. Ti ringrazio. Ti amo. Perdonami se ho sbagliato. Dammi l'energia positiva.

Smile

Each time you give a smile to those who need it—you will feed its need of happiness. With a smile you can change, for free, the day of those whom you meet. When you are in silence and alone do not hesitate to smile in your life and of yourself: you will put out the fire of sadness. By using the power of the smile with others, you will put out the larger fire. When you want to attract a thing and a person, act as a child still not speaking: smile! The world will understand.

I am grateful. I thank you. I love you. Forgive me if I was wrong. Give me the positive power. (Io) Sono grato. Ti ringrazio. Ti amo. Perdonami se ho sbagliato. Dammi l'energia positiva.

Opening the Mind

Open your mind toward the infinity of the universe. It will cease the borders of thought and you will unify in total ecstasy. By having an open and receptive mind toward the promptings of the universe, you, your life, and the others will be changed. Open the mind and listen; the universe will talk and the miracle of Life will spread around you. Do not listen to the false beliefs and the unnecessary superstitions. They will shut down the door of infinity and they will guide your mind into the trap of the dark. When you feel lost, close your eyes and imagine a beautiful light and bring it inside of you: when you open your eyes again your mind will open, and you will look the right way.

I am grateful. I thank you. I love you. Forgive me if I was wrong. Give me the positive power. (Io) Sono grato. Ti ringrazio. Ti amo. Perdonami se ho sbagliato. Dammi l'energia positiva.

Thank You!

Always you have to give thanks for what you are and how you are; you will discover the uniqueness of your person. Saying "Thank you" is not an act of kindness but is a ritual to say to the world that something has been done or made. Always give thanks to others and to yourself and you will receive in exchange the gift of energy and positivity. If you give a gift to someone, do not expect in exchange gratitude, or you will fall down in deception of fulfillment. If someone gives you something, always say thanks with sincerity and you will be always aware of your life. To say thanks or be thanked will confirm our existence. "You have to be awake in every moment, here and now, because only in this way you will not fall asleep and you will not lose the spectacle of life."

Conclusion

To conclude this small diary of positivity: When you get up in the morning, when you go to bed, when you are in a queue at the post office, cinema, or supermarket, or when you feel sad or in other cases during the day, even at work, in the bathroom, while you eat or expect someone, you have to repeat always within you this little phrase:

I am grateful. I thank you. I love you. Forgive me if I was wrong. Give me the positive power. (Io) Sono grato. Ti ringrazio. Ti amo. Perdonami se ho sbagliato. Dammi l'energia positiva.

Finally I want you to reflect on a small but very powerful thing:
"There is only one of you; you are unique! No one can be the same, identical, nor could there be a copy, so think and be proud of yourself because this universe needs your uniqueness."

—Nicola Balestri, Italy

FOR THE WAY
THAT STRETCHES
IN FRONT OF US,

WE SAY
THANK YOU.

FOR THE WAY
THAT LIES BEHIND US,

WE SAY
THANK YOU.

FOR THE WAY
THAT WE WILL
BECOME,

WE HOPE WITH
THANKFUL
HEARTS.

—Erice Fairbrother
Aotearoa/New Zealand

6 ❀ Words of Going Forth

Rini Templeton

BENDICIÓN TERNURA DE MADRE/
BENEDICTION OF A MOTHER'S TENDERNESS

Que el Dios de la Vida
sea tu guía en el camino de cada día,
sea tu refugio en momentos de inseguridad,
y sea tu descanso en tiempos de fatiga.
Que el Dios de la Vida,
te fortalezca cuando te sientas débil,
te consuele cuando estés triste,
y te abrace cuando te sientas sola.
Que el Dios de la Vida,
que te quiere y te conoce,
te cubra con su ternura de Madre.
Por siempre.
Amén.

May the God of Life
be your guide on the road every day,
be your refuge in times of uncertainty,
and be your rest in times of fatigue.

May the God of Life
strengthen you when you feel weak,
comfort you when you feel sad,
and hug you when you feel alone.
May the God of Life,
who loves you and knows you,
cover you with the tenderness of a Mother.
Forever.
Amen.

—Gerardo Oberman, Argentina

BENEDICERE

May your home always be too
small to hold all your friends.

May your heart remain ever supple,
fearless in the face of threat,
jubilant in the grip of grace.

Many your hands remain open,
caressing, never clenched,
save to pound the doors of all who
barter justice to the highest bidder.

May your heroes be earthy,
dusty-soled and rumpled,
hallowed but unhaloed,
guiding you through seasons
of tremor and travail, apprenticed
to the godly art of giggling amid
haggard news and portentous circumstance.

May your hankering be
in rhythm with heaven's,

> whose covenant vows a dusty
> intersection with our own:
> when creation's hope and history rhyme.
>
> May hosannas lilt from your lungs:
> God is not done;
> God is not yet done.
>
> All flesh, I am told, will behold;
> will surely behold.

—Kenneth L. Sehested, USA

BENEDICTIONS FROM AOTEAROA/NEW ZEALAND

Community Blessing

You whom God has called,
Keep listening.
You whom Christ has fed,
Live simply.
You whom the Spirit has filled,
Love completely.
And receive the blessing that awaits you. Amen.

Disciples Blessing

God has spoken to you,
Speak well of others.
Christ has fed you,
Feed others.
The Spirit lives in you,
Live for others. Amen.

Genesis One Blessing

The Wisdom who presided at creation watch over you,
she yearns for you;
The Christ who rose with the dawn awaken you,
she calls to you;
The Spirit that came like a flame fire you,
she lives in you. Amen.

Dismissal for Service

ONE: Go now to love and serve.

ALL: Amen. We go in the name of Christ.

Dismissal in Justice and Peace

ONE: Go now to love and serve your neighbour.

ALL: Amen. We go in the name of justice and peace.

Dismissal in Truth

ONE: Go now; let your eyes see, your hearts care and your tongues speak.

ALL: Amen. We go with courage and in truth.

Dismissal in Wonder

ONE: Here there is wonder, astonishment, and more
They are gifts
Together we have experienced them
Take them with you
Give them to everyone you meet.

ALL: Amen. We go taking all we have received to bring new life in the world.

—Erice Fairbrother, Aotearoa/New Zealand

Du Gott,
möge die Kühnheit deines Geistes uns wandeln,
möge die Güte deines Geistes uns leiten,
mögen die Gaben deines Geistes uns zurüsten und in die Welt aussenden,
durch Jesus Christus, deinen Sohn und unseren Bruder.

ALLE: Amen

God,
may the boldness of your Spirit transform us,
may the goodness of your Spirit guide us;
may the gifts of your Spirit prepare us,
as we go out into the world,
through Jesus Christ, your Son, our brother.

ALL: Amen

—Detlev Knoche, Germany

BENEDICTION FOR AN ISLAND PEOPLE

May the love of God surround you like the constant song of the sea.
May the chuckle of little waves encourage you in joy.
May the boom of great breakers remind you of the power of God's love.
May the crisp salt breeze bring you energy and the flying spray fill you with exhilaration.
May the lullaby lapping of calm seas bring you peace.
May the pull of the tides draw you always to the heart of God. Amen

—Beverley L. Osborn, Aotearoa/New Zealand

We pray to you, living God,
continue working in this world,
fulfill what you have begun.
We pray to you, saving God,
incline yourself to us,
so that we might sense the breath of life and freedom.
We pray to you, God of the future,
come and meet us,
with each step that we take.

—Uwe Boch, Germany

SUNG BENEDICTIONS

Dear Saviour, bless us as we go our way:
be with us all until we meet again.
Help us in wisdom and in faith to grow:
your grace, your power,
your boundless love to show,
we pray. Amen. (*Tune: "It Passeth Knowledge"*)

Walk with us, we pray, Lord Jesus,
out into the world again.
Help us care for those who need us:
show us how and where and when.
Help us fill our lives with kindness,
grace and truth and love. Amen. (*Tune: "Regent Square"*)

O Lord, give your blessing on all here today:
may your love surround us forever, we pray.
May your arms enfold us, whenever we fall.
Enlighten, inspire us: O God, bless us all. (*Tune: "St Denio"*)

—Jan Chamberlin, Aotearoa/NewZealand

BENEDICTION AND SENDING FORTH

We dedicate our lives, God of Love.
Send us to serve you, where your love needs to be known.
We open our hearts, Spirit of Life.
Take us where life needs to be announced, recreated and shared.
We offer to you, God of the way, the Camino,
our feet and our hands.
Lead us to new paths, mature hope,
full of dreams and visions,
that we may enjoy the company
and the encounter with others.
We pray, God of Love, Life, and new trails,
that you sustain us with your blessing,
and renew us with your strength,
that you encourage us with your presence,
and embrace us with your grace,
today and every day, forever. Amen.

—Gerardo Oberman, Argentina

It is God who shapes us; we just wait in silence in the presence of God, and God will do all things in our life in due season.

—Ruan Enrong (Peter), China

WE OFFER TO YOU,
GOD OF THE WAY,
THE CAMINO,

OUR FEET
AND
OUR HANDS.

—Gerardo Oberman
Argentina

YA RAB MUBAREK KIL/
GRANT BLESSINGS, O GOD

Ya Rab mubarek kil
Sinirim genislet
Elin benimle olsun
Beni serden korusun

Ya Rab mubarek kil
Yollarim genislet
Ruhun benimle olsun
Beni serden korusun

Grant blessings, O God.
Expand my limits;
May your hand be with me;
May it shield me from evil.

Grant blessings, O God.
Widen my paths;
May your spirit be with me;
May it shield me from evil.

*(An original hymn from the pastor of the
Istanbul Presbyterian Church in Turkey, it is in
the musical tradition of the mystics of Anatolia.
As such, its style is familiar to several
subcultures of today's Turkey.)*

—Turgay Ucal, Turkey

ONE: Where are we going?

ALL: Where Christ leads us.

ONE: That sounds kind of vague.

ALL: We're going to Alouette Lake's still waters and the Pacific's raging storms.
We're going to Stanley Park's dreams and the Downtown Eastside's nightmares.
We're going where Christ leads us.

ONE: *That* sounds kind of frightening.

ALL: Sometimes it is.
Sometimes it's overwhelming and wonderful.
And the most wonderful thing of all—

ONE: Yes?

ALL: No matter where we go,
no matter what we do—
     Christ is with us.
     Christ is with all.
We are not alone!

ONE: Alleluia!

ALL: Alleluia!

—Richard Bott, (Vancouver) Canada

Lord God, we thank you for calling us into the company
of those who trust in Christ and seek to do his will.
May your Spirit guide and strengthen us
in mission and service to your world,
for we are strangers no longer but pilgrims together
on the way to your Kingdom. Amen.

—The Swanwick Declaration, England

TWO BLESSINGS

Blessing at New Year

God's love to you now and always.
God's love to you each and every moment of this year. Amen

Blessing for Trinity Sunday

Hear us our God of threeness and oneness
Hold us in the breadth of your parental wisdom
Love us in the love of the living, dying, rising Christ
Enfold us in your empowering, sustaining Spirit
This day, this week, and always. Amen

—Elaine E Bolitho, New Zealand (*member of Parish Council and of
the Worship and Education team at Ngaio Union Church, Wellington*)

BENEDICTION IN A TRINITY OF BIRDS

As the whirr of unseen wings tell us of the flight of the *keruru**, may the blessings that
surround us speak of God's love.

As the call of the *morepork** sounds in the loneliness of the night, may we recognise the
companionship of the Christ in our dark times.

As the song of the *tui** peals melody to hills and sky and bush, may your joyous spirit
sing through us into the world around us.

Amen

**keruru = Maori word for a bird also called the New Zealand Pigeon; morepork = Maori word
for a small brown owl also called the Southern Boobook; tui = Maori name for honeyeater bird with
two voiceboxes, which can, like a parrot, imitate human speech)*

—Beverley L. Osborn, Aotearoa/New Zealand

YOU WHOM GOD HAS CALLED,
KEEP LISTENING.

YOU WHOM CHRIST HAS FED,
LIVE SIMPLY.

YOU WHOM THE SPIRIT
HAS FILLED,
LOVE COMPLETELY.

AND RECEIVE THE BLESSING
THAT AWAITS YOU.

—Erice Fairbrother
Aotearoa/New Zealand

7 ❀ PERSONAL PRAYER PRACTICES

A PRAYER WITH MOVEMENT

(Begin the movement prayer by standing together in a circle. Practise the movements first, then say the prayer all together.)
God, you ask us to love one another *(arms stretched out, palms up, into centre of circle)*
as much as we love ourselves. *(cross hands over own heart)*
Sometimes we forget who is our neighbour, *(turn around so now facing outwards)*
And we forget about loving. *(fold arms tightly, bow head down)*
Help us to love one another as much as we love ourselves *(turn around, join hands)*
and as much as you love us. *(lift arms up high, keeping hands joined)* Amen.

—Alyson Huntly, Canada

THE HANDS OF PRAYER

"I will lift up my hands and call on your name." (Psalm 63)

How do you use your body in prayer? Life in Turkey provides many answers.

The dominant Muslim practice incorporates various postures for the ritual of prayer: standing, bowing, and prostrating. The several Christian groups use their hands and arms.

But whatever your religious background in Turkey, there is a posture for prayer recognized by all: arms bent to front at the elbows, with palms facing upward. This is the iconic stance of petitioning, praising, or thanking God. It's as though the hands are held out to receive God's blessing. It's a biblical posture. You'll find it not only in the Psalms but also in the early Christian church (1 Timothy 2:8). This prayer position is as recognizable to everyone in Turkey as Albrecht Durer's image "Praying Hands" is iconic among European Christians.

Muslims in Turkey normally conclude the prayer by moving the open palms up to cover the face and then drawing them straight down, as if washing the face with the prayer. In Syrian Orthodox worship people often exit the praying stance by touching the fingertips of both hands to their lips and forehead. So if a prayer has been said, or a scripture passage read, this "Amen" movement of the hands seals the words into your mouth and mind.

PRAYER: O God we lift up our hands to you, the author of our lives. We spread our hands toward heaven to plead for your mercy. We hold out our arms in need of your support. All good things that you have granted we gratefully clasp within our bodies, minds, and souls. Amen.

—Kenneth Frank and Elizabeth W. Frank, Istanbul, Turkey

PRAYER FOR MIDDAY

Wir beten:
Gott, in der Mitte des Tages
sammeln wir unsere Gedanken.
Wir denken an dich.
Wenn wir Hunger haben
auf halbem Weg,
bist du da
und stärkst uns.
Auf den Durststrecken mitten am Tag bist du da,
erfrischst uns
und trägst uns weiter.
Wir legen dir die Menschen ans Herz, die uns lieb sind.
Sei mit ihnen.
Sei mit allen, denen etwas fehlt. Amen!

Let's pray:
God, in the middle of the day
we gather our thoughts.
We think of you.
When we become weary
halfway through the day,
you are there
to strengthen us.
When we are filled with longing
in the midst of our tasks,
you are there to refresh us
and carry us on.
We bring our loved ones before you. Be with them.
Be with all those who are in need. Amen!

—Detlev Knoche, Germany

I PRAY SHALOM
FOR YOU
THAT YOU WAKE
EACH DAY
EAGER TO MEET
WHATEVER
COMES.

—Isobel De Gruchy
Cape Town, South Africa

FOUR DIRECTIONS PRAYER (participants stand facing in the direction of the prayer, starting in the East and ending in the North)

Creator God, we look to the East where the day begins. We give thanks for the rising sun that warms, nourishes, and brings life. We thank you for children, precious gifts of your Spirit. We are grateful for the responsibility you give us for their care.

Creator God, we look to the South where the waters of the Great Lakes flow. We thank you for water, life sustainer. We pray for those who protect our water. We thank you for our youth, who challenge and enliven us. We are grateful for the responsibility you give us for their care.

Creator God, we look to the West where the sun sets and night begins—the time of resting and renewal. We thank you for our adults who work to provide for others, build homes, create industry, and nurture families. We are grateful for the responsibility you give us to respect and care for them.

Creator God, we look to the North, the white country, where in the long evenings of winter we dream dreams and see visions that transform us. We thank you for our elders, whose wisdom, knowledge, and laughter sustain us all through our life's journey. We are grateful for the responsibility you give us for their care.

Creator God, you are powerful in this circle of life. Accept our gratitude and thanksgiving we pray,

in the name of the One who showed us the kingdom,

so that we may embrace each other without shame or glory,

so that we may look upon our errors with regret and seek forgiveness,

so that we may move forward in hope of new life in you. Amen

—Pat Rodgers, Canada

I PRAY SHALOM FOR YOU

I pray shalom for you—
That you wake each day eager to meet whatever comes,
That you look in the mirror and are pleased with what you see,
That you accept with courage any limitations on your abilities,
That you accept with humility, but develop creatively, your special talents,
That you know which things take priority,
That you are not stressed by having to set some things aside,
That what you do illuminates who you are,
and that you find joy in all you do.
I pray shalom for you—

That your face is turned towards God,
That you are secure in the forgiveness of Christ,
That your life is infused with the presence of the Holy Spirit,
That your whole being is daily transformed and integrated into oneness with Christ,
        And hence wholeness and wellness,
That in having died to self you are alive to your true self,
That love is your prime motivation.
I pray shalom for you—
That you have a soul-friend to walk life's journey with you,
That you are surrounded by a community of support,
That you are a builder of community,
That you are able to transform difficult or destructive relationships through love,
That you may live in a society of justice, peace, and harmony,
But if not, that you may be able to absorb whatever suffering comes your way,
        And transform it, for yourself and for society.
I pray shalom for you—
That the beauty of God's creation enthralls you,
That your love and way of life enhance that beauty and do not deplete
    the resources of the earth,
That the rhythm of your life may be in harmony
        With the rhythm of other's lives and of all creation,
        To be part of God's plan of restoration and renewal.
I pray shalom for you—
That your faith may grow,
That you be filled with love,
And that hope never dies.

—Isobel de Gruchy, South Africa

Jesus and the Samaritan Women   He Qi

8 ❀ Healing and Reconciliation

MY PRAYER AS ONE LIVING WITH PARKINSON'S DISEASE

My legs and my hands may be shaky,
　　But may my courage and my faith be firm.
My muscles may become stiff and hard to move,
　　But may my mind not become inflexible, nor my heart unmoved.
I might lose my balance,
　　But may I continue to be balanced in outlook and personality.
My hand-writing may become small and squiggly,
　　But may I never become small- or woolly- minded.
My face may take on a deadpan look,
But may I always be able to express joy, love, and peace.
My movements may become slower and slower,
　　And may I also become slow to get irritated and lose my cool.
My voice may become very soft and croaky,
But may I not give up on communicating with others.

—Isobel de Gruchy, South Africa

COMPROMISO SHALOM/ SHALOM COMMITMENT

The following is the commitment prayer that we all say together at the Shalom Center/Centro Shalom of the Pentecostal Church of Chile to seal our community covenant. We use the words for peace in English (peace), Spanish (Paz), Hebrew (Shalom), and Guarani (Py'aguapy), each with their special cultural view and context of peace. The Guarani word (Guaraní is the language of Paraguay) literally means "tranquil stomach." Think of the first place one feels the lack of peace! It is also a word that points to justice and community: when all of us are well fed and our stomachs are at ease, then we know peace.

Paz, peace, py'aguapy.
Me comprometo, Señor, a buscar:
    La sanidad de mi relación contigo.
    La sanidad de mi relación conmigo misma.
    La sanidad de mi relación con otros.
    La sanidad de mi relación con toda tu creación.
¡SHALOM!
Paz, peace, py'aguapy.
I commit, Lord, to searching for:
    The healing of my relationship with you.
    The healing of my relationship with myself.
    The healing of my relationship with others.
    The healing of my relationship with all your creation.
¡SHALOM!

—Elena Huegel, Chile

PRAYER FOR CHANGED PHYSICAL CONDITIONS

Oh, God, my get up and go seems to have got up and gone.
Strengthen, I pray, my weak hands, make firm my feeble knees, and make strong my fearful
    heart for what I need to accomplish.
And grant me the grace to accept help where it is necessary in such a way that my gratitude
    is a gift to my helpers. Amen.

—Beverley L. Osborn, Aotearoa, New Zealand

A HEALING STORY

We thought we went to Nicaragua to build houses and get to know about the country and people. We discovered God had a lot more in store for us. We built the better part of three houses and had fun exploring the countryside: swimming on white sand beaches, horseback riding, and boating on the lake. We made friends at the work sites, sharing simple feasts of freshly caught fish. In the end we learned a lesson of humility concerning how God can use each of us in powerful and unexpected ways.

The presence of our mission team gave the local pastor an opportunity to hold a revival. We provided preaching and special music—a little intimidating for members of our group. Four days into our stay, I was approached by a middle-aged man. With the help of the interpreter his story unfolded. The night before, a member of our group had preached about the power of Christ demonstrated by the raising of Lazarus. This man came to believe through the revival and observing us taking time as a group each morning to pray that our group was truly filled with God's Spirit. He wanted us to pray over Carlos, his son, who had epilepsy.

No one in the group had participated in a service like this before, but we took it very seriously. We sang. We prayed. We read the scripture from James that tells us to anoint with oil those who need healing. We asked Carlos to come forward and be anointed with the only oil we had access to: the cooking oil from the community kitchen. Then to my surprise one of the members of our own group stepped forward and asked to be anointed as well. As the team leader I was aware that this person had epilepsy too, but few of the other members were aware of this.

We anointed two people whose lives were worlds apart but at the same time united by a bond few would desire. They both knelt, while the other members of the team and the boy's family laid hands on them, as we prayed fervently for God's healing to touch them. The bond the two shared provided them with the knowledge that they were not alone with their malady, which was a form of healing by itself, even if nothing else occurred.

PRAYER: (Psalm 133) God, heal us and make us healers. Anoint us with the oil of kindred spirit across all our differences. Amen.

—Janice L. Burns-Watson USA, Nicaragua

Mis Manos están dispuestas, Señor　　　　　Elena Huegel

FOR A HEALING SERVICE OF THE ORDER OF ST. LUKE, IN MULGRAVE, VICTORIA, AUSTRALIA

ONE: Gracious God, loving parent, you watch over us like a mother with her children. You have created a world for us with a richness, a beauty that beggars description. As another spring blossoms around us we are awed again by the splendour of the renewal of life. The trees leaf out, the cups of the daffodils reach up to the sky in supplication, the wisteria is heavy with blossoms and heavenly with a heady aroma. Make our hearts to bloom like the spring, with all the richness of the newness of life that you have created for us. Lord, in your mercy . . .

ALL: Hear our prayer.

ONE: Holy Spirit, you blow like the wind. Where you come from and where you are going, we know not, and yet we know that you are always with us, as near to us as our hands and the very air we breathe. We pause this afternoon to sense your presence, to remember your mighty power and your meek gentleness. You are slow to anger and quick to forgive. We are grateful, thankful for your mercy, for we are not perfect people. We have failed to do things we should have done, and we have done things which we should not have done. Forgive us our sins and help us to forgive others. Let us not harbour grudges, for with grudges in port there is no shelter from the storm of resentments which tear at our souls. Lord, in your mercy . . .

ALL: Hear our prayer.

ONE: O Prince of peace, we pray for peace this afternoon. We pray for peace in our world. Not just the peace of no warfare, but the peace, the shalom, the salaam, that is peace with justice for all people. We pray for a world where children get the food and health care they need. We pray for a world where resources are shared equitably with all. We pray for a world where our swords are beaten into plowshares, a place where war is studied no more. Lord, in your mercy . . .

ALL: Hear our prayer.

ONE: We pray for our country. May our land be one that is free and fair. May this be a country where we remember all who have gone before us. May we respect its indigenous people, flora, and fauna. May we be good stewards of this sun-burnt land that we call home. Lord, in your mercy . . .

ALL: Hear our prayer.

ONE: We pray for our communities. May we be good neighbours. May we open our hearts to those around us in need of a helping hand, an encouraging word, a pat on the back. Lord, in the silence of this moment we lift to you the prayers of peace weighing upon our individual hearts. Lord, in your mercy . . .

ALL: Hear our prayer.

ONE: This afternoon we close with these words of challenge to all of us in the words of St. Francis:

ALL: Lord, make us instruments of your peace. Where there is hatred let us sow love; where there is injury, pardon; where there is discord, union; where there is doubt, faith; where there is despair, hope; where there is darkness, light; where there is sadness, joy. Grant that we may not so much seek to be consoled as to console; to be understood as to understand; to be loved as to love. For it is in giving that we receive; it is in pardoning that we are pardoned; and it is in dying that we are born to eternal life. In Christ's name we pray. Amen!

—Theodore Gobledale, USA, Australia

9 ❁ EVENING . . . VESPERS

Sleeping Elijah   He Qi

Dear God, open my heart,
Fill me with your spirit,
Holy Spirit, come upon me now!

Dear God, open my heart,
Fill me with your wisdom,
Holy Spirit, forgive me with your grace!

Dear God, open my heart,
Fill me with your love,
Holy Spirit, transform me into wholeness!

(repeat several times with a loud voice)

—Jae Hyung Cho, Korea

In the silence of the departing day,
we seek your presence, O God.
We come to give you thanks
for your care and your companionship.
And also to beg your forgiveness
for those things still left undone, for our mistakes,
and for the pain we've caused our fellow beings.
We beg you that, at the end of this workday,
you calm the waves of our anxiety
and permit us the repose
that both body and soul require.
We have moved along on the road,
we have exerted ourselves on the march,
and now we need you
to quench our thirst,
to feed our spirit,
to nourish our life,
to sustain our faith,
to show us a place of rest.
Tomorrow the new day will bring
new challenges.
We ask you, God, to wait for us there,
so that we may walk with you on the path
and not lose the way;
so that we may seek, by your hand,
the dawn of justice,
the sun of solidarity,
the joy of human encounters,
a horizon of plenty,
the life of truth.
May the gentle breath of your spirit
watch over our sleep
and may you invite us, tomorrow,
to serve, to follow you and to love you
in everything and in everyone.

—Gerardo Oberman, Argentina

ONE: In all times and all places, your name, O God, is echoed far.

ALL: Holy is your name.

ONE: In many sounds and in many languages, your name, O God, is echoed far.

ALL: Holy is your name.

ONE: In sorrow and in delight, in despair and in hope, your name, O God, is echoed far.

ALL: Holy is your name.

ONE: In darkness and in light, your name, O God, is echoed far.

ALL: Holy is your name.

ONE: As the night draws near and we prepare for rest, your name, O God, is echoed far.

ALL: Holy is your name.

ONE: In silence, and in stillness, we bring ourselves into the presence of the Holy one. *(silence)* Your name, O God, is echoed far.

ALL: Holy is your name.

ONE: May our thoughts, our words, and all that we do with our lives be an acceptable and living sacrifice to the one whose name is echoed far. Amen.

—Lynne Frith, Aotearoa/New Zealand

Part Two

OUR HANDS LIFT UP

Celebrations of Seasons and Days

10 ❀ ADVENT, CHRISTMAS, AND EPIPHANY

AN ADVENT PSALM

Blessed is the God of Heaven and Earth
who gives us the bread of hope
when we are in despair.

For too long we have been lulled to sleep,
our senses numb from fears of war,
terrorism, pestilence, scarcity,
global warming, danger lurking everywhere,
on every newscast, on every TV screen
and radio call-in show.

Sleepers awake. Look around and see. God
is doing a new thing like a spider's web woven in the dark,
coaxing out the best in us, calling forth people in our midst to manifest
the courage to lead, being the change we seek, showing us

through small victory after small victory
the wisdom of compassion
the strength of listening
the joy of practicing respect
the valiance of peace
the blessing of mercy.

The day is coming
as a child being born in Bethlehem,
bringing to birth a new era, a new dawn.

All you who walk in the land, have faith and live in hope.
O taste and see that our God is good. Give thanks and praise
to God who leads us on with stars and angels and carol song.

O Blessed is the God of Heaven and Earth.

—Ray McGinnis, Canada

COME EMMANUEL—AN ADVENT PRAYER FOR AFRICA

May be used in conjunction with the hymn, "O Come, O Come Emmanuel"
May be read by a single voice, responsively, or antiphonally

"How long, O Lord?"
"How long?" they ask in Africa.
In camps where homeless hungry wait,
in towns where rebels rape and loot,
in fields where women pull the plows
designed for oxen dead of thirst,
in queues where many wait long hours
to see uncaring bureaucrats,
in streets where congregate young men
for whom a job's a distant dream,
in chanceries where clerks add up
the debts owed nations far away—
"How long?" they ask in Africa.

In ancient days the prophets gave
to such a query harsh reply:
"Till cities crumble, mighty fall,
till millions die of hunger, plague,
and all the land lies desolate."
Is that the word for Africa?

"O Come, Emmanuel," we respond.
"O come, O Shoot of Jesse, come."
Sprouting Branch, shooting out
from a stump we took for dead,
grow tall and strong, branches spread
to shelter all who seek repose.

"O Come, O Key of David, come."
Key to every door that's closed
against the quest for fullest life,
open wide those portals grim
and free the captives waiting long.

"O Come, O Dayspring, come."
Morning Star, eternal Light,
rise wherever darkness reigns.
Let day break upon the foes
of peace, the purveyors of pain.

"O Come, O come Emmanuel."
Come, lift the weight of weariness.
Bring in the awaited age of hope.
Set all free to sing your praise,
to offer service all our days.

How long? Not long.
Emmanuel is come to us, to Africa.

—Allen Myrick, USA, South Africa, Zimbabwe

ADVIENTO DE PAZ/ADVENT OF PEACE

Adviento de paz y esperanza,
luz de armonía y plenitud,
Vida que anuncia vida,
acompáñanos en nuestro trabajo hoy y cada día.
Tierno brote de nuevas ilusiones,
semilla de eternidad,
sabia de infinita sabiduría,
nutre nuestros pensamientos, afirma nuestras decisiones.
Sol de justicia y de gracia,
calida llama de perdón,
transparente mirada de misericordia,
envuélvenos con la seguridad de tu presencia.
Anuncio de buenas noticias,
Evangelio de perdón,
Palabra que crea y que sana,
háblanos al corazón, afirma nuestra fe.

Dios con nosotros y nosotras,
Padre y Madre desde el comienzo hasta el final,
promesa, realidad, alfa y omega,
abrázanos con tu bendición y danos tu paz.

Advent of peace and hope,
light of harmony and abundance,
Life that proclaims life,
accompany us in our work today and every day.
Tender bud of new dreams,
seed of eternity,
sage of infinite wisdom,
nourish our thoughts, affirm our decisions.
Sun of justice and of grace,
warm flame of forgiveness,
clear gaze of mercy,
wrap us in the security of your presence.
Announcement of good news,
Evangelist of pardon,
Word that creates and restores,
speak to our hearts, affirm our faith.
God with us,
Father and Mother from the beginning to the end,
promise, reality, alpha and omega,
embrace us with your blessing and give us your peace.

—Gerardo Oberman, Argentina

Texto utilizado en el devociónal de apertura del encuentro preparatorio de la Vida Espiritual de la Convocatoria Ecuménica Internacional por la Paz, en Jamaica, Mayo de 2011 (Text used in the opening devotional of the preparatory meeting of the Spiritual Life of the International Ecumenical Peace Convocation, Jamaica, May 2011)

NO ONE KNOWS MY NAME

I am the girl whom no one's heard of,
no one remembers, no one cares,
no one even knows my name.
Could it be that I never lived?
Yet that far-off day seems more real
now than many another.

Early spring light, soft and pink on the shutters,
was suddenly shadowed by the imposing form
of a stranger tall and serious.
"Greetings—the Lord is with you."
And seeing I trembled,
"Do not be afraid,
I have a message for you,
you will bear a son and he will inherit
his father David's throne."

The Visitation   He Qi

I stood still as a statue,
while my thoughts
whirled and jangled.
I was not married.
I was too young. It must be a joke?
Who was this man anyway?
Was I really hearing this word,
or imagining it?
He stood waiting
and I cried out, "Oh, no,
I'm not the one, don't ask me!
there must be someone else."
The light in his eyes dimmed
not of vision surely,
but of deep sorrow.

You know, don't you, where he went?
And that is why no one knows my name.

—Isobel de Gruchy, South Africa

TWO WOMEN SPEAK AT CHRISTMAS

The following meditations give imaginative voice to two women who must have been there. . . . Step back from the familiar traditions, consider other possibilities, and open your hearts and minds to receive Christ afresh.

WORSHIP LEADER: We have walked with the women who witnessed the beginnings of the Christmas story.

We open ourselves to new possibilities.

Let us pray together:

ALL: Birthing God, bringer of joy, hope, love, and new beginnings, keep our imaginations active and our hearts generous. Help us to meet this Christmas with deeper appreciation of all that Christmas means. Keep us mindful that the work of Christmas is never done. We offer ourselves as Christmas people. Amen

WOMAN TRAVELER (Luke 2:1–5): Jolly silly idea if you ask me—having to travel to the town where your husband was born just to be counted. Why couldn't they count you where you are living now? You could say which tribe you are from. However, it's not every day we get to go on a journey. We are going on a holiday, I told the girls. You are going to see your grandparents.

It was no small task organizing everything. I turned the children's bedrolls into bags to wear on their backs with spare clothes tucked inside. Luckily mine are old enough to walk. Martha's son is heavy for a three-year-old. She made a sling to carry him in. Her Tim took him on his back at times. It was the girl, Mary, I felt sorry for, she was almost due. Joseph made her a stout walking stick. What she needed was a donkey, but landless people don't have donkeys.

We got quite friendly on the way. Well you do, don't you, all traveling together. She was such a pleasant person. My girls just loved her. She wasn't worried about the birth. Said the baby would come in God's good time. Easy to tell it was her first, but far be it from me to scare a young woman. I'd helped deliver Martha's son; now that was a difficult birth, such a big baby. She's lucky to have him, the first two didn't go full time, stillborn, both of them.

When we arrived at Bethlehem the place was fair humming and quite booked out. Of course we were going to Tim's parents. Martha and Saul had family too, but Joseph's parents had died. They intended staying at an inn. Every inn we passed had a no vacancy sign up. Mary told us not to worry. She was a calm one, that Mary—in my opinion, a woman of faith.

INNKEEPER'S WIFE (Luke 2:6–14): What a night! We were chocker! Not a bed anywhere. Not so much as a blanket to spare. The guests were all calling for ale. I was run off my feet. Not that I minded. This census thing is certainly good for business. It's not often Quirinius does anything useful.

Anyway, Dan had barred the door but people kept knocking. When someone pounded with a stick Dan unbolted the door with a curse. It was lucky I was nearby because I saw these travelers. The man was supporting a young woman. She was heavily pregnant. Dan was in no mood to give directions but I couldn't just shut the door on a pregnant woman. I moved over to tell them about the Three Mile Inn, being on the far side of town it was always last to fill. Then I saw the woman clutch her husband. She was more than merely pregnant.

I took charge. Got Dan to move a couple of horses out of the stable and tether them 'round the back. Sent the boy to open a fresh bale of hay. We made a reasonable bed. I asked among the guests for a midwife and sure enough there was one. I gave her a lantern.

It wasn't very dark considering it was midwinter. Strange really as the moon was only a slender crescent. The light was coming from a star. I'd never seen this star before. But, as you know, I was busy. When finally all the guests had bedded down I checked the window for another look at that star and I'll swear to my dying day that the whole sky lit up, bright as day it was, and I heard music! A moment later the midwife came in wanting more hot water. I blurted out, "The child's been born!" "It's a boy," she said.

I took them some breakfast late in the morning. The couple were so gracious in their thanks. Lovely people. Her name was Mary. You'd never guess where the baby was sleeping.

—Rosalie May Sugrue, Aotearoa/New Zealand

BENDICIÓN DEL OTRO MUNDO POSIBLE/BLESSING FROM ANOTHER POSSIBLE WORLD

Que cada día: Dios te acune en sus brazos.
Que Su voz tierna te arrulle, y que en el día y la noche, guíe tú caminar.
Que el Jesús del Pesebre, solidario y humilde,
nos siga dando esperanza y consuelo.
Que el Espíritu de amor, de vida y paz, nos siga levantando y animando.
Que sigamos viviendo la vida junto a Dios, por que así, la vida tiene sentido, pasión,
valor, justicia, perdón y dignidad.
Porque otro mundo es posible, porque hay buena vida,
porque ya es tiempo de compartirla.
Y porque, con todo esto, podemos dar vuelta a la historia.

That every day: God may cradle you in his arms. That God's tender voice lull you to sleep, and that day and night God may guide your way.
That the Jesus of the manger, humble and alone,
may continue giving us hope and consolation.
May the spirit of love, of life and peace, continue raising us up and giving us life.
May we continue living life at God's side, because this way life has meaning, passion,
courage, justice, forgiveness, and dignity.
Because another world is possible, because there is a good life,
because now is the time to share it.
And because, in doing all this, we can turn the course of history.

—Joel Eli Padron Ibanez, Church of Peniel, Mexico

Based on phrases of songs by Gerardo Oberman, Argentina

THAT EVERY DAY:
GOD MAY CRADLE YOU
IN GENTLE ARMS,

THAT JESUS OF THE
MANGER,
HUMBLE AND ALONE,

MAY CONTINUE GIVING US
HOPE

AND CONSOLATION.

—Joel Eli Padron Ibanzes
Mexico

TWO CHRISTMAS PRAYERS FROM INDIA

1. Lord, it is Christmas,
and I have traced my way
to a manger
by the light of a beam
from a teardrop,
of a new born child
crying
for love,
for peace,
in a war-torn
broken world,
filled
with greed and lawlessness,
with violence and destruction,
draping
this beautiful earth
in clouds
of despair,
of disunity.

Lord,
this Christmas,
Give us
new hope and strength,
new meaning and power
to Change
with love,
with understanding,
to face challenges
with courage
believing that
a life centered in Thee
will never fail
to build a world
of Peace
of Brotherhood
of Love.
The Love that was born at Christmas. Amen.

2. Lord, It is Christmas,
and my shattered mind
wings its flight,
through flames of terror and injustice
through clouds of poverty and ignorance
through cries of pain and suffering,
searching for life
in the debris of human forms
destroyed
    by deathblows of destructive technology,
    by furies of nature,
    by human unkindness.
And my down-trodden spirit
struggles to soar to mystic groves of Hope,
    to star speckled skies
    of my deathless dreams
    for Faith
    for Love
to the straw-lined cradle
with its gift at Christmas
of a new life,
in this new era of untold challenges.

Lord,
rekindle in us the dying embers of Faith
with the power
    of the Incarnation
    of the Cross
    of the Resurrection
to rebuild our broken world
with friendship and laughter
with music and dance
with your Life-giving Spirit,
to weave all creation
and all nations
in your garland
of changeless Love. Amen.

—Savithri Devanesen, India

CHRISTMAS BENEDICTION

Go with us, Lord, throughout this Christmas tide:
be our protector, brother, friend, and guide.
Give us your peace and keep us in your care:
help us your love and grace with all to share.

(May be sung to tune "Eventide")

—Jan Chamberlin, Aotearoa/New Zealand

EPIPHANY CALL TO WORSHIP

ONE: Look to the East! What do you see?

ALL: A wall.

ONE: (shaking head) Sometimes you're just too literal!
Look *through* the wall. What do you see?

ALL: Our communities—Maple Ridge, New Westminster, Vancouver—
children, women, men, living in this place.

ONE: Look farther.

ALL: Our country—provinces bound by land,
provinces bordered by water.

ONE: Look farther!

ALL: A great ocean.
People and places of all lands and races!

ONE: Look farther!
If you look far enough, right around the globe, you see—

ALL: Ourselves!
Christ's people in *this* place,
gathered to worship God.

ONE: All of creation—the high mountains, the deep waters—and beyond,
joyfully singing, as Epiphany fills our lives.

ALL: Joyfully singing, as God touches our souls.

ONE: Joyfully singing—

ALL: as we worship God!   Alleluia!

—Richard Bott, Canada

CHRISTMAS SERVICE (PERAYAAN NATAL)
Prayer of Dedication (Doa Persembahan)

MAGI I (MAJUS I): O Baby Jesus, with this gold I give my thanks to you. Joy/sadness, laughter/crying, success/failure are "gold"—valuable experiences in my life. Please receive my life as my offering to you.

(Ya Bay Yesus, dengan emas ini kupersembahkan syukurku kepadamu. Suka/duka, tawa/tangis, keberhasilan/kegagalan adalah "emas"—pengalaman/pengalaman yang berharga bagi hidupku).

ALL (J): Take our life as our gold of offering to you, O Lord.

(Terimalah kehidupan ini sebagai sebagai persembahan emas kami untukMu, ya Tuhan)

MAGI II (MAJUS II): O Baby Jesus, with this incense I give my thanks to you. My story of life: the failure and the success that come and go are the incense that smelled beautifully in my life. So take my incense of life, O Lord!

(O Bayi Yesus, dengan kemenyan ini kupersembahkan hidupku. Cerita kehidupanku: kejatuhan dan sukses yang silih berganti adalah kemenyan yang harum bagi hidupku. Terimalah kemenyan kehidupanku ini, ya Tuhan!).

ALL (J): Take our life as our incense of offering to you, O Lord.

(Terimalah kehidupan ini sebagai persembahan kemenyan kami untukMu ya Tuhan).

MAGI III (MAJUS III): O Baby Jesus, with this myrrh I give thanks to you, O Lord. When I was weak, you strengthened me; when I fell, you came and picked me up. Your love and care are the myrrh that healed my wounds of life.

(O Bayi Yesus, dengan mur ini kupersembahkan syukurku kepadaMu, ya Tuhan. Ketika aku lemah, Engkau menguatkanku; ketika aku jatuh, engkau datung menggendongku. Cinta dan kepedulianMu adalah mur yang menyembuhkan setiap luka hidupku).

ALL (J): Take our life as our myrrh of offering to you, O Lord

(Terimalah kehidupan ini sebagai persembahan mur kami untukMu, ya Tuhan).

—Sandra Pontoh, Indonesia

11 ❊ LENT, HOLY WEEK, AND EASTER

Supper at Emmaus   He Qi

ONE: Let us pray

As we start on our Lenten journey we remember travellers:.

Those who are travelling by choice: for work, to see friends and family, to experience
    new cultures and see the world,

Those who are forced to travel: to leave their homes because of fire or flood or war,

Those who must leave their countries due to fear of violence and who hope to resettle
    in another country.

For all travellers, we ask your blessing.

ALL: Lord, give them strength for the journey.

ONE: As we start on our Lenten journey we remember travellers.

Those whose journey involves giving something up in order to deepen
    their relationship with you,

Those on a journey away from self-destructive habits such as dependence
    on cigarettes, alcohol, or drugs,

Those who haven't chosen to give things up but have had them taken away from them:
    their belongings, their homes, their freedom.

For all travellers, we ask your blessing.

ALL: Lord, give them strength for the journey.

—Penny Guy, Aotearoa/New Zealand

HOSANNA!

¹We join the crowd, who, on this day,
sang praise to Christ along the way;
their theme renewed we gladly sing:
Hosanna to the Lord, our King!

²Yet, when the homage has been paid
and all the acclamations fade,
may we be found with Jesus still
beneath his cross on Calvary's hill,

³Keep watch with him through all his shame,
the taunts, the insults and the blame,
his lonely agony, his doubt,
his brokenness, his life poured out.

⁴Then come with wonderment to see
how great his love for you and me:
he takes the vicious cross of wood,
and turns its evil to our good.

⁵Henceforth no darkness, no despair,
but light from Christ is shining there:
the precious Passion of the Lord
brings hope renewed and joy restored.

⁶Accepting all his love will give,
for him and others let us live,
and come prepared to sing and pray,
with greater cause, on Easter Day.

L.M., sung to tune "Agincourt" or "Tallis Canon"

—Norman J. Goreham, Aotearoa/New Zealand

PALM SUNDAY SERMON BY A CONFIRMAND—THE DONKEY

Donkeys are known as lazy animals. You can expect to see them in a field probably eating grass and napping. I think this particular donkey in this story was chosen by Jesus himself. Out of thousands of donkeys that special one was chosen. Wow, I want to be that donkey. That donkey went from being in a field to being ridden by Jesus through a crowd of people.

I think of myself as a donkey sometimes. I can be lazy and stubborn, like when it's Sunday and I have to wake up to get ready for church. I'd rather stay in bed sleeping. I think some youth in our world today would rather be out with their friends than sitting in church. They probably think that learning about church is pointless and sometimes stupid; others think that kids who go to church are stupid for going.

I want to be like the donkey mentioned in that passage. I want to be the donkey that Jesus picked. I want to give myself to good and not just attend church but be more included in this ministry. I mean—wouldn't you feel special if you were chosen by Jesus himself? I definitely would be ecstatic.

—Virginia Risakotta, Indonesia, USA

READING FOR PALM SUNDAY

(While it is being read, carry in, very slowly, a candle,
which symbolizes the presence of Jesus in the midst of the people.)
Lord, we greet your presence in our midst,
as on that day when you entered,
riding a borrowed donkey,
into that city in which you were acclaimed and hated,
received and rejected, praised and insulted.
We raise our hands to heaven,
as a sign of gratitude, in the same way that, on that other day,
many placed their own clothes on the road
and waved palms as you passed
to welcome you,
to express their joy,
to show their hope . . .
Each extended arm
was a symbol of freedom,
a desire for peace,
the dream of a better tomorrow,
a desire for peace.
And each shout raised up to the heavens
contained the longings of generations
of men and women
injured by injustice
and wounded by scorn.
Today we,
each from our own situations
of pain or disillusion,

or sadness or frustration,
greet you with faith,
we receive you with love,
we give to you all that we are
and promise to accompany you
on the road that you choose for us.
Welcome, Lord Jesus, to your home . . .
Thank you for coming to us.

—Gerardo Oberman, Argentina

TASTE OF FREEDOM AND POWER OF THE TOWEL MAUNDY THURSDAY SERVICE
With the Washing of Feet and the Eucharist in the Tradition of the Church in Georgia

(Wherever it is possible a circle of chairs is made with an altar in the centre. On it are twelve large white candles and one red or purple candle.. The red one is either in the middle of two sets of six candles or is placed separately in front of Christ's icon, which dominates the altar. Also on the altar are a white towel, a jar with water, a larger bowel, a cup of wine, and a paten with bread).

ONE: Grace of our Lord Jesus Christ and the Love of God the Father and the Communion of the Holy Spirit be with you all.

ALL: And with your Spirit.

ONE: Let us lift our hearts.

ALL: We lift them to the Lord.

ONE: Let us give thanks to our Lord.

ALL: It is right indeed to worship Father, Son and Holy Spirit: the Most Holy Trinity, one in essence and undivided.

ONE: It is right to hymn you, to bless you, to praise you, to give thanks to you, and to worship you here and in all your churches around the world, for you are the true God: invisible, inconceivable, incomprehensible, ineffable, ever existing, and eternally the same.

SECOND VOICE: You have brought us from nothing into being. And when we had fallen away you did raise us up again and did not cease to do all things until you have brought us up to heaven and did grant us your kingdom which is to come. For all these things we give thanks to you, to your only begotten Son, and to your Holy Spirit for all good things that have been done for us, whether known or unknown, whether manifest or hidden.

ONE: We thank you for the incarnation of your begotten Son Jesus Christ, our Lord, who during the last supper, knowing that you have given all things into his hands, and that he had come from you and was going to you, got up from the table, took off his outer robe, and tied a towel around himself. Then he poured water into a basin and began to wash the disciples' feet and to wipe them with the towel.

ALL: We beseech you to grant us the same mind that was in your son Jesus Christ, who, though he was in the form of God, emptied himself, taking the form of a slave, being born in human likeness. He humbled himself and became obedient to the point of death—even death on a cross.

ONE: Therefore you also highly exalted him and gave him the name that is above every name.

ALL: So that at the name of your son Jesus Christ every knee should bend, in heaven and on earth and under the earth, and every tongue should confess that Jesus Christ is Lord.

Washing of Feet

(Here the celebrant takes towel and jar of water and starts washing feet and drying with towel, being assisted by somebody who could help him or her moving the bowl. Then the celebrant returns to the table and says:)

ONE: After having washed his disciples' feet your son returned to the table and said: you call me Teacher and Lord. So if I, your Lord and Teacher, have washed your feet, you also ought to wash one another's feet.

ALL: We thank you for your son Jesus Christ, who set for us an example of humility and serving. Help us to follow his example in our lives and ministries.

Continue with Holy Communion.

—Reverend Ala Kavtaradze and Archbishop Malkhaz Songulashvili,
  Evangelical Baptist Church of Georgia (country)

Washing Disciples' Feet   He Qi

MODERN DAY MARIA: A MAUNDY THURSDAY PORTRAIT

When the judge read my son's sentence, "guilty," I could not contain my screams. It was as though that fast, forceful gavel pounded straight down on my head.

I stood. I screamed. They eventually had to usher me out of the courthouse because my cries could not be consoled. They put me out on the curb, and it was so cold on the outside of that stone building. It was fitting that they read such a verdict to me surrounded by such stone. "They are stone; their hearts are stone!" I screamed. The wind was strangely still. All I could hear was my own frantic breath.

My son's sentence: death. Execution. My baby! How dare I be given another breath as they take his away? Months have passed—what feel like years—since that moment. Now, the time of my son's execution is tapping my shoulder. Here, in Texas, they execute some with lethal injection. Tomorrow, they will fill my son's veins with their vile hate and kill him. Why? Because my son has been too honest for their taste. He's been too outspoken about the injustice of the authorities on the Mexico–United States border . . . of the way they shoot us down. He's fought the authorities too vocally. He's been telling them that no human is "illegal" and that our families and children crossing the border have real economic hardship that needs to be remedied. He's called them on their greed! And for this, they will kill him tomorrow!

From the time he was young, he's always had that fire about him. He would speak his mind anywhere and to anyone, even to our priest. Some weeks I would be nervous to bring him to mass, fearing what he might say. Fearing, almost admiring his boldness. And now they're going to snuff that fire because they can't handle the heat of his truth. They can't handle the mirror he holds up to them!

No amount of poetry, of prose, of appeal, can come from my pen to stop them. I have visited the judge's home, again and again, with candle vigils and photos of my son in hand. I stopped this when they threatened me with arrest. I can't afford to go to jail and leave the others at home alone. But home, our home, will be shattered by their cruelty. By his honesty. They are murdering my son. Yes—he is guilty. Guilty of love. Guilty of telling them the truth.

—Laura Markle Downton, USA, Mexico

TENEBRAE

Tonight somewhere someone
Marries unseasonably
While downtown the young
Released to holiday
Round lampposts dance.

Above the hills
The old goddess
Soon to be displaced except
To sign the time for resurrection
Coldly stares and
Slides behind strange clouds
Piled up like boats or serpents
Backlit, waiting
For Friday's darkness.

—Janet Chambers, Aotearoa/New Zealand

GOOD FRIDAY REPENTANCE

A dying rebel turned to see
the Saviour one dark day;
and by Christ's blood, his cruel scorn
and sins were washed away.
For when the scoffer saw the King
a-dying by his side,
he came to love the very Name
of Jesus crucified—
Love Jesus crucified!

"Yes, I fear God, deserve to die;
but Christ did nothing wrong."
"My Saviour King, remember me
when comes your reign along."
Said Jesus, turning with a smile:
"To Paradise you'll go;
with me and like me, there you'll be
In Love's eternal glow!
To Paradise you'll go!"

(Luke 23:38–43. Tune: "Vox Dilecti," starting with C, not D)

—Gordon Piesse, Aotearoa/New Zealand

THE CRUCIFIXION LAMENT

Why did he even so willingly die
Knowing that I would reject the price?
Why did he my life buy
Knowing that I would refuse the prize?
Why did he not leave my side
Knowing that I would betray him more than thrice?
Why did he not lie
That he was not king and prove himself wise?
Why did he not fly
And escape to Paradise?
Why did he, on the Cross, heave a relieving sigh
Knowing that I would still doubt him to rise?
Why did he not eye
To bring down his purpose to my tiny size?
Why does he still stand denied
When all he ever did was to lift us to eternal skies?

—Eyingbeni Hümtsoe, India

EASTER SUNRISE SERVICE

This is part of a short Easter morning sunrise service over Waddington Fell in the Trough of Bowland, Lancashire. It was a clear blue sky with just a whisper of cloud on the eastern horizon. The grass was covered in a thin film of silvery ice and there was no sound. It was 6:15 in the morning as sixteen of us gathered to welcome the risen Christ.

Welcome

We wait
and . . .
we wait . . .

Time creeps onward . . .
The long night is nearly over . . .
No sound disturbs the waiting dawn.
Will it ever end?

we wait . . .
(silence)

Without warning
The gold of resurrection
quietly seeps over the horizon
gently melting away the black and grey
transforming the icy cold,
as rays of light
start to invade our world
revealing a tapestry of colour,
flooding the world with a warm glow,
pulsating with your life blood,
breathing eternal life
into all creation.

Christ is risen!

Scripture reading

John 1:1–5

Blessing

May God bless us in this New Day,
the love of the cosmic Christ fill our hearts
and the wind of God's Spirit
guide us into eternal life.

—Michele Jarmany URC Minister at Clitheroe, Barrow, and Newton, England

SWING INTO SPRING, A LATVIAN EASTER TRADITION

The northerly country of Latvia, located on the Baltic Sea, experiences large changes in the position of the sun during the year, and the spiritual customs are very much based on the passage of the sun. The Spring Equinox traditionally was called "Big Day," but pre-Christian equinox customs now have become associated with Easter.

One of the traditional rituals of this occasion is the hanging of swings, large and small, in towns and in the country. Swings can be as simple as a single board suspended by ropes from a tree branch, or more complex structures with solid frameworks to carry several people. The swings can be erected in a town square, or anywhere, for that matter. Ready made swing sets, sturdy structures of bolted together logs, are available for instant deployment in house yards or parking lots.

It is expected that swinging will bring good crops, and no doubt is an aid to courtship, as young men take young women for rides, show off their prowess at driving the swings higher and higher. And all ages get to ride, as children or older folks are taken as passengers on larger swings.

The swing, like other passages of seasons or stages of our lives, is governed by laws of nature. Its period has to do with distance from the fulcrum to the center of gravity, and we cannot change that. We get on the swing, and someone gives a gentle shove to start us off. We slightly manipulate the center of gravity by shifting our weight, and make the swing go higher and higher, until we see over the onlookers or the treetops, and feel the excitement, the thrill, and even trepidation as we hang on to the ropes or the frame.

Eventually, we slow down, come to a stop. We relinquish our place to the next couple, and give them a gentle push to start off . . .

For Christians, this time of life's renewal is marked by the resurrection of Jesus, and as the old customs of Latvia merged with the new, the Easter observation appropriately took on the name of "Big Day."

—Indulis Gleske, Latvia, USA

REFLECTION ON EASTER

The singing of evening prayers emanates from the fourth cottage of the orphanage at Vellore, India. I glance at my watch; they are unusually early today. Children crowd near the inside of the door. This seems odd since they usually sit in orderly rows. Leaving my shoes and bag outside, I squeeze into a space in the doorway and see the children, cottage mothers, and warden sitting in a circle that touches the edges of the room.

"Jabom. Prayer," the Warden announces, and the children rise to kneel on the smooth cement floor. They reach out, clasp hands, and connect the circle. The Warden prays. Then Rajesh, the little boy next to her, lifts his voice in prayer, followed by Indumathy next to him, followed by Sujeeth and so forth around the circle, each person lifting a prayer to God. The children, some as young as five years old, kneel and pray for an hour, trying not to let their stiff knees or the swarming mosquitoes disturb them. These special prayers are for Mathan Kumar, a four-year-old from our nursery who is very sick and currently in the Pediatrics Intensive Care Unit at Christian Medical College (CMC) Hospital in Vellore.

Mathan died two days after I visited him in the hospital. He never reopened his eyes or spoke another word. He will never again sit in his mother's lap or recite the A-B-C's during playschool with the other nursery children. He will never again play on the swings at Pannai or play tag with his friends. His diagnosis? Measles: a disease for which an inoculation is available; a disease from which no child need suffer or die.

Where is God in a world where an innocent child is allowed to die of an easily preventable disease? How can God let this happen? My understanding of God is that God does not let something happen and, likewise, God cannot do anything to change the situation. Instead of a God that does, I believe in a God that IS: a God that is present with us in times of trouble and pain as well as in times of joy and celebration, a God in which and through which all being and life exists.

From the cross, Jesus cries out to God, "My God, my God, why have you forsaken me?" But God has not forsaken Jesus. God is with him on the cross just as God was with him throughout his life. God was with Madhan and all of us as we experienced the tragedy of his death. At Easter time we so often focus on the resurrection without remembering the pain and grief of death. Death is as much a part of life as birth. At Easter, hope is faith that God is with us now and always . . . that for everything there is a time and that through all those times, God is ever present.

—Thandiwe Gobledale, India

EASTER BENEDICTION

Risen Lord Jesus, give us your blessing:
Help us to bring peace in our world's strife.
Death has been conquered—you are the victor!
Come and transform us—give us new life.

(Could be sung to tune "Bunessan")

—Jan Chamberlin

¡JESÚS ESTÁ RESUCITANDO!/JESUS IS RISEN!

Tres noches de oscuridad
te tragaron como queriendo
enterrar los sueños
del pueblo oprimido,
de la gente que ama.
El imperio y la religión insensible
creían que matándote,
mataban las esperanzas
de los humildes.
Tres días de oscuridad no bastaron
para matar la esperanza de la humanidad
Te querían silenciar los que le daban al cesar
lo que era de Dios y del pueblo.
Te asesinaron los que predican
y no practican sus discursos.

Te quería matar el imperio para eliminar
los ideales de libertad de los pueblos invadidos,
y masacrados.
Te mataron,
maltrataron tu cuerpo,
pero no pudieron matar tu espíritu,
tus ideales.
Te enterraron para borrar tu recuerdo,
porque el imperio siempre le teme
a las ideas que resucitan
en la conciencia de la gente.
El imperio huyó despavorido
a la señal de tu resurrección,
abandonaron la tumba encadenada,
¡Como te temían Jesús!
¡Le pusieron cadenas a tu tumba!
Tenían miedo de tus palabras de amor,
de tu contacto con los pobres,
tenían miedo de tu sonrisa.
Resucitaste,
porque tu proyecto es vida,
solidaridad.
Los ricos y sacerdotes
te odiaban,
siempre andabas con los marginados,
con los excluidos,
hablabas con prostitutas
y hasta te contaron con malhechores.
¿Como podías llamarte maestro?
¿Como pretendías ser un Rabino?
Tenias que morir,
Tenían que matarte,
Había que desaparecerte.
Los llamaste Hipócritas,
Sepulcros blanqueados.
¿Quien te dio esa autoridad?
Los sacerdotes que se vendieron al imperio,
te acusaron de traidor,
porque querías tumbar al imperio,

porque tumbaste las mesas
de las ganancias del templo.
Te habías proclamado Rey
y solo rey era el Cesar,
el extranjero opresor.
Te odiaban los ricos comerciantes,
¿Como te atrevías a regalar el pan
y brindar salud de forma gratuita?
¿Sabes cuanto cuesta el trigo?
¿Cuanto cuestan las patentes
de los medicamentos?
No sabes Jesús cuantos hambreadores
deseaban tu muerte.
Jesús,
resucitaste,
rompiste las cadenas que pusieron
en tu tumba.
Resucitaste,
te mostraste a los pobres,
a los bienaventurados
y bienaventuradas,
a los que sufren, a los ciegos,
a los oprimidos,
a los encarcelados.
Tres noches no bastaron,
todavía hoy estas resucitando
en los pueblos,
en las mujeres.
Todavía el imperio te teme,
e intenta matarte,
pero si te vuelven a matar
seguirás resucitando una y otra vez,
y cada vez que sea necesario
te resucitaremos,
porque resucitas en mi,
en mis hermanos y hermanas,
en los niños y niñas,
en los que aprenden a leer,
en los que luchan,

MAY GOD BLESS US
IN THIS NEW DAY,
THE LOVE
OF THE COSMIC CHRIST
FILL OUR HEARTS,
AND THE WIND
OF GOD'S SPIRIT
GUIDE US
INTO ETERNAL
LIFE.

—Michele Jarmony
United Kingdom

en nuestros pueblos autóctonos
de Bolivia, Ecuador y Perú.
En nuestra gente afro descendiente.·
Estas resucitando
y resucitaras
cada vez que sea necesario.
¡Este es el tiempo de resurrección!
¡Aleluya,
Jesús esta resucitando!

Three nights of darkness
tried to swallow you up,
burying the dreams
of the oppressed people
who loved you.
The empire and the insensible religion
believed that killing you
would kill the hopes
of the humble.
Three days of darkness were not enough
to kill the hope of humanity.
Those who gave you to Caesar wanted to silence you,
who belonged to God and to the people.
Those who preach and do not practice their preachings
killed you.
The empire wanted to get rid of you to eliminate
the ideals of freedom from the invaded
and massacred people.
They killed you,
mistreating your body,
but they couldn't do away with your spirit,
your ideals.
They buried you to erase your memory
because the empire always fears
the ideas that revive
the conscience of the people.
The empire fled in terror
at the sign of your resurrection,
abandoned the chained tomb.

How they feared you, Jesus!
They put chains on your grave!
They were afraid of your words of love,
of your relations with the poor—
they were afraid of your smile.
You have risen,
because your project is life,
solidarity.
The rich and the priests,
they hated you.
You were always walking with the marginalized,
with the ostracized.
You talked with the prostitutes
and after that you talked with criminals.
How could you call yourself teacher?
How could you claim to be a rabbi?
You had to die,
they had to kill you,
you had to go.
You called the hypocrites
whitened tombs;
who gave you that authority?
The priests who sold themselves to the empire
accused you of treason
because you wanted to overthrow the empire,
because you overthrew the tables
of the Temple earnings.
You had proclaimed yourself King
and the only King was Caesar,
the foreign oppressor.
The wealthy merchants hated you,
how did you dare to take the bread
and offer health for all for free?
Don't you know how much wheat costs?
How much the patents
for the medicines cost?
You don't know, Jesus, how many starving people
wish for your death.
Jesus, rise,

break the chains they put
on your grave.
Rise!
You showed yourself to the poor,
to the blessed,
and you blessed
the suffering, the blind,
the oppressed,
the imprisoned.
Three nights were not enough,
even today you are resurrecting
in the villages
in the women.
Even now the empire fears
and tries to kill you
but if they do,
you will rise again
and whenever necessary
you shall rise,
because you are risen in me,
in my brothers and sisters,
in the children,
in those who learn to read,
in those who fight,
and in the indigenous villages
of Bolivia, Ecuador, and Peru.
In the people of African descent
you are risen
and you rise
every time it's necessary.
This is the time of the resurrection!
Hallelujah!
Jesus is risen!

—Obed Juan Vizcaíno Nájera, Venezuela

CARRIED BY WINGS OF GRACE: ECUMENICAL EASTER SERVICE IN THE PHILIPPINES

I participated in an Ecumenical Easter Sunrise Service in the greater Manila area right beside one of the big military camps—either Bonifacio or Aguinaldo. It was the height of martial law and I decided the Word I had to deliver should speak of the hope, the courage, and the power that the resurrection gives to believers in any situation, but especially in days of darkness and despair. So when I mounted the pulpit to preach, I compared the situation into which the disciples were thrown by the crucifixion of Jesus to the hopelessness martial law had brought upon the Filipino people. However, the deeper truth was that the faith given to us by the crucified and risen Lord empowered his followers to see through the deceit and hypocrisy of the present regime, resist its inhuman policies and actions, and be open to the indwelling of the God's Spirit that alone could deliver them from the inhuman regime.

About ten minutes into my sermon, we heard a rumbling sound that shook the earth. Six or seven tanks surrounded our gathering, training their machine guns at the gathered assembly. One was directly pointed at me! I am not a brave man, but, strangely, fear did not take hold of me, and I felt I was not myself anymore. Carried by a power far greater than I, I continued to speak. Death had become an entrance to a far more glorious reality, and I thought I was about to enter it—death was no longer an enemy, it became a friend! I think my mind was caught up in the logic of martyrdom and my spirit was caught up in the movement of God's Spirit itself. I no longer remember what I said at that point; it could be that I spoke the truth in love and the tank commander heard it and ordered his group back to the camp. The power of the resurrection came down upon us. It was one of the most meaningful and powerful Easter services I ever experienced.

—Levi Oracion, Philippines

12 ❀ CELEBRATING SPECIAL DAYS

PENTECOST

Today is Pentecost Sunday
It was festival time
when wind, flame, and spirit
enveloped timid disciples in that upper room
We remember this ancient story
as dark clouds gather in our city
icy winds disturb decaying autumn leaves
and we retreat to the cosy warmth of our homes
Where is our Pentecost?
Where is wind, flame, and spirit in our city?
In our houses we feel the warmth from ducts—
down there somewhere is flame
While the wind howls
we listen
we wait
we take a jacket and walk into the night
we feel wind and rain on our face
moonlight glows behind a cloud
we walk; we remember

The wind and flame of Pentecost is surely here
stirring in our hearts
glowing in the faces of those we love
in the still, small voice
of compassion for those on the margins
of passion for justice
many candles and flames quietly and resolutely burning

in distant places
in our own neighbourhood
within our small community of faith
Who will shout, "look here it is" or "there it is"?
There is no need
because Pentecost is within us

—Digby Hannah, Australia

PENTECOST READING FOR SEVERAL LANGUAGES

This Pentecost reading bathes the sanctuary in the sounds of language, as in Acts 2:1–6. It can be done effectively with as few as three readers, but seven readers makes for a fuller, more chaotic, sound at the end. It also can be done with more readers, if you wish to add more languages.

The reading is done this way: the first time through, each reader reads one verse in English. The second time through each will read a verse in the same order but using one of the different languages. The third time through all read, all at the same time, with each speaking in his or her own language. The first read-through will sound coherent. The second time through will be slightly incoherent, and the last time will sound like babbling. Don't worry, that's the point. We have occasionally done this with Cambodian and Vietnamese readers, and that adds a lot.

Just in case the individual readings are confusing, here is the order of readers for the service below. Reader 1 is English, Reader 2 is French, Reader 3 is Spanish, Reader 4 is Latin, Reader 5 is German, Reader 6 is Portuguese, Reader 7 (who comes in only in the last reading) is Greek (a transliterated version of the original Greek text, United Bible Society edition).

It is even more effective when the readings can be made from all points around the sides of the sanctuary. When the sounds are coming from all sides, the sense of being surrounded with the sounds of many different languages is heightened.

First Reading: English

READER 1: When the day of Pentecost had come, they were all together in one place.

READER 2: And suddenly from heaven there came a sound like the rush of a violent wind, and it filled the entire house where they were sitting.

READER 3: Divided tongues, as of fire, appeared among them, and a tongue rested on each of them.

READER 4: All of them were filled with the Holy Spirit and began to speak in other languages, as the Spirit gave them ability.

READER 5: Now, there were devout Jews from every nation under heaven living in Jerusalem.

READER 6: And at this sound the crowd gathered and was bewildered, because each on heard them speaking in the native language of each.

Second Reading: Individual Languages

READER 1, ENGLISH: When the day of Pentecost had come, they were all together in one place.

READER 2, FRENCH: Tout à coup il vint du ciel un bruit comme celui d'un vent impétueux, et il remplit toute la maison où ils étaient assis.

READER 3, SPANISH: Y se les aparecieron lenguas repartidas, como de fuego, asentándose sobre cada uno de ellos.

READER 4, LATIN: Et repleti sunt omnes Spiritu Sancto et coeperunt loqui aliis linguis prout Spiritus Sanctus dabat eloqui illis.

READER 5, GERMAN: Es wohnten aber in Jerusalem Juden, die waren gottesfürchtige Männer aus allen Völkern unter dem Himmel.

READER 6, PORTUGUESE: Correndo aquela voz, ajuntou-se uma multidão, e estava confusa, porque cada um os ouvia falar na sua própria língua.

Third Reading: All Languages at Once

READER 1, ENGLISH (New Revised Standard Version): When the day of Pentecost had come, they were all together in one place. And suddenly from heaven there came a sound like the rush of a violent wind, and it filled the entire house where they were sitting. Divided tongues, as of fire, appeared among them, and a tongue rested on each of them. All of them were filled with the Holy Spirit and began to speak in other languages, as the Spirit gave them ability. Now, there were devout Jews from every nation under heaven living in Jerusalem. And at this sound the crowd gathered and was bewildered, because each on heard them speaking in the native language of each.

READER 2, FRENCH (La Sainte Bible, Édition Revue, Alliance Biblique Universelle, 1998): Le jour de la Pentecôte, ils étaient tous ensemble dans le même lieu. Tout à coup il vint du ciel un bruit comme celui d'un vent impétueux, et il remplit toute la maison où ils étaient assis. Des langues, semblables à des langues de feu, leur apparurent, séparées les unes des autres, et se posèrent sur chacun d'eux. Et ils furent tous remplis du Saint-Esprit, et se mirent à parler en d'autres langues, selon que l'Esprit leur donnait de s'exprimer. Or il y avait en séjour à Jérusalem des Juifs, hommes pieux, de toutes les nations qui sont sous le ciel. Au bruit qui eut lieu, la multitude accourut, et elle fut confondue parce que chacun les entendait parler dans sa propre langue.

READER 3, SPANISH (Dios Llega al Hombre, Versión Popular, 3ra edición, 1983, Sociedades Bíblicas Unidas): Cuando llegó el día de Pentecostés, estaban todos unánimes juntos. Y de repente vino del cielo un estruendo como de un viento recio que soplaba, el cual llenó toda la casa donde estaban sentados; y se les aparecieron lenguas repartidas, como de fuego, asentándose sobre cada uno de ellos. Y fueron todos llenos del Espíritu Santo, y comenzaron a hablar en otras lenguas, según el Espíritu les daba que hablasen. Por aquellos días había en Jerusalén judíos cumplidores de sus deberes religiosos, llegados de todas partes del mundo. La gente se reunió al oír aquel ruido, y no sabía qué pensar, porque cada uno oía a los creyentes hablar en su propia lengua.

READER 4, LATIN (Vulgate): Et cum conplerentur dies pentecostes erant omnes pariter in eodem loco et factus est repente de caelo sonus tamquam advenientis spiritus vehementis et replevit totam domum ubi erant sedentes et apparuerunt illis dispertitae linguae tamquam ignis seditque supra singulos eorum et repleti sunt omnes Spiritu Sancto et coeperunt loqui aliis linguis prout Spiritus Sanctus dabat eloqui illis erant autem in Hierusalem habitantes Iudaei viri religiosi ex omni natione quae sub caelo sunt facta autem hac voce convenit multitudo et mente confusa est quoniam audiebat unusquisque lingua sua illos loquentes.

READER 5, GERMAN (Luther's Die Bibel): Und als der Pfingsttag gekommen war, waren sie alle an einem Ort beieinander. Und es geschah plötzlich ein Brausen vom Himmel wie von einem gewaltigen Wind und erfüllte das ganze Haus, in dem sie saßen. Und es erschienen ihnen Zungen zerteilt, wie von Feuer; und er setzte sich auf einen jeden von ihnen, und sie wurden alle erfüllt von dem heiligen Geist und fingen an, zu predigen in andern Sprachen, wie der Geist ihnen gab auszusprechen. Es wohnten aber in Jerusalem Juden, die waren gottesfürchtige Männer aus allen Völkern unter dem Himmel. Als nun dieses Brausen geschah, kam die Menge zusammen und wurde bestürzt; denn ein jeder hörte sie in seiner eigenen Sprache reden.

READER 6, PORTUGUESE (Bíblia Sagrada, Alfalit, Brasil, 1996): Sete semanas já se haviam pasado desde a morte e a ressurreição de Jesus, e com isto chegou o Dia de Pentecoste. Quando os crentes se reuniram naquele dia, de repente apareceu um som semelhante ao rugido de um poderoso vendaval no céu por cima deles, e aquilo encheu a oasa onde estavam reunidos. Então, viu-se algo parecido com labaredas ou lígias de fogo que pousaram sobre as cabeçdeles. Todos os presentes ficaram cheios do Espírito Santo, e começaram a falar em línguas que não conheciam, porque o Espírito Santo deu a eles esta capacidade. Em Jerusalém estavamhabitando judeus, homens religiosos, de todas asnações que estão debaixo do céo. Correndo aquela voz, ajuntou-se uma multidão, e estava confusa, porque cada um os ouvia falar na sua própria língua.

READER 7, GREEK (transliterated from United Bible Society text, 2nd ed., 1965): Kaì èn tô sumpleroûsthai tèn hèméran tês pentekostês san pántes ómoû èpì tò aùtó. Kaì ègéneto áphno èk toû oùranoû êchos h sper pheroménes pnoés biaías kaì éplérosen h`ólon ton oíkon hoú esan kathémenoi kaì öphesan haútoîs diamerizómenai glôssai hòseì pyròs kaì hékáthisen éph' h`èna hékaston aútôn. Kaí éplésthesan pántes pneúmatos hàgío kaì ërzanto laleîn hètérais glóssais kathòs tò pneûma èdídou ápophthéggesthai haútoîs. Esan dè eìs Ierousalèm katoikoûntes Ioudaîoi, ändres eùlabeîs àpó pantòs ëthnous tôn ùpò to oùranón; Genoménes dè tês phonês taútes sunêlthen tò plêthos kaì sunechúthe ti ëkouon eîs ëkastos tê idí dialékto laloúnton aùtôn.

—Stan G. Duncan, USA

A LITURGY FOR ALL, REGARDLESS OF LABEL—RESOURCES FOR DISABILITY SUNDAY
Call to Worship

To the God who walks on wounded feet and heals with wounded hands,
To the God who stands beside us wounded, all knowing and all loving,
To the God of imperfections
We offer our imperfect praise,
Trusting in the perfect love of the God who knows what it is to be truly human.

Prayer of Approach

God of pain and God of peace, Mother and Father of us all,
Created in your image we inherit what makes us human,
The ability to think, communicate, reflect, record, and create.
These gifts are precious and we give you thanks.
Though we have gifts in common, we are not all alike,
Each of us is a different individual, unique and special,
We come before you rejoicing in difference.
We come before you knowing each child is given a different blend
of gifts and experiences that shape, and keep shaping, the adult.
Every person in your world is differently abled.
Every person in your world is differently disabled.
Help each of us use what we can to enhance our lives and your world. Amen

Reflection on Scripture—Luke 13:10–17—Regardless of Label

Imagine the synagogue with its bustle of religious men performing their religious duties. This particular Sabbath a visiting preacher captures a large audience. Behind a grill, women, children, and slaves gather to watch. One person, more outcast than the rest, slouches alone. Children stare and mothers pull them away. She bears the stigma of sin— a curse that renders her a cripple. She exists with the burden of living bent over for eighteen years, denied easy glance to sky and faces. Her wretched and painful world is that of feet, dust, and mud. She must have done something terrible to merit this. She survives by begging. Her only hope is to be as religious as possible.

Anticipation mounts as the speaker mounts the rostrum. He gazes over the crowd. He is young and confident. His eyes light upon the misshapen shadow beyond the grill. "Woman," he calls, "Come here." The crowd is astounded and shocked. Men do not speak to women in the synagogue and women do not enter the men's court. Despite only wanting to remain unnoticed, the outcast dares to obey. Feel her hating the gaze of the public; imagine her pause in panic as the public moves back. See the disgust in the faces. She does not twist to look but feels the disdain. An unpleasant murmur ripples the crowd and over it comes the voice of Jesus saying, "Come unto me." The woman musters all the courage she posses and limps forward. Jesus stoops and touches the untouchable one. The touch is warm, human, tender, and strong. "Woman," he says, "You are freed from your infirmity." She straightens to his words and looks into the face of the Christ. The crowd is transfixed, and angry.

Not only has an unclean woman entered a sacred part of the synagogue, the healer is "working" on the Sabbath. The young preacher dares answer his elders and betters with a ring of authority. He calls them hypocrites, reminding them they tend animals on the Sabbath.

Then Jesus refers to the deformed woman as a "'daughter of Abraham." Abraham! The greatest of the Patriarchs, the founder of the Nation, the "great one" prepared to follow God to the end of the world, the person of perfect faith with whom God made a holy covenant. To be called a daughter of Abraham elevates her to undreamed of status.

Those present witnessed more than mere healing. All were confronted with the fact that this woman was their equal. Jesus further reminded the people it was not sin but Satan that bound their kinswoman. The people understood and were ashamed. And then they were able to rejoice.

Offering

ONE: God, help us to know the truth of your love in our lives;

ALL: Enable us to grow in the grace we need . . .

ONE: . . . to be agents of change for a better world.

ALL: We dedicate ourselves and our gifts to your service. Amen.

Prayer of Intercession

God of our yesterdays and God of our tomorrows,
we ask that you be with us now, God of our today.

We are an Easter People!
We have experienced the resurrection,
Yet often we behave like your pre-Easter followers,
uncertain and unprepared.
Help us claim our Easter heritage
and live with confidence.
Equip us for what is to come.
Help us to travel light,
carrying what is best from the past to the future.

God of Vision and New Possibilities,
open our hearts and minds to the reality of your presence.
God of Light, illuminate the dark places of our lives.
We are not perfect people.
Come through the cracks of our imperfections and fill us with your light.

We pray for all marginalized people:
Those who suffer discrimination because of gender, race,
sexual orientation, physical or mental impairment.
Give them strength and belief in their worth.
We pray for those active in discrimination,
and those who allow it to happen.
May they know what they do.
May they understand the hurts they cause.

We gather our thoughts in this sacred place,
knowing that you have heard each sincere desire.
We long for a time when all people are valued.
May our unconditional love flow from us to others.
May it swirl and curl through this year,
embracing all who seek a better life. Amen

Hymn suggestion:"Who is my mother . . ." by Shirley Murray, music by Ian Render, no. 158 in the songbook Alleluia Aotearoa

Affirmation

ONE: With your help, O God:

ALL: We reject victim mentality—we will live as survivors.
We will do the best we can—we will be people of faith.

Benediction/Commission

ONE: For the God who walks on wounded feet and heals with wounded hands,
For the God who stands beside us wounded, all knowing and all loving,
For the God of imperfections,

ALL: We go into our wonderful and imperfect world to reflect God's perfect love,
and in so doing, claim what it is to be truly human.
(Disability Sunday in New Zealand, third Sunday in June; UN International Day of Persons with Disabilities, third of December; Access Sunday in the USA, second Sunday in October)

—Rosalie May Sugrue, Aotearoa/New Zealand

INTERCESSIONS FOR PLANET EARTH (EARTH DAY)

ONE: On this Earth Sunday, let us pray for planet earth and for all living things.
We pray that there will be careful use of the earth's resources, that forests, waters, soil, and air may be kept clean and that life in all its abundance will flourish.
May blessing and peace abound.

ALL: This is our prayer.

ONE: Let us pray for those countries where people continue in conflict with each other—fighting over land and resources, fighting for freedom of speech, religious or cultural expression. We pray especially for . . . (*name concerns*)
May blessing and peace abound.

ALL: This is our prayer.

ONE: Let us pray for those communities suffering as a result of natural catastrophe—flood, drought, earthquake, fire—where lives, homes, and livelihoods have been destroyed, especially . . . (*name concerns*)
May blessing and peace abound.

ALL: This is our prayer.

ONE: Let us pray for emergency workers—fire fighters, search and rescue personnel, aid workers, peacekeepers and peacemakers—and all those who respond to crisis situations.
Especially we pray for those committed to the rebuilding and restoration of broken community. May blessing and peace abound.

ALL: This is our prayer

—Lynne Frith, Aotearoa/New Zealand

YACHANA* (for Earth Day)

In the rainforest deep in Ecuador
There's a place for you and me
Called Yachana, place of learning
There we learn just how to be
How to live free.

Thick and lush are our surroundings
Filled with new sounds in the night
Equal time for day and evening
Equal time to make things right
Together, in God's sight.

Rini Templeton

Meeting people from each community
Along the river's many miles
Bringing children lots of color
Lots of children with beautiful smiles
Friendship in those smiles.

Finding ways to reach each other
Community to community
Radios talking to Yachana
Building a system of family
Making connections to you and me.

So we greet and we meet each other
We from the North have ventured here
We'll go home to share with others
Bringing your stories and presence near
Finding others to come here.

Oh Yachana, place of learning
Teaching us just how to care
For God's earth and all its creatures
For God's children everywhere . . .
Everywhere.

(Quichua word meaning "place of learning")
This piece is set to music by its author.

—Barbara W. Van Ausdall, USA, Ecuador

BLESSING THE GIFTS OF CREATION (for Earth Day)

This service is a reaffirmation of the sovereignty of God, the creator of heaven and earth. Through this service we thank God for the creation, all the gifts bestowed upon us daily. In our gratitude to our Creator we will bless soil, water, wine, oil, grains, and other fruits of the earth *(which have been placed on the altar in larger bowls. There should also be placed on the table a basket with fragmented bread and a separate jar with wine)* and bless the sharing of these gifts by the people God has created in God's own image and likeness. God's saving work in Christ through the power of the Holy Spirit is for the transfiguration of the whole cosmos into the new heaven and the new earth, therefore by this service the entire creation is blessed.

Preparation

ONE: Blessed is our God at all times:
now and for ever and to the ages of ages. Amen

ALL: Heavenly King, Comforter, the Spirit of truth
present in all places and filling all things;
treasury of good things and giver of life,
come and dwell in us
and purify us from every stain,
and of your goodness, save us.

ONE: All Holy Trinity, have mercy on us,
Lord, cleanse us from our sins.
Master, pardon our iniquities.
Holy God, visit and heal our infirmities
for your name's sake.
Lord, have mercy, Lord, have mercy, Lord, have mercy.
Glory to the Father and to the Son
and to the Holy Spirit, now and for ever
and to the ages of ages. Amen
As our Saviour Jesus Christ taught us so we pray:

ALL: (The Prayer of our Saviour)

The Word of God

ONE: (First reading: Genesis 8:15–22)

ALL: Let there be respect for the earth, peace for its people;
Let there be love in our lives, delight in the good;
Let there be forgiveness for past wrongs,
and from now on a new start. Amen.

ONE: Let us listen to the Holy Gospel. Peace be with you.

ALL: And with your spirit.

ONE: The reading is from the Holy Gospel according to St. Mark.
Glory to you, O Lord. (Mark 8:1–9)

ALL: Praise to you O Christ.

Litany of Intercessions

ONE: Again we pray for all those with responsibility
for our churches and communities,
for all brothers and sisters in Christ
and for every Christian soul afflicted and weary,

in need of God's mercies and help.
Hear our prayer and have mercy.

ALL: Kyrie eleison

ONE: Lord Jesus Christ, our God,
you have said, "Apart from me you can do nothing."
In faith we embrace your words, Lord,
and entreat your goodness.
Help us, O Lord, to grasp and discern your will
while seeking to work
with the secular structures of society
while remaining countercultural.
We acknowledge in prayer
that you are our help and refuge
and that we can do nothing right
without your guidance and help.
Bless us, enlighten and strengthen us, Lord,
so that not our will but your will be done.
Guide us to bring about fruits of goodness
to your service and glory, we diligently entreat you, hear our prayer and have mercy.

ALL: Kyrie eleison

ONE: O Lord Almighty, the healer of our souls and bodies,
who by word alone did heal all diseases
who is able to put aside every malady and infirmity,
do you now, in your great mercy
visit our sisters and brothers who are sick.
Stretch forth your hand that is full of healing and health
raise them from their bed of pain
and send down upon them your great mercy
and if it is your will
give them health and a complete recovery,
for you alone are the Physician of our souls and bodies,
we pray, hear our prayer and have mercy.

ALL: Kyrie eleison

ONE: Hear us, O God, our Saviour
the hope of the ends of the earth
and be gracious, be gracious, O Lord,
unto us sinners and have mercy on us.
For you are a merciful God who loves humanity

and all your creation
and unto you we give glory,
to the Father and to the Son and to the Holy Spirit,
now and for ever and to the ages of ages.

ALL: Kyrie eleison

Prayer of Blessing

Five loaves and two fish are placed prominently on a table along with red and white grapes. There are also bowls with grain, oil, wine, soil and water and a larger bowl with fragmented bread, which is to be sprinkled with wine. The minister censes all the gifts and then continues:

ONE: Lord Jesus Christ, our God! As you blessed the five loaves and two fish,
and satisfied the five thousand hungry people in the wilderness,
so now, bless this bread, fish, wine, oil, grain, and all the fruits of the earth;
sanctify the faithful who partake of them,
and let there always be plenty
not only for us, here present,
but for all your people everywhere.
For you are the one who blesses
and sanctifies all things, Christ our God,
and we give glory to you,
your eternal Father
and the all-holy, good and life-giving Spirit.
Now and forever and to the ages of ages.

ALL: Amen

(The minister sprinkles the fragmented bread with the wine. The participants receive blessed bread and are anointed by the minister on their forehead with oil).

ONE (as he/she anoints): May the blessing of the Lord
descend upon you by his grace and love,
now and forever and to the ages of ages. Amen

—Archbishop Malkhaz Songulashvili, Evangelical Baptist Church of Georgia (country)

QUATRE DIRECTIONS: une liturgie de la Justice pour Jour de la Terre ou d'autres occasions (FOUR DIRECTIONS : A Liturgy of Justice for Earth Day or Other Occasions)

Ce temps de prière est un temps privilégié pour reconnaître que le chemin, le mouvement et le processus de la vie prennent leur origine dans le Dieu créateur et libérateur. Il est présent dans toute la création, dans tous les peuples et en nous. Il est agissant à l'est, à l'ouest, au nord, au sud, et au centre, chez ceux et celles qui luttent pour un autre monde, et un autre avenir. Cet avenir est décrit en terme poétique dans le livre du Deutéronome. N'est-il pas le fidèle reflet des aspirations légitimes des peuples?

Lecture: Deutéronome 8:7–18 (traduction Bible en français courant)

Est—Couleur Rouge

Dieu Mère et Père, nous te saluons depuis l'est, lieu où naît le soleil, nous te remercions pour le don de la vie car c'est toi qui es la vie, que le sang des martyrs de la libération soulève notre coeur pour qu'ensemble nous puissions défendre la vie que tu veux pour toute la création. Nous te demandons de bénir les peuples autochtones, tous ceux et celles qui vivent en orient, tous ceux et celles qui luttent pour la vie. Soutiens ceux et celles qui travaillent pour que le soleil de la justice se lève encore et dans ce mouvement: un autre monde est possible, un autre avenir est possible.

Nous allumons le cierge. Silence.

Ouest—Couleur Noire

Dieu Mère et Père, nous te saluons depuis l'ovuest, lieu où se couche le soleil, lieu où la vie semble disparaître et où apparaît la nuit, l'obscurité. Il y a plusieurs événements qui font que la vie et l'espérance disparaissent devant nos yeux. C'est un temps de souffrance, de dépouillement, de deuil, de questionnement sans issue. La capacité de rêver, de faire des projets n'est plus présente. Fortifie notre espérance et notre lutte contre tous les signes de mort. Soutiens ceux et celles qui luttent contre l'économie de mort, contre les violences faites aux femmes et aux enfants. Nous te demandons de bénir tous ceux et celles qui vivent à l'ouest sous le souffle de ton esprit. Soutiens ceux et celles qui travaillent dans ce mouvement: un autre monde est possible, un autre avenir est possible.

Nous allumons le cierge. Silence.

Nord—Couleur Blanche

Dieu Mère et Père, nous te saluons depuis le nord. Le blanc évoque le deuil, la mort. Nous nous souvenons de ceux et celles qui nous ont précédés dans la foi, nos ancêtres. Donne-nous la grâce de goûter à ta sagesse et qu'elle nous conduise à l'option pour la vie, malgré les forces de mort. Nous te demandons de bénir tous ceux et celles qui vivent au Nord et qui luttent contre les forces de la mort quand elles sont nourries par l'injustice et la guerre. Soutiens ceux et celles qui ouvrent leurs églises aux réfugiés et qui interpellent le gouvernement. Soutiens ceux et celles qui travaillent dans ce mouvement: un autre monde est possible, un autre avenir est possible.

Nous allumons le cierge. Silence.

Sud—Couleur Jaune

Dieu Mère et Père, nous te saluons depuis le sud, symbole de la fécondité, des fruits et de la femme. Tu donnes tant de vie! Nous te remercions pour les femmes prophètes en leur milieu, tisserandes de paix et pour toutes les femmes qui optent pour la vie au milieu dans tant de signes de mort. Bénis toutes les femmes et tous les hommes qui optent pour une paix juste. Nous te demandons de soutenir tous ceux et celles qui vivent au sud, tous ceux et celles qui sont victimes des politiques des puissants, les réfugiés et les abandonnés. Soutiens ceux et celles qui travaillent dans ce mouvement: un autre monde est possible, un autre avenir est possible.

Nous allumons le cierge. Silence.

Centre—Couleur Bleue et Couleur Verte

Dieu, coeur du ciel et de la terre, en Jésus-Christ, en qui s'enlace le divin et l'humain, tu nous vois et par lui, nous te voyons Père et Mère. Fais que chaque jour soit un moment de prise de conscience de ta présence agissante et un temps d'action pour l'avancée du projet de ton règne. Nous te saluons avec Jésus en qui tu bénis toute la création. Nous te demandons de bénir tous ceux qui vivent au centre parce que ton règne est au centre de leurs projets et leurs préoccupations. Soutiens ceux et celles qui travaillent dans ce mouvement: un autre monde est possible, un autre avenir est possible.

Nous allumons le cierge. Silence.

En Nous—Couleur Terre

Dieu, Mère et Père, voici notre réseau qui, par ses membres, est enraciné dans différents milieux. Nous sommes un réseau qui, parmi d'autres, opte pour la justice, la paix et l'intégrité de la création, pour la libération des personnes et des peuples. Soutiens-nous dans les moments difficiles et donne-nous de te remercier dans les moments de joie. Que nous soyons une de ces petites minorités abrahamiques, comme le disait Helder Camara, prophète des pauvres,—ces hommes et ces femmes qui incarnent l'universalité à l'encontre de la privatisation du monde—pour qu'un autre monde soit possible, qu'un autre avenir soit possible!

Nous allumons le cierge. Silence.

Oui un autre monde est possible, un autre avenir est possible. Comme disciples du Christ, nous sommes invités à faire fructifier nos talents pour nourrir, soutenir les autres dans cette venue d'un nouveau monde. C'est pourquoi dans le chapitre 24 et 25, on trouve deux paraboles sur le serviteur fidèle. Vous remarquerez que le serviteur fidèle n'est pas celui qui pille, exploite mais celui qui fait fructifier, qui nourrit, qui soutient, qui donne. Écoutons deux extraits; le premier éclaire le second.

Lecture: Matthieu 25:14–21, Matthieu 24:45–46

LEADER: Par ce credo des prophètes pour un monde nouveau, nous sommes conscients du travail que le Seigneur confie à ses serviteurs.

Four Directions: A Liturgy of Justice for Earth Day or Other Occasions

This time of prayer is a moment especially conducive to recognizing that the path, the activities, and the process of life take their origin in the God who is Creator and Liberator. God is present in the whole of creation, in all peoples and in each one of us. God's activity is felt in the east, in the west, in the north, in the south, and at the center, among those men and women who are struggling to bring about another world and another future. This future is described in poetic terms in the book of Deuteronomy. Is this not the faithful reflection of the legitimate aspirations of the nations?

Reading: Deuteronomy 8:7–18

East—Red Colour

Mother and Father God, we greet you from the east, the point where the sun rises; we thank you for the gift of life, for it is you who are Life; may the blood of the martyrs for liberation so stir our hearts that, together, we may come to the defense of the life you have willed for the whole of creation. We ask you to bless the indigenous peoples, all those who live in the east, all those who fight for the cause of life. Support those men and women who labor so that the Sun of Justice may rise once more in this movement, "another world is possible; another future is possible."

We light the candle. Silence.

West—Black Colour

Mother and Father God, we greet you from the west, point where the sun sets, point at which life seems to disappear and darkness and night appear. There are many events that cause life and hope to disappear before our eyes. It is a time of suffering, of stripping down to bare essentials, a time of mourning, of questioning that has no answers. The ability to dream, to make plans, is no longer present. Strengthen our hope, our resistance against all that stands for death. Support the men and women who struggle against the economy of death, against violence inflicted on women and children. We ask you to bless those who live in the west who are guided by your Spirit. Support the men and women who work in the movement "another world is possible, another future is possible."

We light the candle. Silence.

North—White Colour

Mother and Father God, we greet you from the north. White evokes mourning and death. We recall those who have gone before us, our ancestors in the faith. Grant us the grace to taste your Wisdom and may it lead us to choose life, despite the forces of evil. We ask you to bless all men and women living in the north and who fight against the forces of death, when these are nourished by injustice and war. Support those who open their churches to refugees and who challenge government policies. Support the men and women involved in the movement "another world is possible, another future is possible."

We light the candle. Silence.

South—Yellow Colour

Mother and Father God, we greet you from the south, symbol of the fecundity of fruits and of women. You give life in such abundance! We thank you for women who are prophets in their milieu, weavers of peace, and for all women who choose life in the midst of so many signs of death. Bless all women and all men who make just peace their option. We ask you to support all men and women who live in the south, all who are victims of the policies of the powerful, the refugees and those who have been abandoned. Support all the men and women who work in the movement "another world is possible, another future is possible."

We light the candle. Silence.

Centre—Blue and Green Colour

God, you who are the heart of heaven and of earth, you look upon us in Jesus Christ, in whom the divine and the human are interwoven, and through Him we look upon you as Father and Mother. Grant that our every day may be a moment of awareness of your active presence and a time for action on our part to advance the plan of your Kingdom. We greet you in Jesus in whom you bless the whole of Creation. We ask you to bless all those who live at the centre because your Kingdom is at the centre of their plans and their preoccupations. Support the men and women who work in the movement "another world is possible, another future is possible."

We light the candle. Silence.

In Us—Earthen Colour

Mother and Father God, look down on our network, that, through its members, is rooted in many different milieux. We are one network that, among others, is working for Justice, Peace, and the Integrity of Creation and for the liberation of individuals and of nations. Support us in difficult times and grant that we may give thanks to you in moments of joy. May we be one with those Abrahamic minorities, as Helder Camara, the prophet of the poor, used to say, those men and women who incarnate universality in the face of worldwide privatization, "so that another world may become possible, another future become possible!"

We light the candle. Silence.

Yes, another world is possible, another future is possible. As disciples of Christ, we are invited to develop our talents in order to nourish, to support others to prepare the coming of a new world. That is why, in chapters 24 and 25 of Matthew, we find two parables about the faithful servant. You will note that the faithful servant is not the one who pillages and exploits, but the one who earns more with his talents, who nourishes, who supports, who gives. Let us listen to two extracts: the first casts light on the second:

Reading: Matthew 25:14–21, Matthew 24:45–46

ONE: Through this credo of the prophets of a new world, we become aware of the work the Lord entrusts to his servants.

Translated from the French original by Sr. Bernadette Ward, FMM. Original text by the members of the ROJeP Réseau œcuménique justice et paix, Québec, with particular thanks to Renaude Grégoire. Copyright: ROJeP, 2004

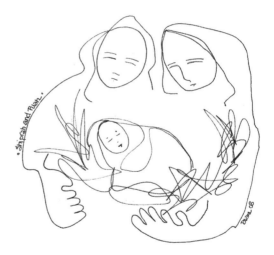

MOTHERS' DAY LITANY

ONE: We walk in the company of the women who have gone before, mothers of the faith both named and unnamed, testifying with ferocity and faith to the Spirit of Wisdom and Healing. They are the judges, the prophets, the martyrs, the warriors, poets, lovers, and saints who are near to us in our memory and our dreaming.

ALL: We walk in the company of Deborah,

ONE: who judged the Israelites with authority and strength.

ALL: We walk in the company of Esther,

ONE: who used her position as queen to ensure the welfare of her people.

ALL: We walk in the company of you whose names have been lost and silenced,

ONE: who kept and cradled the wisdom of the ages.

ALL: We walk in the company of the woman with the flow of blood,

ONE: who audaciously sought her healing and release.

ALL: We walk in the company of Mary Magdalene,

ONE: who wept at the empty tomb until the risen Christ appeared.

ALL: We walk in the company of Phoebe,

ONE: who led an early church in the empire of Rome.

ALL: We walk in the company of Perpetua of Carthage,

ONE: whose witness in the third century led to her martyrdom.

ALL: We walk in the company of Saint Christina the Astonishing,

ONE: who resisted death with persistence and wonder.

ALL: We walk in the company of Julian of Norwich,

ONE: who wed imagination and theology, proclaiming wellness as reality.

ALL: We walk in the company of Sojourner Truth,

ONE: who stood against oppression, righteously declaring her womanhood in 1852.

ALL: We walk in the company of the Argentine Mothers of the Plaza de Mayo,

ONE: who turned their grief to strength, standing together to remember the disappeared children of war with a holy indignation.

ALL: We walk in the company of Alice Walker,

ONE: who named the purple hue of womanish strength.

ALL: We walk in the company of you mothers of the faith,

ONE: who teach us to resist evil with boldness, to lead with wisdom, and to heal.

ALL: Amen.

—Laura Markle Downton, USA

THINKING ABOUT DAD

My dad died today
He left a heritage
It's called "evangelical"
If that sounds as though it could mean revival rallies and angels
in a way, it does
For us it meant reading the Bible at meal times
praying at the end of the day and in the car before driving
and sitting through religious meetings
listening to missionaries with slides
It meant not talking about sex

and, if possible, not thinking about sex
It also meant being hugely generous, though not wealthy
and giving, without keeping accounts or seeking recompense
It assumed a hospitable lifestyle
with all sorts of people staying for meals overnight
It implied honesty, the scrupulous kind, with no exceptions
even when disadvantaged
and it demanded selfless, hard work
for the sake of others and for God

My dad died today, just hours ago
He was old and he was ready for death
as he knew where he was going
Knowing death would be hastened he had refused his medication
allowing his body of skin and bones to die
but not his mind or spirit
Nor his evangelical heritage—
the same traditions his own father had left him
In those straightforward days "evangelical" was a familiar word
"coke" was for stoking fires not for drinking
and a "joint" only smoked when your house was on fire
Then, "evangelical" meant believing the Bible without question
memorising its pages and doing what it said
While recovering from TB during the war my dad memorised
the entire book of Romans

My dad died today
Even if I survive to the same age
my life is already more than half spent
Times have changed
My children are captivated by video stars, sports heroes
and the products of global marketing
They talk about sex
To them "evangelical" is a strange sounding word
Sometimes they remember their story
and sometimes they ask about God
about the future . . . and about death
When I die, will I leave a heritage?

—Digby Hannah, Australia

A REFLECTION FOR ANZAC* DAY

Today is a very special day:
It is Sunday, the day we come to the Lord's House to honour Him, to praise Him
  and offer prayers.
It is the day we meet members of our church family and spend time with them
And it is April 25th—Anzac Day—the day we remember the sacrifice of lives in war.

There was a box of poppies at the door as you came in to church today. The red poppy
has become a symbol of Returned Services Associations everywhere; perhaps it has
become a symbol of war. Certainly it represents remembrance.

A remembrance of many things:
the courage of young men who became soldiers, sailors, and airmen
  and left their homes to fight and die
the courage of young women who worked in field hospitals, many just behind
  the fighting positions
the courage of people who were repulsed by war and spoke against it, refusing to serve
  in the armed forces or work in industries such as munitions. Many went to prison,
  others became stretcher bearers
the courage of those who stayed at home, shouldering bigger burdens of work, fundraising,
  training in case of invasion, enduring long silences of news of loved ones.

During World War I, in the fields of Flanders in Belgium, a fierce battle raged where
many soldiers were killed and more and more crosses were erected in a cemetery where
the wild red poppies bloomed. The tragic scene inspired a Canadian medical officer,
Major John McCrea, who tended the wounded and dying soldiers, to write a poem that
immortalized the red poppy of Flanders. For many years now Poppy Day has raised
funds for the work of the Returned Services Association (R.S.A.), and every year there
are commemoration services in many parts of the world. For fifteen years my husband
and I lived in 17th Avenue, not far as the wind blows, from the Tauranga R.S.A., and at
dawn on Anzac Day each year we could hear the Last Post played and the Reveille and
we knew that at the service the poem about the fields of Flanders would be read.

*ANZAC = *The Australian and New Zealand Army Corps*

—Barbara Murray, Aotearoa/New Zealand

13 ❁ SEASONS OF THE NATURAL WORLD

A GATHERING PRAYER ON A FIRST SPRING MORNING

G'zhem-mnidoo (Creator God), Creator of all things great and small:

This morning I saw him—just where you called him to be! He wasn't very big, actually kind of scrawny looking. But when the frost leaves Omizakamigokwe's (Mother Earth's) breast he will grow plump again. Here in the time of Ziisbaakdoke-Giizis (Sugar Moon Month) he will welcome growing stronger.

His bright red chest caught my eye. When I looked there was Opichiinh (Male Robin) standing quite alert on a patch of open grass between the last remaining snow drifts. His cheerful colour is such a contrast to all the muddier hues, that even though he was quiet, he made my heart sing. After this long winter season he is a welcome guest.

He is a tough one, this brave little warrior. He has survived winter, and so he must have taken well the teachings that only Gaa-biboonikaan (Winter Maker spirit) can provide. I don't see his wiiwan (wife), but then her feathers are so much more subdued, that my tired old eyes may have missed her. I hope she also survived the winter, for she too will be a welcome guest.

G'zhem-mnidoo, it is good to be alive on this day. Soon the ziinzibaakwadaaboo (tree sap) will begin to flow in the sugar maples, and we will taste again the sweetness of life. The Zhaganaash (English speaking people) calendar may call this time "spring," but my returning robin friend and I know that soon fresh ziinzibaakwad (maple sugar) will be a welcome flavour on our tongues.

And so it seems, Creator of all things, that we too have survived another winter. Do you ever wonder if your sentient creatures have learned much from the harsh lessons that Gaa-biboonikaan teaches? Did you called our winged brothers and sisters to our land to remind us of transforming new life, and teach us to sing again? That is a welcoming thought.

We come into our church circle around you, G'zhem-mnidoo, beginning to thaw from our self-imposed frostiness by the little signs you have shared with us. In our worship this morning may our words and songs be as genuine and honest as the robin's melody. May we lift our heads high to the heavens, fill our lungs with life-giving air, and raise our voices in a harmonious chorus of thanks and praise. Surely that will also be a welcomed sound.

Chii-miigwech (literally "great/many thanks," but also "Amen"), G'zhem-mnidoo.

(As a person of Aboriginal heritage, I was privileged to serve many years as a minister within First Nations communities. Also regarded as an elder, I sought to blend our traditional Native spiritual heritage with the Christian practices of the United Church of Canada. I find total harmony between the quintessential spirituality of both traditions, and so reintroduced many of our symbols and approaches to the church service. As many of my congregants had suffered through Residential Schools, where missionary types literally beat into them a residual fear of any Native ways, the reintroduction had to be done very gradually and carefully. There were then very few resources to turn to, so, although I am by no means a liturgist, I wrote some of my own.)

—R. Matthew Stevens, Canada

HYMN FOR SPRING

Bare branches reach toward the winter sky,
a chilling wind blows from the southern snow,
the frozen pastures bleak and barren lie;
we yearn for warmth and life to come once more.

By bush-clad coast we wait for signs of spring:
the budding grape vine and the kowhai* bloom;
in celebration, hymns of praise we sing,
as symbols of new life, bright flowers we share.

Life-giving Spirit, through your people move!
Awaken gifts which in us dormant lie;
may each one blossom in your caring love,
revived by you like sun and gentle rain.

Now help us face the pain that growth may bring:
and overcome the fears that hold us back;
around us and within we welcome spring,
the promise of a faithful God fulfilled.

(Tune: "Sursum Corda")
**Kowhai is a legume tree famous for its golden springtime blossom, the national flower of New Zealand.*

—Viv Whimster, Aotearoa/NewZealand

Diane Wendorf

A GATHERING PRAYER ON A FIRST SUMMER MORNING

Gizhe-manidoowiwin,

Indeed your divine nature is revealed and evident to us on this, the longest day of the year. In the pre-dawn darkness we light our sacred fire, and we are ready to welcome mooka'am (spirit of the sunrise) with prayers. Our waabini manidookewin (sunrise ceremony) is meant for celebrating this special day with hearts full of thanks for all you give your people.

All around us Omizakamigokwe (Mother Earth) sings her summer song of activity. Our four-legged brothers and sisters bring forth their oshki-ayaansag (literally "new ones," figuratively "newly born"). They venture from their burrows and lairs under the watchful eyes of their parents, with so many teachings yet to learn, and yet so much playfulness in their learning. Even the way wabooz (rabbit) mirthfully hops through the tall grass reminds us that it is good to celebrate this day.

We look up, G'zhem-mnidoo (Creator God), and our winged sisters and brothers are soaring and swooping, their tiny hearts bursting with the song of freedom. In their nests mottle feathered little ones stretch wide their beaks, endlessly seeking more nourishment to flourish and mature. Soon they too will dance in the skies, joining their parents in celebrating all you give to all living things—great and small.

The Zhaganaash call this day "Summer Solstice," and celebrate it with thoughts of the warm days to come. Those who are growers look to be on the land, turning the rich dark soil, planting seeds redolent with promise, and tending the delicate shoots that are even now burgeoning forth from Omizakamigokwe's (Mother Earth's) breast. Already we can recognize the first mandaamin (corn plants) embarking upon their journey toward the sun, and our mouths water at the remembrance of how sweet those kernels will taste. Oh yes, it is a good day to celebrate.

Do you ever wonder, Creator of all things, with all this joyful activity prospering in nature, why your sentient creatures often seem so sluggish and listless in the summer warmth? How often you must ponder, that quick as we are to moan and complain when a few things don't go as we suppose they should, we silently take all multitude of good things for granted as if they were somehow our due?

G'zhem-mnidoo, we come together this morning in the circle of our church, brimming over with awe for all of your creation. Even though we can be such facile and fickle creatures, we also have more than sufficient capacity to be filled with amazement and appreciation for your wondrous gifts. In our worship this providential morning, hear our words and songs as celebration from hearts overflowing in thanks and praise, for all you give your people.

Chii-miigwech (literally "great/many thanks," but also "Amen"), G'zhem-mnidoo.

—R. Matthew Stevens, Canada

PERFECT TIME

Water falls from the ledge,
Cascading rhythm.
Marking time, pacing life,
Upstream, downstream.
Flowing shower, rainbow maker.

Sunshine splinters, renegade drops
That glitter on leaves, flowers, ferns
And plunge roaring into the depths
Where waves pulse the shore
Dancing to the tune
Of your perfect time.

Summer flower birthed from the spring button
Warmth and light call forth the brilliance
Of budding synchronized with the season's race.
Opened glory, exuberant joy
Dying slowly as winter comes round the bend.

Life is too short to mourn or grieve,
Death's an instant in eternity
When the petals drop to earth,
Each one departing with the wind,
Each good-bye foretells the welcome
Of your perfect time.

If water measures in ebb and flow,
If seasons follow the spinning earth,
If flowers bloom and wither in a moment,
If stars, moon, and sun cling opposite on the merry-go-round,
If clouds swing by holding hands with the breeze,
If children skip and hop to each day of birth,
If each of these tells time within God's mind,
Then how do seconds fill infinity

And do years become of age?
What clock ticks with the fidelity
Of your perfect time?

—Elena Huegel, Chile

THE GLEANERS

In the time between
the baler's thump
and the lifter`s rattle
In the spaces
between the bales
the gleaners claim
their ancient right.

In this evening moment
of butterscotch light
there is peace between tribes.
Plover will sift straw with starling
finch will peck beside thrush.
They shall not hurt or destroy
in all my holy field.

—Robin List, Aotearoa/NewZealand

Rini Templeton

A GATHERING PRAYER ON A FIRST AUTUMN MORNING

Gizhe-manidoowiwin,

Oh yes, I felt it this morning! It actually caused me to turn back into my home for a sweater, and a secret tingle of delight when I had slipped it on. Autumn is most definitely here again with morning air that is sharp, clearing idle thoughts from my head. For that I am thankful.

It's time to check the wood pile, and split more for the coming cold weather. I've been meaning to do that, but those hot summer days called me to less strenuous activities. Time to also find the spade again, and dig up the mounds of badakaan (potatoes) tucked under the soil. We should have a good supply, and for that too I'm thankful, Generous Creator.

This is the season, G'zhem-mnidoo (Creator God), for which you save your best colours and hues. The sugar maples are already subjects of your artistry, and on a nearby hill one has burst overnight into a fiery red. By the creek the rose hip have grown fat, and once touched with gentle frost they'll be ready to pluck. It's a busy time, for the bright red apples also call to be picked. It feels good to gather in the autumn bounty, and for that I am thankful.

Our four-legged brothers and sisters sensed the coming of autumn long before us, and they have been busy filling their hidden cachés for some time. Just the other day I stopped to watch brother amik (beaver) rebuilding part of his lodge. He and I seem to compete for the most suitable poles—and he generally wins. That I accept, but I'm not really thankful.

Many of our winged relations will soon venture to their southern homes. They bulk up with all the nourishment they'll need to sustain their long journey. A wedge of nikag (literally "goose," locally "Canada goose") noisily practice formation flying, and the young learn they still need to strengthen if they are to pace their elder's flight. For the bagwa-janoomin (wild rice) in the marshlands, both they and I will be thankful.

This is also the season for thoughts of transition, for one day it will be our time to cross over to be with our ancestors and you, G'zhem-mnidoo. Do you ever wonder why your sentient creatures are so reluctant to consider their crossing-over? Do you sometimes ponder the acceptance of the nikag to their journey, and hesitancy of humans to affirm your presence throughout the cycle of life?

We come together in the circle of our church, a little more pensive than on other Sabbath mornings. We have been taught that part of Sabbath derives from "peace," and so perhaps today would be a good time for all of us to make our peace with all others. In our worship may you hear in our words and songs our commitment to be in harmony with your plan for our mortal existence.

Chii-miigwech (literally "great/many thanks," but also "Amen"), G'zhem-mnidoo.

—R. Matthew Stevens, Canada

IN THIS
EVENING MOMENT
OF
BUTTERSCOTCH
LIGHT,
THERE IS
PEACE
BETWEEN
TRIBES.

—Robin List
Aotearoa/New Zealand

A PRAYER WHEN PARCHED AND WAITING

At this time of autumn,
the snow is thin,
the mountain slopes bare.
But the cold is coming,
with the touch of frost,
and the fog on the shore.
We need it because the earth is dry,
and the trees hold their hands high for rain.
Like us, they are parched, waiting for water.

In places the lake is warm,
fed by hot springs from below,
with energies of unimagined power.
We harness some of it with our pipes,
but we cannot control what is under the surface.

We forget the strength of creation,
when the volcano blew ash in our faces.
The sun was gone and the air was cold.
It can bring a sense of insignificance,
and a search for our foundations.

Created in your image,
open our eyes to find you
in the volcano and the tree—
The volcano and the tree. Amen

—John Howell, Aotearoa, New Zealand

THE VISITORS

Sometimes you look at a black pond
like this and the water is filled

with stars. And ancient apple trees
gnarled branches in search of

something. Out of the woods three fauns
with their mother stare at you 'cross

meadows, motionless as the trees,
then lower their heads to nibble

a long time. And something as
imperceptible as stardust

fills you, whispers yes, then passes.
The deer gone, the meadow empty.

—Ray McGinnis, Canada

A GATHERING PRAYER ON A FIRST WINTER MORNING

G'zhem-mnidoo, great and kindly Creator:

We awoke this morning to find that overnight Gaa-biboonikaan (Winter Maker spirit) had made a first visit. A thin blanket of white stretched out before us, and in the light of the brilliant rising sun we saw that the trees had been glazed in a crystal sheen. It was surprising.

We step outside, and recall the sound of new frost crunching under our feet. Now we move carefully, for suddenly we recollect the pain that comes from slipping and falling. As we rediscovered our "winter legs" we regained forgotten confidence, and ventured further in this glacial wonderland. It was sensational.

Our first deep breath fills our lungs with the crisp clarity of frigid air. It's so sharp it almost burns, and yet in a matter of seconds we are certain that we're fully conscious and completely alive. Yes, it is as you ordained it, G'zhem-mnidoo (Creator God)—and it is good.

How like our relationship with you, great and kindly Creator, is this early winter morn. When we are warm and relaxed like a summer day, we are too often sluggish in expressing our chii-miigwech for all you gift us with each and every day. We put down our semma (ceremonial tobacco) too casually without reflection, simply performing through ritual rather than sincerity. This is not good!

Then comes a cold wind of unexpected intervention into our lives, and now we are fully conscious and aware of the potential peril it brings. We remember that were it not for your ancient teachings we might slip and fall, and we recollect the pain of past occurrence. It is then that we rediscover our "prayer legs" and that you ordained challenge that we might grow. We know, this too is good.

As you witness the foolishness and forgetfulness of your sentient creatures, do you, G'zhem-mnidoo, ever ponder when we will accept the teachings of the seasons? Do you wonder about how clearly you must need to draw the circle of life, before we gain what our winged and four-legged brothers and sisters know by instinct? Is this disappointing?

We have come together this morning in the circle of our church, asking only that you, great and kindly Creator, continue to be patient with us. In our worship hear our words and songs as our rededication to transformation. This is a commitment from us all, to follow in a good way the path to which you've called us. And that will be good!

Chii-miigwech (literally "great/many thanks," but also "Amen"), G'zhem-mnidoo.

—R. Matthew Stevens, Canada

Winter
Elena Huegel

Part Three

OUR HANDS TOUCH GOD
Sacraments, Ceremonies, and Transitions

14 ❀ SACRAMENTS AND CELEBRATIONS—BAPTISM

Baby Moses   He Qi

THE COVENANT OF BAPTISM

(outdoor service in a homestead in northern Saskachawan)

Welcome:

Hear what Jesus thought about the importance of welcoming children: "People were bringing little children to Jesus in order that he might bless them; and the disciples spoke sternly to them. But when Jesus saw this, he was indignant and said to them, 'Let the children come to me; do not stop them; for it is to such as these that the kingdom of God belongs. Truly I tell you, whoever does not receive the kingdom of God like a little child will not enter it.' And Jesus laid his hands on the children, and blessed them." Mark 10:13–16.

Presentation of Candidates

On behalf of _____, I welcome and present for baptism: _____, son of _____ ; _____, son of _____ ; _____, daughter of _____ ; _____, son of _____ .

Profession of Faith

ONE: Do you believe in God, who is the creative force for good in the universe, who has come in Jesus to show us what God is like, and who works in us and others by the Spirit?

PARENTS: We do, by the grace of God.

ONE: Will you follow Jesus, resisting evil, seeking justice, and acknowledging God's love for all creation, including yourselves?

PARENTS: We will, God being our helper.

ONE: Will you join with your brothers and sisters in this community of faith to celebrate God's goodness, to live with respect in creation, and to love and serve others?

PARENTS: We will, God being our helper.

ONE: In baptism, these baptismal candidates mark an important step in their journey. Do you promise to love and care for these children, and to seek to work with them as they grow into what it means to be a Christ-follower in this world?

PARENTS: We do, God being our helper.

Congregational Commitment

The people stand, as able, to pledge love and support.

ONE: Recognizing that it takes a whole village to raise a child, will you do all in your power to love and be respectful of these baptismal candidates and their families?

ALL: We will, God being our helper.

ONE: Do you commit yourselves to support and nurture this family within a community that is Christian with one another, that seeks justice, and that resists all behavior devoid of love and kindness?

ALL: We do, by the grace of God.

Act of Baptism

ONE: _____, baptism is the promise that you are welcome in God's church; you are gifts of God to us in the church, to your parents and family, to the world, and to yourselves. Baptism encourages you to wrap your arms around yourself and your world with enthusiasm and love, knowing you are each a child of God, loved and cherished.

Let us pray: Divine Companion, pour out your Holy Spirit on us. May this water of baptism bless and seal the love and goodwill present here today. Amen

We baptize you, _____ in the name of the Father, the Son, and the Holy Spirit. May the blessing of God, who shelters us like a mother hen her chicks, be with you today and always. Amen

_____, let your light so shine before others, that they may see the good in you and give thanks to God for you. Amen

Into the household of faith, we welcome you!

—Suzanne E. Edgar, Canada

SELECTIONS FROM A SERVICE OF ADULT BAPTISM

Baptismal candidates are given candles. While the candles are being lit, the minister takes up the censer, goes to the baptismal place, which can be a baptistery, pool, or river, and censes around it. Baptism is by total imersion in the water.

ONE: Blessed is the Kingdom of the Father, and of the Son, and of the Holy Spirit, both now and ever, and to the ages of ages. Amen.

The Blessing of the Baptismal Waters

Great are you, O Lord, and wondrous are Your works, and no word will suffice to praise your wonders. You have created this planet and have crowned the cycle of the year with the four seasons; the sun praises you; the moon and the stars, the springs of waters and the seas, winds of the air and clouds, the flowers of the earth, and the birds of the sky, all the creatures of your creation glorify you; the choirs angels and archangels worship before you; the many-eyed cherubim and the six-winged seraphim, as they stand and fly around you, veil themselves with fear of your unapproachable Glory; for you, being without bounds and beginning came down on earth, emptied yourself taking the form of a servant, being made in the likeness of human beings; for you, Lord, because of your limitless mercy, could not endure our suffering by the sin and fear and came to save us. We confess your Grace and thank you for setting us free. You sanctified the streams of Jordan, sending down from the Heavens your Holy Spirit, and crushed the head of evil.

Therefore we beseech you, our loving king and great high priest, be present with us now and bless this water so it becomes for us the water of liberation, adoption, healing, and sanctification.

You have bestowed upon us the gift of regeneration from on high by water and the spirit. Manifest yourself, Lord, in this water, and grant that he (she) who is to be baptized may be transformed through the baptism. Help him (her) to put away the old person, which is corrupt according to the deceitful lusts, and to put on of the new person, which is renewed according to the image of Him who created him (her), that, being planted in the likeness of your death through baptism, he (she) may become a sharer of your glorious resurrection; bless him (her) that by this holy baptism he (she) may be accounted among the number of the first-born, whose names are written in heaven.

CHOIR: Amen.

ONE: Let us pray. *(The minister, singing "Alleluia" thrice with the people, makes three crosses with the oil upon the water.)*

CHOIR: Alleluia, alleluia, alleluia.

ONE: Blessed is God who enlightens and sanctifies every man and woman that come into the world, both now and ever, and to the ages of ages.

CHOIR: Amen.

The Prayer of Laying on Hands and Anointing

Blessed are you, Lord God Almighty, Fountain of Blessings, Sun of Righteousness, who made to shine forth for those in darkness a light of salvation through the manifestation of your son and our Saviour, Jesus Christ, our God.

Who now also has been well-pleased to regenerate this your servant and disciple newly enlightened through the baptism. Now we beseech you, our sovereign Lord and most intimate friend, compassionate King of All, bestow upon him (her) also the seal of your Holy Spirit; keep him (her) in your sanctification; confirm him (her) in the faith of the One, Holy, Catholic, and Apostolic church. In the faith of unconditional love, forgiveness, reconciliation, and peace.

Deliver him (her) from the evil one and all his devices; preserve his (her) soul, through your saving love, in purity and righteousness, that in every work and word, being acceptable before you, he (she) may become a child and heir of your heavenly Kingdom.

For you are our God, the God of Mercy and Salvation, and to You do we send up glory the Most Holy Trinity: Father, Son, and Holy Spirit, both now and ever, and to the ages of ages. Amen.

(After this prayer, the minister anoints the baptized and makes on the person the sign of the cross with the oil on the forehead, the eyes, the nostrils, the mouth, the ears, the breast, the hands, and the feet. At each anointing and sealing is said, "the seal of the gift of the Holy Spirit," . . . then he/she lays hands on the baptized and says, "I bless you in the name of the Father, Son, and Holy Spirit.")

The seal of the gift of the Holy Spirit: the disciple of Christ _____ is anointed with the "oil of gladness" in the name of the Father, Son, and Holy Spirit.

(As he/she anoints the forehead) May God enlighten your mind with his wisdom.

(As he/she anoints the ears) May God almighty let you always hear his voice.

(As he/she anoints the eyes) May God almighty let you see his truth.

(As he/she anoints the lips) May God almighty inspire you to proclaim the gospel of salvation.

(As he/she anoints the palms of the hands) May God almighty bless every work that you undertake for the sake of the love of God and neighbour.

(As he/she anoints the feet) May God almighty lead you in the ways of peace and justice.

(Then he/she lays his/her hand on the baptized and says):

I bless you in the name of the Most Holy Trinity, Father, Son, and Holy Spirit.

ALL: Amen.

The baptized is invested with in a new white robe:

Clothed is the servant of God and the disciple of Christ _____ with the garment of righteousness, in the name of the Father, and of the Son, and of the Holy Spirit. Amen.

As many of you as have been baptized into Christ, have put on Christ. Alleluia. Alleluia. Alleluia.

Glory to the Father and to the Son and to the Holy Spirit. Both now and ever unto ages of ages.

—Archbishop Malkhaz Songulashvili, Evangelical Baptist Church of Georgia (country), and Rev. Benjamin Bakuradze

FOR A BAPTISM SUNDAY—CALL TO WORSHIP OR COMMISSIONING

ONE: If Jesus had been baptised in the waters
 the Anisnabeg (*Ah-nish-na-bey*) call
 Gii-dzhii Ojibwe-gah-meeng (*Gi-chee Ojib-weh-ga-mey*),—
would the Holy Spirit have been seen in the snow-white of a Dove?

ALL: Or in the red-black flash of a Woodpecker,
 the standing grey of a Heron,
  the blue lightning of a Jay?

ONE: If Jesus had been baptised in the waters
 we call "Lake Superior"
would the Holy Spirit have been heard in the coo of a Dove?

ALL: Or in the hoot of a Great Horned Owl,
 in the laugh of a Whiskey Jack,
  in the scream of a Gull?

ONE: The voice of Spirit is not always gentle.

ALL: The wings of the Spirit are both great and small.

ONE: The flight of the Spirit carries us to forever.

ALL: If only we look and listen—
 to the unexpected *and* the everyday.

ONE: Let us open our eyes to the Holy Spirit's passage . . .
Let us open our ears to the Holy Spirit's song.
Let us open our lives to the Holy Spirit's yearning.

(if a Call to Worship):
ALL: Let us worship God!

(or if a Commissioning/Benediction):

ALL: Let us go into the Creator's world,
knowing the Spirit is with us.
Let us be Christ's people,
following the Spirit's call.
    Alleluia! Amen!

—Richard Bott, Canada

CALL TO WORSHIP FOR BAPTISM OF JESUS SUNDAY

ONE: *(Water is poured into the font.)* Water.

ALL: Life making.
Body filling.
World changing.

ONE: *(Water is poured into the font.)* Spirit!

ALL: Life making.
Soul filling.
World changing!

ONE: *(Water is poured into the font.)* Child of God!

ALL: Life making.
Spirit filling.
World changing!

ONE: Blessed—

ALL: and blessing.

ONE: Water. Spirit. Children of God.

ALL: Together in this place.
Remembering who we are.
Remembering whose we are.
    Worshipping God.

ONE: Alleluia!

ALL: Alleluia!

—Richard Bott, Canada

REMEMBERING OUR BAPTISM

ONE: *(Water is poured into the font.)*
The sea-salt tang of the Strait of Georgia,
the milky glow of a glacier's melt,
the icy runoff from the Golden Ears mountains,
the earthy warmth of Harrison Hot Springs—
    Gift-of-God—water!

ALL: Flowing across the land, flowing in our lives.

ONE: *(A candle/the Christ Candle is lit.)*
The mist-gentled glow of a Victoria street-lamp,
the star-studded sky of a boat on the sea,
the blue-orange warmth of a dawn on Mount Seymour,
the noon-bright reflection coming off English Bay—
    Gift-of-God—light!

ALL: Bringing warmth to creation, bringing warmth to our lives.

ONE: *(The Bible is opened in front of the people.)*
Shared by an Elder on the shore of the Fraser,
shared by a child on the porch of a home,
shared by the glow of the PNE* Ferris Wheel,
shared by a blanket on a Vancouver street—
    Gift-of-God—faith!

ALL: Lived between neighbours, lived in our lives.

ONE: With water, with light, with faith—

ALL: we remember our baptism.

ONE: With water, with light, with faith—

ALL: we remember Christ's call.

ONE: And as we remember—

ALL: we worship God!
    Alleluia!

Pacific National Exhibition—held each year in Vancouver, British Columbia

—Richard Bott, Canada

15 ❁ SACRAMENTS AND CELEBRATIONS—COMMUNION

Diane Wendorf

BREAD, BROKEN AND SCATTERED

The ears of wheat are broken and scattered
on the hillside to grow.
Gathered, they are broken again
and scattered through the city to make bread.
The bread is scattered to each home
and broken to give nourishment.
Broken and scattered, broken and scattered,
and some becomes the Lord's body broken for us
as we are the people of God scattered throughout the city
and, perhaps, broken to give nourishment to others.

—Isobel de Gruchy, South Africa

BRIEF ORDER FOR THE SACRAMENT OF HOLY COMMUNION

An Invitation

ONE: *(raising the bread)* This is the bread we have offered;
With thankful hearts we have blessed it,
With open hands, come and receive it.

ALL: Amen

ONE: *(raising the cup)* This cup is full; like our hearts
It overflows, with a thirst for justice,
Come and drink from it.

ALL: Amen. With open hands and hearts overflowing, we come.

An Offertory

If there is a divine spark
That is in me,
Let it flame;
That I might be consumed
For peace.

If there is anything holy
That is in me,
Let it be as breath;
That I might carry it
Lightly.

If there is any wisdom
That is in me,
Let it cry out;
That justice be heard in
My speaking.

If there is any love
That is in me,
Let it sing;
That love might be the song
Of my heart.

If any of these gifts
Be found in me,
Let them bring life;
Fill all of me, and become
My offering.

Be a Blessing

Let us: Take care of this world,
it is a gift to us
Find love in all people,
they share it with us
Make peace unconditionally,
all life depends on it
And be a blessing. Always. Amen.

—Erice Fairbrother, Aotearoa,/New Zealand

WORDS FOR INVITATION AND ADMINISTRATION OF COMMUNION

The Invitation

The bread is lifted up
The bread is blessed and broken:
It calls us to make the vulnerable,
The poor and hungry, our priority.

The cup is lifted up
The wine is poured and the cup full:
It calls us to be filled with compassion,
An outpouring of justice and peace

All are called. Come.

The Administration

All surround the table. The passing of communion is in silence. The plate is offered to each person by the person next to him or her. Each person takes a portion from the plate and holds it. Then it returns to the presider, who also takes a portion and holds it up saying: "this is bread for all who are hungry."

Together the people respond: "Amen." The people eat their portions together.

The person next to the presider takes the cup, raises it and drinks from it.

The cup then passes to the next person, and so it continues around, given and received in silence. When all have received, the presider, receiving it last, holds it before them and says: "this is the cup of justice and peace."

The people respond by saying together "Amen."

—Erice Fairbrother, Aotearoa/New Zealand

CALL TO WORSHIP FOR COMMUNION SUNDAY

ONE: Jesus said, "I am the bread of life."

ALL: What did he mean?

ONE: Jesus said, "Whoever eats this bread
  will live forever."

ALL: How could he make such promises?

ONE: Jesus said, "Whoever comes to me
  will never be hungry,
whoever believes in me will never thirst."

ALL: In our bodies?

ONE: In our souls!
This is the bread that fills the hunger
  that the world cannot fill.
This is the bread that feeds our spirits
  as we walk the journey of life.

ALL: Jesus Christ is our manna—
  gift of God forever and ever!

ONE: In that gift, with that gift, through that gift—

ALL: we worship God. Alleluia!

—Richard Bott, Canada

WELCOMED AT THE TABLE—A STORY OF COMMUNION IN SOUTH AFRICA

Micah, my son, was unsure about attending the *inkonzo* (worship) with me at Umzumbe. It was a church, far away, two hours away, mostly on a dirt road. He would not understand much, as the worship is conducted in isiZulu. Besides, in his opinion, I, the *umfundisi* (minister), usually preached the *intshumayelo* (sermon) for too long! He did not need to hear more of me. Also, Micah knew that Sunday school would be much different. He would not know the other children. He feared would not know the songs. He thought he would probably just sit and be bored.

Well, the trip to Umzumbe was far more beautiful than he expected, and it was fun turning on the winding roads. Instead of sitting and being bored, he helped the chief deacon set up the communion table. They could not understand each other, but the deacon used his hands to show Micah what to do. The old man's eyes and smile showed his approval. Micah felt good to be useful while I prepared for worship. Micah enjoyed looking outside of the church, seeing the river far down below. Micah was surprised the window he looked out from was actually an open cross in the wall of the church. That was cool! After church was a great meal. He had never had lunch at church after worship.

As Micah rode home from Umzumbe, he realized that he can worship God in a new place, in a different language, with people he didn't know, and in different ways. Despite the fact that worship was different at Umzumbe, Micah knew God felt that "it was good"!

—Scott Couper, South Africa

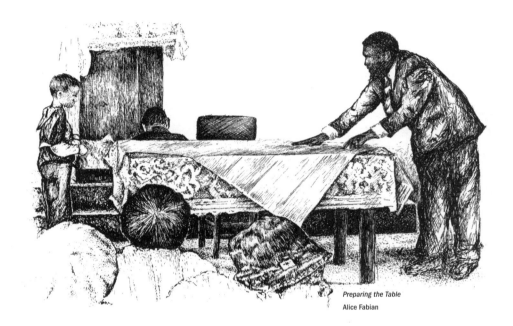

Preparing the Table
Alice Fabian

A COMMUNION LITURGY

ONE: God is with you.

ALL: And also with you.

ONE: Lift up your hearts.

ALL: We lift them up to God.

ONE: Let us give God thanks and praise.

ALL: Let us give God thanks and praise!

ONE: Alleluia.

ALL: Alleluia!

ONE: With all of our hearts, we thank you, God.
In love, you created all things.
In curiosity, you continue to live with your creation.

In hope, you promised to be with it—and with us—
to the end of the ages.
    And so we say,

ALL: Alleluia.

ONE: And so we cry,

ALL: Alleluia!

ONE: And so we shout,

ALL: ALLELUIA!

ONE: For all that keeps life going—
    the touchable—water, light, air, food—
    and the intangible—love, friendship, and care—
we thank you God.
In the stories of the people Israel,
in the stories of peoples around the world—
    place to place, generation to generation—
we have heard of your overwhelming love for all:
    for the tall cedars, whose roots grow deep into the earth,
    for the flowing waters, and the salmon that swim them,
    for the eagles above and the earthworms below,
    for all that creeps and crawls and walks . . .
        and for us—
            human beings of every shape
                and size and colour;
            people of every land and race;
            people of all places and times.
    Thank you, God!

ALL: Thank you, God!

ONE: Your love for us is incomprehensible, God!
Even when we do damage—
    to ourselves, to other humans,
        to the rest of your creation—
even when we do damage
    that *we* see as unforgivable—
you call us back to your Love.
    Again and again—and again.
Through wise women and men,
    through teachers and preachers and prophets,
    through singers and dancers and storytellers,

and through Jesus—the Christ—
you call us back to your Love.
Thank you, God!

ALL: Thank you, God!

ONE: With all of your creation, we sing praise!

ALL: Holy, holy, holy Lord,
God of love and life,
heaven and earth are full of your glory!
HOSANNA in the highest!
Blessed is the one who comes in God's name.
HOSANNA IN THE HIGHEST!

ONE: We remember, and in our remembering,

ALL: we ask for your forgiveness.

ONE: We remember, and in our remembering,

ALL: we ask for your Wisdom.

ONE: As we come to your table, God,
we remember those who have sinned against us—
    and we release them. *(Pause)*

ALL: We release them.

ONE: As we come to your table, God,
we remember those whom we have sinned against—
    and we ask your forgiveness. (pause)

ALL: We ask forgiveness.

ONE: As we come to your table, God,
we remember the night that Jesus sat with his friends and disciples.
We remember that they gathered together,
    for a meal of celebration and hope.
As they were eating, Jesus looked at these folk who had walked with him.
He picked up the bread, gave thanks to you, God most holy,
    and he broke it—and looked at them.
With all their eyes on him, listening intently, they heard him say,
"This is my body, given for you. Eat this and remember me."
He took a cup, filled with wine.
He gave thanks to you, God most holy, and held that cup close.
He looked at his friends and said, "This cup is the new covenant, in my blood.
Each time you drink it—remember me."
And so we eat, we drink, and we remember.

ALL: We eat the bread of life.
We drink the cup of hope.
We remember Jesus the Christ.
Alleluia!
Come, Christ Jesus!
Come into our hearts.
Come into our lives.
Come into our love.

ONE: God of the delta, that feeds our bodies,
God of the mountains, that remind us of our youth,
God of the waters, the sustainer of life—
    God of all creation—
we ask your blessing on this bread and this cup.
We ask your blessing on all gathered here.
We ask your blessing on all creation.
In this moment,
    may your Holy Spirit make us one with Christ,
        with all.

ALL: Alleluia, amen!
(Bread is broken, wine is poured.)

ONE: Jesus Christ, the bread of life!

ALL: Jesus Christ, the cup of hope!

ONE: The gifts of God for the people of God.

ALL: Thanks be to God!

(Communion is shared)

Prayer after Communion

ALL: Thank you, God:
for the bread and the cup,
for the life and the Love,
    for the Wisdom to walk into your world.
With your strength, our faith is strengthened.
With your love, our love grows.
    Help us to share that love, strength, and faith.
    Help us to accept when others share it with us—
that it might change the world.
In Christ's name, we ask it. Amen.

—Richard Bott, Canada

POST COMMUNION PRAYERS

We thank you, Lord,
that you have strengthened us through your nearness
and we pray: grant that the ears that have heard your Word
may be closed to the voice of discord;
that the eyes which have seen your great love
may see the blessedness which you have promised;
that the tongues which have sung your praise
may testify henceforth to the truth;
that the hands which have received your gifts
may do good to your honour;
that the feet which have come into your house
may not stray from the way of light;
that the bodies which have had a share
in your living body
may change into a new life.
To you be glory for ever. Amen.

—Adapted from Agenda I, edited by Church Office of the Evangelical Church
of Kurhesses-Waldeck, Kassel, Germany

Dear Father in heaven,
you have been our host at the table of your Son
may his life, his death, and his resurrection
strengthen us now in our lives.
Your Word is greater than our anxieties,
your hope is stronger than our despondency,
your presence is more certain than our doubts.
Lead us that we may become the image of your creation,
which waits for you.
Lord Jesus Christ, we pray:
lead us with your hand,
so that from the many may come one whole,
from the diversity, a richness,
and from the barrenness of the everyday, fruitful life.
You are Lord over all power and force

in heaven and on earth,
bring us together and protect us in your community.
God, Holy Spirit,
Lead us to a knowledge of your truth,
Let us grow together in one body and give us strength
for each day of our lives,
so that we might praise the Father with one mouth
each morning and at the approach of night
that we might be strong in readiness for the day
when you will lead us
to eternal light. Amen.

—Achim Reinstadtler, Germany

Rini Templeton

AN AGAPE LITURGY

Agape meals were part of the worshipping life of the early church. They took up the banquet imagery present in a number of Jesus' parables, and expressed powerfully some of the distinctive characteristics of the coming of God's kingdom. They were occasions of joy and festivity, as the community celebrated the meaning of resurrection. They were boundary markers, enabling the community to affirm its identity as those who belonged to Christ. And they were places of economic justice, enabling a sharing and redistribution amongst the community. These themes are taken up in this liturgy.

Opening Sentences

Come! If you are hungry there is food to eat.
Come! If you are thirsty there is water to drink.
It is food for those who hunger for justice,
and water for those who long for life in all its fullness.

Come! Eat and drink to proclaim the feast of God's kingdom
where all are welcome
and no one is left out.

Prayer Offering Praise

God, our Mother and Father,
You have given us this earth rich and vibrant.
Its renewing life sustains us.
Its unfailing goodness nourishes us.
Blessed be your name.

Jesus, our Saviour and Healer,
You ate with friends and enemies.
At a meal you brought the gift of hope.
At a meal you gave the word of life.
Blessed be your name.

Spirit, our Comforter and Disturber,
You do not leave us on our own.
Here are companions to know our joy.
Here are companions to share our sorrow.
Blessed be your name.

Prayer Seeking Renewal

ONE: As we gather together, around this table where all are welcome, we seek God's peace and renewal—
From regret and fear:
ALL: Give us peace, loving God.
ONE: From anger and mistrust:
ALL: Give us peace, vulnerable God.
ONE: From pain and brokenness:
ALL: Give us peace, healing God.
ONE: From division and conflict:
ALL: Give us peace, reconciling God.
ONE: From violence and injustice:
ALL: Give us peace, gentle God.
ONE: Welcoming God, come and renew us
Name us as your people.
Name our world as yours.
And give us peace. Amen.

Sharing Scripture

A passage of scripture is read, followed by a simple comment or a period of silence for quiet reflection.

Sharing the Day

An opportunity for those present to offer the day to God, whether it is naming what has already happened or what still lies ahead.

Sharing Concerns

ONE: Around a table of feasting and festivity, where we are all invited to find life-giving gifts, we hold in love the struggle and the pain of the world.
Where a child experiences abuse and neglect:

ALL: Come, Holy Spirit, make us impatient for change.

ONE: Where the hungry cry out for food:

ALL: Come, Holy Spirit, make us impatient for change.

ONE: Where people live with advancing sickness and disease:

ALL: Come, Holy Spirit, make us impatient for change.

ONE: Where communities fail to care for the weak and ignore the stranger in their midst:

ALL: Come, Holy Spirit, make us impatient for change.

ONE: Where those in power listen to the demands of the rich and ignore the needs of the poor:

ALL: Come, Holy Spirit, make us impatient for change.

ONE: Where the church is preoccupied with its own
rightness and ceases to be the hope of good news:

ALL: Come, Holy Spirit, make us impatient for change.

ONE: Create in us and all people a holy discontent with the way things are, and a holy desire for the ways of peace and justice.

Words of Hope

The Prophet Isaiah writes: "On this mountain the Lord Almighty will prepare a feast of rich food for all peoples, a banquet of aged wines—the best of meats and the finest of wines. On this mountain he will destroy the shroud that enfolds all peoples, the sheet that covers all nations; he will swallow up death forever. The Sovereign Lord will wipe away the tears from all faces; he will remove the disgrace of his people from all the earth. The Lord has spoken. In that day they will say, 'Surely this is our God; we trusted in him, and he saved us. This is the Lord, we trusted in him; let us rejoice and be glad in his salvation.'"

Sharing

Eat this fruit.
It is the wonder of creation held in our hands;
the gift of sun and soil, wind and rain.
It speaks to us of the work of human labour,
of the longing of the poor,
of the promise that in the kingdom
we will all share in the feast of life.
Eat this fruit.
For it is the sweet taste of liberation.

(Fruit is distributed and eaten.)

Drink this water.
It is the wonder of creation held in our hands;
the gift of cloud and rain, river and spring.
It speaks to us of cleansing,
of the longing of all creation for its renewing,
of the promise that in baptism
we are all invited to a new and living hope.
Drink this water.
For it is the refreshing taste of life.

(Water is distributed and drunk.)

Offering *(Hands are joined for the offering of one another to God.)*

We are God's people.
Shaped and formed by water and Word.
Sustained and nourished by the fruit of love.
Together we will live as God's people.

Closing Sentences

We must not stay here.
Our purpose is among those who cry out for peace.
Our place is alongside those who search for justice.
Let us go with trembling hearts and joyful spirits,
to sow the seeds of God's kingdom.

—Graham Sparkes, Anthea Sully, England

WORLD COMMUNION SUNDAY RESOURCES

ONE: Welcome, my friends! A feast has been spread here before us, and the Risen Christ, our host, gathers us together as guests around one table.

ALL: Our table is an altar that reaches around the world as Christians from every country on earth share the bread of life and the cup of blessing.

ONE: Can you hear the voices of parents, grandparents, and care-givers near and far calling their children home for supper? Listen now as people from around the world call us home for supper:

(Here names and languages can be listed for people from the congregation who have agreed to share typical words that would call children in for supper: "Supper's ready!" "Vengan niños a comer," "A comida esta pronto," etc. The more languages, the better!)

ALL: We hear God's voice in many languages. Let us praise God in song as we prepare to gather around the Communion table this day!

—Christina J. Del Piero, USA

ALL PEOPLE, COME

All people spread across the Earth
sing to our God with awesome mirth;
serve in the Light with hand and voice;
come now with us, learn to rejoice.

O sense the Mind behind the World:
see the great Maker's flag unfurled.
We are the flock God wants to feed;
but others also are in need.

Let's enter then the Sphere of Grace,
and learn to serve God all our days,
in deeds and words, in works and ways:
through trials learn to dance in praise!

Tune: "Old 100th" Psalm, in G-flat

—Gordon Piesse, Aotearoa, New Zealand

A LITANY OF HOPE AND CONNECTION FOR WORLD COMMUNION SUNDAY

ONE: In a world of difference God reminds us that we are deeply alike.

ALL: We seek sustenance in bowls of rice and loaves of bread.

ONE: We laugh when lotus flowers bloom and autumn leaves dance in the wind.

ALL: We eat with knives and forks and chopsticks and remember that there are people who have no food.

ONE: We celebrate new friendships and the ties of love that connect us across the globe.

ALL: We weep when the suffering of our sisters and brothers becomes real for us.

ONE: We hope for a world of peace and justice for all of creation and remember that . . .

ALL: We are God's strong back and work-weary arms.

ONE: We are God's callused hands and muscled legs.

ALL: Through us, with us, God loves and suffers, laughs and cries.

ONE: God calls all of us to do justice, to love kindness, and to walk humbly with God.

ALL: God calls us to be God's co-creative partners in the redemptive work of justice.

ONE: United in faith, working in love, we are the hope for the world.

ALL: God is with us through it all. We are not alone. Amen.

—Frances A. Bogle, USA, *written after a visit to China*

CALL TO WORSHIP FOR WORLD COMMUNION SUNDAY

ONE: Today we celebrate World Communion Sunday. With Christians everywhere, we gather at Christ's welcome table to share in simple elements of bread and cup. In our unity, Christ is alive. In this sacrament, Christ is made known throughout the earth.

PEOPLE: We come to this World Communion table to unite our hearts with brothers and sisters in every nation who seek to know Christ's presence in the breaking of the bread.

NORTH AMERICA: I represent North America, and I come bringing corn bread from Mississippi and sourdough rolls from California and tortillas from Mexico and bagels from New York.

ALL: Praise God for the bread of life, gift of the earth
Bless, O God, all those who dwell upon the earth.

ASIA: I represent Asia, and I come bringing rice cakes from Japan and wontons from China and na'an from India.

ALL: Praise God for the bread of life, gift of the earth.
Bless, O God, all those who dwell upon the earth.

AFRICA: I represent Africa, and I come bringing fufu from the Congo and pounded yam from Nigeria and chin chin from Ghana.

ALL: Praise God for the bread of life, gift of the earth.
Bless, O God, all those who dwell upon the earth.

EUROPE: I represent Europe, and I come bringing baguettes from France and sweet rolls from Portugal and foccacia from Italy and black rye from Russia.

ALL: Praise God for the bread of life, gift of the earth.
Bless, O God, all those who dwell upon the earth.

SOUTH AMERICA: I represent South America, and I come bringing pao de coco from Brazil and empanadas from Colombia and cassava bread from Venezuela.

ALL: Praise God for the bread of life, gift of the earth.
Bless, O God, all those who dwell upon the earth.

MIDDLE EAST: I represent the Middle East, and I come bringing pita from Turkey and challah from Israel and lavash from Armenia.

ALL: Praise God for the bread of life, gift of the earth.
Bless, O God, all those who dwell upon the earth.

CENTRAL AMERICA: I represent Central America, and I come bringing bulla cakes from Jamaica and ozzies from the Dominican Republic and cheese bread from El Salvador.

ALL: Praise God for the bread of life, gift of the earth.
Bless, O God, all those who dwell upon the earth.

LEADER: Many grains were gathered together to make this bread.
So we who are many, and come from many places, are one in Christ.
May the peace of Christ be with you.

ALL: And also with you.

This is a creative way to begin World Communion Sunday for a congregation in the United States. You can invite the children, youth, and adults in the church to dress in native attire from around the world and enter the sanctuary carrying these many varieties of breads from across the world. Then lay the many baskets of bread on the communion table. A visit to your local international foods store or ethnic grocery store can yield many treasures of grains from around the world—you can substitute for these named breads others you find.

—Jennifer Mills-Knutsen, USA

16 ✿ Celebrating the Transitions in Our Lives

**BIRTHDAY SERVICE FOR AN INDONESIAN CONGREGATION/
TATA IBADAH HARULANG TAHUN**

Preparation (Persiapan)

Hymn

Opening Prayer (Doa Pembukaan)

ONE: We come to you, O Lord, to thank you for being constantly present in the years of our life. (Kami datang kepadaMu, ya Tuhan untuk mensyukuri rahmat, kasih dan kehadiranMu yang tak putus-putusnya di dalam tahun-tahun kehidupan kami).

ALL: More years of life, more blessings we received from you. (Semakin tahun usia kami bertambah, semakin kami merasakan kehadiran berkatMu).

THE BIRTHDAY PERSON: Thank you, Lord, for your abundant love that you have poured out into my life. Glory and honor to you, O my Lord! (Terima kasih Tuhan untuk kelimpahan cintaMu yang Engkau curahkan dalam hidupku. Pujian dan hormat ku persembahkan untukMu, O Tuhan).

ONE: This thanksgiving fellowship is in the name of God the Father, Son, and Holy Spirit. (Persekutuan syukur ini adalah di dalam nama Allah Bapa, Anak dan Roh Kudus)

**Prayer of Confession and Assurance of Pardon
(Doa Pengakuan Dosa Dan Berita Anugerah Allah)**

THE BIRTHDAY PERSON: O Lord, who am I that you so care so much about me? Am I worthy to glorify you while I live in sin? (Ya Tuhan, siapakah aku ini sehingga Engkau begitu peduli? Layakkah aku memuliakan Engkau di sementara aku hidup dengan dosaku?)

ALL: Who are we your people that you so love us so much? Are we worthy to honor you while we grumble and live with stubborn hearts? (Siapakah umatMu sehingga Engkau begitu mengasihi kami? Adakah kami layak menghormatiMu di sementara kami hidup bersungut dank eras kepala?)

ONE: This is the word of God, "Where sin increased, grace abounded all the more, so that, just as sin exercised dominion in death, so grace might also exercise dominion through justification leading to eternal life through Jesus Christ our Lord." Rom. 5:20b–21 (Di mana dosa bertambah banyak, di sana kasih karunia menjadi berlimpah-limpah, supaya sama seperti dosa berkuasa atas alam maut, demikianlah kasih karunia akan berkuasa oleh kebenaran untuk hidup yang kekal oleh Yesus Kristus, Tuhan kita" Roma 5:20b–21).

Hymn: "Betapa Indah Harinya" (O Happy Day)

Reading Scripture and Message (Pembacaan Alkitab Dan Renungan)

Music Ministry (Puji—Pujian)

Offering (Pemberian Persembahan)

Prayer of Thanksgiving (Doa Syukur)

Charge and Benediction (Pengutusan Dan Berkat)

ONE: My brothers and sisters, you may fall but do not stay down. Get up and move forward to the days that await you. May the grace of Jesus Christ, the love of God, and the communion of the Holy Spirit be with you all." (Saudara-saudaraku, kamu bias saja jatuh tetapi janganlah engkau tinggal dalam kejatuhanmu. Bangkit dan majulah menuju hari depan yang menantimu. Maka kasih karunia Yesus Kristus, kasih Allah dan persekutuan dengan Roh Kudus menyertai kamu.)

Each month in Indonesian churches the birthdays of the month are celebrated with this service. It is an important part of congregational practice.

—Sandra Pontoh, Indonesia

PRAYER LOOKING BACK ON A MARRIAGE

For the day of our marriage
and the years we have shared together,
we praise and thank you, Lord

For faithfulness and friendship,
for love and security,
we praise and thank you, Lord

For the hours of happiness and joy,
for the hours of sadness and tears,
we praise and thank you, Lord

For difficulties shared,
and problems overcome,
We praise and thank you, Lord

For your gift of children,
and all that you have blessed us with,
we praise and thank you, Lord

For your protecting power,
and your presence in our home,
we praise and thank you, Lord

For the love you have shown us,
and your peace and grace given us,
we praise and thank you, Lord

Almighty and heavenly Father,
for all that lies ahead of us,
we trust and praise you.

For the future together without fear,
we trust and praise you.

For our love to deepen and strengthen,
we trust and praise you.

For the anticipation of grandchildren,
we trust and praise you.

For the hope in which we look to you,
we trust and praise you.

For the salvation we have in you,
we trust and praise you.

—Pamela Wilding, Kenya

Wedding at Cana · He Qi

SELECTIONS FOR A SERVICE OF LOVE AND CROWNING—A WEDDING SERVICE
The Crowning

The minister says aloud the following (+ indicates the sign of the cross):

O Master, Lord our God, send down Your heavenly Grace upon these Your servants, _____ and _____ , and (+) Bless them. O Lord our God, as you blessed Abraham and Sara. (+) Bless them, O Lord our God, as You blessed Isaac and Rebecca. (+) Bless them, O Lord our God, as you blessed Jacob and all the prophets. (+) Bless them, O Lord our God, as You blessed Joseph and Asenath. (+) Bless them O Lord our God, as You blessed Moses and Zipporah. Bless them, O Lord our God, as You blessed Joakim and Anna. (+) Bless them, O Lord our God, as You blessed Zacharias and Elizabeth.

Preserve them, O Lord our God, as You preserved Noah in the Ark. Preserve them, O Lord our God, as You preserved Jonah in the jaw of the sea beast. Preserve them, O Lord our God, as You preserved the holy Three Children from the fire, when You sent down upon them the dew of the Heavens.

Remember them, O Lord our God, as You remembered Enoch, Shem, and Elias. Remember them, O Lord our God, as You remembered all Your holy martyrs, sending down upon them the crowns from the Heavens. Remember them, O Lord our God, and the parents who have reared them, for the prayers of parents confirm the foundation of houses. Remember, O Lord our God, the best men (*names the best men*), the wedding company that here have come together from various parts of Georgia and also from other parts of the world: Great Britain, USA, Germany, Holland, Denmark, Norway, Sweden, France, Belgium, Jamaica, North Korea, Ukraine . . . to be present at this rejoicing. Remember, O Lord our God, Your servant _____ (groom) and Your servant _____ (bride), and bless them. Give to them fruit of the womb, concord of soul and body.

Exalt them as the cedars of Lebanon, and as well-cultured vine; bestow on them a rich store of sustenance, so that having a sufficiency of all things for themselves, they may abound in every good work that is good and acceptable before you. Let them behold their children's children as newly planted olive trees round about their table; and, being accepted before you, let them shine as stars in the heavens, in you, our Lord, to whom are due all glory, honor, and worship as to your eternal Father, and your all-holy, Good, and life-creating Spirit, both now and ever, and to the ages of ages. Amen.

MINISTER: Let us pray to the Lord.

ALL: Lord have mercy.

MINISTER: Holy God, Sovereign Lord, stretch forth Your hand from Your holy dwelling place, and join (*When this is said, the minister joins their right hands*) together this your servant _____ and your servant _____ , for by you are a husband and a wife joined together.

Join them together in oneness of mind; crown them with wedlock into one flesh; grant to them the perfect love and the fruit of the womb, for yours is the dominion, and yours is the Kingdom, and the Power, and the Glory: of the Father, and of the Son, and of the Holy Spirit, both now and ever, and to the ages of ages. Amen.

After the Amen, minister, taking up the crowns, crowns first the bridegroom, saying:

The servant of God _____ is crowned for the servant of God _____ in the name of the Father, and of the Son, and of the Holy Spirit. Amen. Amen. Amen.

And the minister crowns the bride, saying:

The servant of God _____ is crowned for the servant of God _____ in the name of the Father, and of the Son, and of the Holy Spirit. Amen. Amen. Amen.

MINISTER: O Lord, our God, crown them with glory and honor.

O Lord Almighty, God of our fathers, we pray You, listen and have mercy. Have mercy on us, O God, according to your great mercy; we pray you, listen and have mercy. Bless your servants _____ and _____ that they may have mercy, life, health, peace, safety, salvation, pardon, and remission of their sins. For you are a merciful and loving God, and to you do we send up glory: to the Father, and to the Son, and to the Holy Spirit, both now and ever, and to the ages of ages. Amen.

MINISTER: Let us pray to the Lord.

ALL: Lord have mercy.

(The couple kneels, the minister lays hands on the crowned couple)

MINISTER: O Lord our God, who in your saving providence did promise in Cana of Galilee to declare marriage honorable by Your presence, do You Yourself preserve in peace and oneness of mind these Your servants _____ and _____, with whom You are well pleased, should be joined to one another. Declare their marriage honorable. Preserve their bed undefiled. Grant that their life together be with be without spot of sin.

And assure that they may be worthy to attain unto a ripe old age, keeping Your commandments in a pure heart. For you are our God, the God to have mercy and save, and to you do we send up all glory, as to your eternal Father, and your all-holy, good, and life-creating Spirit, both now and ever, and to the ages of ages. Amen.

(Bride and Bridegroom stand)

MINISTER: Account us worthy, O Sovereign Lord, with boldness and without condemnation to dare call on You, the Heavenly God, as Father, and to say:

ALL: *(Recite the Prayer of our Saviour.)*

The Sharing of Cup

Then the common cup is offered. The minister blesses the cup, saying this prayer:

O God, who by your might create all things, and confirm the universe, and adorn the crown of all things created by you, do you, with your spiritual blessing, (+) bless also this common cup given to them that are joined in the community of marriage. For blessed is your holy name, and glorified is the Kingdom of the Father, and of the Son, and of the Holy Spirit, both now and ever, and to the ages of ages.

MINISTER: We let you drink from this cup in affirmation of the principle that from this day forward you will have everything in common.

Then the Minister gives them to drink three times from the cup, first to the man, then to the woman, chanting: I will drink from the cup of salvation; I will call upon the name of the Lord.

Procession around Altar

Then the minister takes the couple and leads them in a circle around the altar thrice as a symbol of joyful dance and God's guidance the couple will need in their lives. The choir and people chant The Dance of Isaiah:

O Isaiah, dance your joy, for the Virgin was indeed with child; and brought to birth a Son, Emmanuel, Who came as both God and man. Day-at-the-Dawn is the name He bears, and by extolling Him, we hail the Virgin as blessed. Hear us, you martyred Saints, who fought the good fight, gaining crowns: entreat the Lord to shed His tender mercy on our souls. Glory to You, O Christ our God, Your apostles' proudest boast and treasure of Your martyrs' joy, Who to all proclaimed the Consubstantial Trinity.

Final Blessing

Then the Minister touches the bridegroom's crown with his hand and says:

Be magnified, O bridegroom, as was Abraham, and blessed as was Isaac, and increased as was Jacob. Go your way in peace, performing in righteousness the commandments of God.

Then he touches the crown of the bride and says:

And you, O bride, be magnified as was Sarah, and rejoiced as was Rebecca, and increased as was Rachel, being glad in your husband, keeping the paths of the Law, for so God is well pleased.

O God our God, Who was present in Cana of Galilee and blessed the marriage there, do You (+) also bless these Your servants, who, by Your providence, are joined in the community of marriage. Bless their comings-in and their goings-out. Replenish their life with all good things. (*Here the minister lifts the crowns from the heads of the bride and groom and places them on the table.*) Accept their crowns in Your Kingdom unsoiled and undefiled; and preserve them without offense to the ages of ages.

PEOPLE: Amen.

The Proclamation

The Minister proclaims bridegroom and bride as husband and wife and congratulates them.

In the presence of God and before this congregation, _____ and _____ made their marriage vows to each other. They have declared by the giving and receiving of rings, by being crowned, by sharing the same cup and by walking together around the altar. With the authority God has granted to his church, I therefore proclaim that they are husband and wife.

The minister joins their right hands together and says:

Those whom God has joined together let no one put asunder.

Benediction

—Compiled after the marriage rites of the Church in the West and in the East by Archbishop Malkhaz Songulashvili, Evangelical Baptist Church of Georgia (country), and the Rev. Canon Hugh Wybrew

THE BLESSING (written for a same gender loving couple)

Living God, Creator of humankind,
Bless _____ and _____ as they go on their way together
in love and unity of purpose.
Loving Christ, Creator of compassion,
bless _____ and _____ as they develop their skills
so that their love will bring wholeness to people.

Refreshing, Resilient Spirit, Creator of vitality,
Bless and encourage them to engage in lively activity
and to seek justice throughout their lives,
to turn disappointments into challenges,
to transform darkness into light,
to root their ideals in the ground on which they walk.

Go in grace
with confidence
and know peace. Amen.

—Geoffrey Duncan, England

EMBRACING OUR SEXUALITY: PRAYERS OF PASSION AND PAIN

"It was you who formed my inward parts; you knit me together in my mother's womb. I praise you, for I am fearfully and wonderfully made" (Psalm 139:13–14).

We pray with gratitude for the gift of our human sexuality. You, our generous God, have made us who we are, rich in body, mind, and spirit, and with our whole humanity we offer to you our praise and our thanksgiving.

> For the touch of tenderness, we thank you.
> For the intimate embrace and the making of love, we thank you.
> For deep and dangerous emotions, we thank you.

With joy we recognise the wonder of our creation, affirming the presence of the holy in the human, and knowing ourselves to be stamped with your image. All that we are and have comes from you, our God. May we accept with gratitude the gift of our human sexuality.

"We have not ceased praying for you and asking that you may be filled with the knowledge of God's will in all spiritual wisdom and understanding" (Col. 1:9).

We pray with desire for the gift of wisdom and understanding. You, our yearning God, call us to seek the narrow path that leads to life, the light that shines in the darkness, the word that brings salvation. Amidst all that is hidden and all that is revealed,

> we pray for wisdom that we may interpret scripture aright;
> we pray for insight to hear the cries of the human heart;
> we pray for understanding as we listen to people's stories;
> we pray for discernment that we may witness to all that is good and true.

Give us the guidance of your Spirit to challenge and provoke, to question and determine, to affirm and deny. From you, our God, comes the word that brings good news. May we seek with desire the gift of wisdom and understanding.

"This is my commandment, that you love one another as I have loved you. No one has greater love than this, to lay down one's life for one's friends" (John 15:12–13).

We pray with passion for the gift of love and friendship. You, our gentle God, who came to us in Jesus to call us friends, come to us in one another that each stage of our life's journey may be enriched through sharing.

> Give us friends with whom we can be ourselves.
> Give us friends with whom we can be intimate.
> Give us friends who will tell us the truth about ourselves.
> Give us friends who will not leave us nor forsake us.

Allow us, our God, to love and to be loved, finding within the depths of our relationships a glimpse of what is holy and eternal. May we receive with passion the gift of love and friendship.

"Out of the depths I cry to you, O Lord. Lord, hear my voice! Let your ears be attentive to the voice of my supplications!" (Psalm 130:1–2).

We pray with concern for the gift of peace in the midst of pain. You, our grace-filled God, know the wounds that we bear, the fears that possess us, and the regrets that haunt us. Our lives are so fragile and faithless. So we offer to you

> those who struggle with their sexuality;
> those whose experience is rejection and ridicule;
> those whose experience is grief and loneliness.

Where lives are scarred by failure, brokenness, and hurt, bring your forgiveness and healing. Bring to each, our God, the assurance of your faithfulness, that they may discover a renewed sense of inner worth and self-acceptance. Together may we search for the gift of peace in the midst of pain.

"There is one body and one Spirit, just as you were called to the one hope of your calling, one Lord, one faith, one baptism, one God and Father of all" (Eph. 4:4–6)

We pray with hope for the gift of true unity in Christ. You, our creator, redeemer, and sustainer, have blessed us with difference and diversity, shaping and forming the minds and hearts of each one of us. From you we have learned to see things differently and believe things differently. Amidst all that might keep us apart, we pray that in Christ we may be one.

> Unite us to be your people, the church.
> Unite us in faithful service and witness.
> Unite us as followers of Jesus.
> Unite us in your love.

In you, God, all barriers and divisions have come down, making us a new community in a new kingdom. May we hold with hope the gift of true unity in Christ. Amen

—Graham Sparkes, Baptist Union of Great Britain

SERVICE OF TEARS AND HOPE—MEMORIAL SERVICE (composed by Archbishop Malkhaz Songulashvili after the death of his son, Benjamin, January 2009)

MINISTER: Blessed is our God, always, now and forever and to the ages of ages.

ALL: Amen.

MINISTER: God, Holy Mighty, Holy Immortal, have mercy on us. *(three times)*

ALL: Glory to the Father and the Son and the Holy Spirit, now and forever and to the ages of ages. Amen.

MINISTER: All holy Trinity, have mercy on us. Lord, graciously forgive our sins. Master, pardon our transgressions. Holy One, visit and heal our infirmities for the glory of your name.

ALL: Lord, have mercy. Lord, have mercy. Lord, have mercy.

MINISTER: Glory to the Father and the Son and the Holy Spirit, now and forever and to the ages of ages.

ALL: Amen.

MINISTER: As our Saviour Jesus Christ taught us so we pray:

ALL: *Pray the Prayer of our Saviour.*

CHOIR (*sung three times while when all the participants are lighting their candles*): "Holy God, Holy and strong, Holy and immortal, have mercy on us."

MINISTER: Let us pray to the Lord our God.

You are the resurrection and the life, Lord, and all of us who believe in you, even though we die, we will live in you and with you, and everyone who lives and believes in you will never die. Strengthen our faith in your resurrection, we beseech thee, our Lord.

ALL: Lord have mercy, Lord have mercy, Lord have mercy.

MINISTER: Since we believe, Lord, that you yourself died on the cross and rose again, it is our faith that God will bring to you all of us when we die so that we will be with you forever. Encourage us with these words, we beseech thee, our Lord.

ALL: Lord have mercy, Lord have mercy, Lord have mercy.

MINISTER: Your steadfast love, O Lord, never ceases, your mercies never come to an end, they are new every morning; great is your faithfulness. Help us to count on your faithfulness in the darkest hours of our life, we beseech thee, our Lord.

ALL: Lord have mercy, Lord have mercy, Lord have mercy.

MINISTER: We bring nothing into the world, Lord, and we take nothing out. You give all the gifts of love, friendship, and comfort and you take them away. Enable us to accept this painful reality, we beseech thee, our Lord.

ALL: Lord have mercy, Lord have mercy, Lord have mercy.

MINISTER: God so loved the world that he sent you to us, our Lord, so that everyone who believes in you may not perish but may have eternal life. Nourish us with this belief until we see you face to face, we beseech thee, our Lord.

ALL: Lord have mercy, Lord have mercy, Lord have mercy.

MINISTER: You told us "do not be afraid", because you are the first and the last, you are the living One. You were dead and now you are alive for ever and ever. Cast out the fear from our hearts and minds in this time of grief and sorrow, we beseech thee, our Lord.

ALL: Lord have mercy, Lord have mercy, Lord have mercy.

Diane Wendorf

MINISTER: *(At this point the minister takes up the censer and censes the icon of Christ, if it is available, a portrait of the departed, and all the participants present in affirmation of the faith that all who are alive and those who went home are a part of the same visible/invisible communion of God in Christ.)* As this frankincense burns and fills this place with its fragrance, may God fill all of us with the fragrance of the knowing of his son Jesus Christ, so that we can also live and die as the aroma of Christ (2nCor. 2:14–15). Let our prayers rise before you and the raising of our hands be as an evening sacrifice. Glory be to the Father and to the Son and to the Holy Spirit now and ever and unto ages of ages.

CHOIR: *Anthem such as "Thine is the Glory"*

MINISTER: O God of spirits and of all flesh, you have trampled upon death and have abolished the power of the devil, giving life to the word you had created. Give rest to the soul of your departed servant _____ in a place of light, in a place of repose, in a place of refreshment, where there is no pain, sorrow, and suffering. As a good and loving God, forgive every sin he (she) has committed in thought, word, or deed, for there is no one who lives and does not sin. You alone are without sin. Your righteousness is an everlasting righteousness, and Your word is truth.

ALL: Within your peace, O Lord, where all your saints repose, give rest also to the soul of your servant _____ , for you alone are immortal, you alone are the Lord of resurrection.

MINISTER: You are indeed the resurrection, the life, and the repose of your departed servant _____ , Christ our God, and to you we give glory, with your eternal Father and your all holy, good, and life-giving Spirit, now and forever and to the ages of ages. Amen.

ALL: Glory to the Father and the Son and the Holy Spirit, now and forever and to the ages of ages. Amen.

MINISTER: Glory to you, O God, our hope and only comfort, glory to you. May Christ our true God, who rose from the dead and who as immortal King has authority over the living and the dead, have mercy on us and save us. May he establish the soul of our beloved _____ departed from us, in the dwelling place of the saints, among the righteous: Mary the spotless Mother of our Lord; all holy, glorious, and praiseworthy Apostles; of our predecessors who love God and people; all of the holy and glorious forefathers: Abraham, Isaac, and Jacob; of his holy and righteous friend Lazarus, who lay in the grave four days; and of all the saints.

May your memory be eternal, dear brother (sister); rest in peace in God until we meet again.

ALL: Amen.

—Archbishop Malkhaz Songulashvili, Evangelical Baptist Church of Georgia (country)

PRAYER ON THE OCCASION OF THE CELEBRATION
OF THE LIFE OF PASTOR DOUG NICHOLLS*

God of creation, imagination and love, we thank you that we are not all created the same, and that you have given us the exciting riches of diversity. We thank you for artists, sculptors, and musicians who continue to tell the story of our shared humanity in all shades of joy and sadness.

Thanks be to God for the gift of peoples of different races, colours, and cultures, people with whom to share stories, remember traditions, celebrate identity, and grieve and repent over opportunity lost.

God of justice and reconciliation, we thank you today for the story and reminiscences of one whom God knew by name, by character, and by calling: Sir Douglas Nicholls.

Thanks be to God for the Gospel hope that he held that all may live in God's grace.

Thanks be to God for his passionate Christian leadership in the pursuit of justice for Aboriginal people.

Thanks be to God for his voice, echoed by many of his brothers and sisters and by many of all nationalities calling for release from exploitation and greed all those who are oppressed.

God who listens and God who empowers, as Pastor Douglas Nicholls followed in the footsteps of Jesus, may this day of memory inspire and point us to a future where his hope, leadership, and voice become a new part of who we are in Australia today, as pastors, politicians, artists, citizens. Would this be Doug's prayer for us today as people who can make a difference?

Let justice be done, O God—

May all children in this country have the same chance for life and health.

Let justice be done, O God—

For an end to prejudice and discrimination in attitudes held and resources shared.

Let justice be done, O God—

So that we may live together in thankful harmony because we have rightly shared the land, generously paid our debts, acknowledged our violence, and recognised the dignity and worth of all people.

And would Doug remind us of the words of the prophet? For what does the Lord require of us but to do justice, love kindness, and walk humbly with our God? Amen

Sir Douglas Nicholls (born 1906) a Churches of Christ minister and Aboriginal activist.

—Alan Andrew Niven, Australia

A RITUAL FOR MOVING HOUSE
Background

During the past few years there have been many members of our inner city church community who, for one reason or another, have moved house. In years gone by, these major changes have occurred almost unnoticed and certainly uncelebrated by the church community. How could this happen? For anyone, and especially for a family, moving house is a significant transition. It often means months of financial planning, trips to the bank to determine the viability of the move, more months poring over the real estate pages and then the tedious business of inspecting highly inflated properties. This leads to the nerve-wracking process of bidding at auctions. Even if only moving to rented accommodation, a person is faced with the tedious search for their new abode and fierce competition from dozens of others keen to prove their credentials to suspicious real estate agents. When the time finally arrives to pack belongings we all realize afresh how burdensome the "necessities of life" have become in our materialistic twenty-first century.

The moment eventually arrives when the last box has been carried in and life can begin to get back to normal—even if the "spare room" is full of unpacked items, which, when needed, are certain to be at the very back and the very bottom. But why is this magic moment so rarely celebrated? In our church community we have tried hard enough. With many an individual or couples who have faced this transition, we have all agreed that as soon as their move is complete we will organise a house- or flat-warming, complete with a "blessing" and a meal to which the whole church community will be invited. In our experience, this event has often failed to actually happen. Why?

The difficulty is that in the aftermath of moving house few people find that they have the energy to do anything but barely survive. Furthermore, moving to a new house can be a process that for many will take years battling feelings of unexpected emptiness from the loss of all things familiar. As a compromise we established the tradition of delivering a bunch of flowers with a note of blessing to people as they moved into their new house or flat. Some were subsequently able to host a "house blessing" and some were not. At least this milestone never passed unnoticed.

When it has happened it has been wonderful. One woman who belongs to our worshipping community has a partner belonging to Sukyo Mahikari, a Japanese-based religion with origins in Buddhism. We wondered if it might be too awkward to concoct a ritual that would respect the strong faith commitments of both partners. The mutual respect already existing within this couple provided the basis for a ritual that affirmed the faith of both partners and celebrated the move to their first real home. A decade later this couple, now with two children, remembers with clarity and fondness their "moving house ritual." This occasion marked an important milestone and cemented for them all the hopes and dreams of the time. They hoped this would be the house in which they would be blessed and would raise children, and it has happened just so.

A Simple Ritual for the Celebration of Moving House

If possible it is certainly good to combine this ritual with a "housewarming" whereby friends are invited to share a common meal. If this is achieved, then a Eucharist could be included as part of the meal.

Sprinkling of water in each room of the house—A bowl of water is placed at the centre of the gathered group. The leader explains what a rich symbol water is:

Water is the basis of our very survival. We are fortunate to live in houses in which the availability of water is taken for granted. Three quarters of the world's population do not enjoy this luxury—or should it be, this right? Let this bowl of water remind us of those who lack the basic necessities of life such as food, water, and shelter. Water satisfies our physical thirst. Jesus offered "living water" to the Samaritan woman at the well. "Those who drink this water," he said, "will never again thirst, for it will become a spring of living water gushing up to eternal life." Let this bowl of water remind us of the spiritual life that comes with knowing Jesus. We also consume water in the bathroom and laundry. All our fancy soaps and detergents would be useless without the water that cleanses our bodies, clothes, and floors. Jesus' living water cleanses out hearts, enabling us to forgive and be forgiven, bringing peace to a household. Let this bowl of water remind us of the forgiveness and inner cleansing that comes with knowing Jesus. There are taps also in the backyard. With these we water plants. Without water there is no growth. Let this bowl of water remind us of the growth our inner lives experience through knowing Jesus. We will sprinkle water in each room of the house and, as we do, we will say prayers of blessing.

Different people may be allocated to say the blessing for the different rooms around the house. Some may add spontaneous prayers of their own—though these would be best kept brief. In some rooms there will not be space for more that a few people.

Dining room: This is the womb of the house. May Jesus be always present, eating and drinking. May this be a place of nutritious meals, good conversation, and hospitality.

Kitchen: Let enticing aromas emerge from this kitchen. May they be produced with love and received with appreciation. May people queue to help with the dishes.

Bathroom: May the shower run only for three minutes, the mirror never admit wrinkles, and the scales deliver good news.

Lounge: Let this be a place for retreat, prayer, reading of good books, and the sharing of wine and conversation.

Bedrooms: May sleep be peaceful and refreshing. (*You may add: May those who sleep here never be too old for stories and bedside prayers . . . or may love be wild and satisfying but not audible beyond the passage.*)

Laundry: Let those who labour here labour cheerfully. May everyone in this house know how to operate the washing machine.

Front Porch: May all who arrive here be warmly welcomed.

—Digby Hannah, Australia

MARANATHA INDONESIAN UNITED CHURCH OF CHRIST—HOUSEWARMING SERVICE

The family of _____

Preparation and Prelude

Hymn: "Bila Yesus Berada" (When Jesus in the Midst of Our Family)

Call to Worship

ONE: When you are in the midst of us, O Lord,

ALL: we are filled with joy.

ONE: When you are in the midst of us, O Lord,

ALL: we are filled with calmness.

ONE: When you are in the midst of our household, O Lord,

ALL: we are filled with peace.

ONE: When you are in my life, I feel safe to walk toward my future.

FAMILY: Please be with us and hold our family in your hands, O Lord.

ONE: This thanksgiving fellowship is held in the name of God the Father, the Son, and the Holy Spirit. Amen.

Hymn: "Tuhan Allah NamaMu" (God the Lord Is Your Name)

Prayer of Confession

ONE: Home is the place where we can rest secure.

ALL: The place where parents and children share love and care.

ONE: Where family can unite in prayer and thanksgiving.

ALL: Where family can reconcile and forgive one another.

FAMILY: That is our dream and hope for this home, O Lord.

ONE: But we must confess that we often fill our homes with anger and profanity.

ALL: We fill them with so much discord that love, care, and forgiveness are pushed out the door.

ONE: O gracious Lord, forgive us and let this house be the house of prayer and thanksgiving for those who live here.

Assurance of Pardon

ONE: "Therefore my heart is glad, and my soul rejoices; my body also rests secure. You show me the path of life. In your presence there is fullness of joy; in your right hand are pleasures forevermore" (Psa. 16:9, 11).

Reading Scripture and Message: Matthew 3:13–17

Music Ministry

Offering

ONE: "But I with the voice of thanksgiving will sacrifice to you; what I have vowed I will pay; deliverance belongs to the LORD!" (Jonah 2:9).

Prayer of Dedication

Charge and Benediction

ONE: Go in peace, the people of God. Share your love and forgive one another. May the grace of Jesus Christ, the love of God, and the communion of the Holy Spirit be with you all.

ALL: Amen, amen, amen.

—Sandra Pontoh, Indonesia

CHANGING JOBS—THE TRANSITION TO A NEW PLACE OF EMPLOYMENT
Background

Have you ever attended an ordination service in which a candidate is accepted into the ordained ministry of his or her particular church? These are very grand affairs attended by a surprisingly large number of church dignitaries and other very important people. Most dignitaries arrive in sartorial splendour, usually attired in robes, possibly carrying

Rini Templeton

crosses or other religious symbols, and certainly wearing the most solemn and awed expressions. Similarly when a minister is inducted into a new parish, this is an occasion for the gathering of multiple dignitaries, pretentious ceremony, and verbose adulation followed by an interminable, soporific sermon. Why should these transitions be afforded such pomp and ceremony? The reason derives from the high view of calling that underlies the office of church ministry. The assumption is that this man or woman (though some churches still disallow the contribution of women) has listened to the call of God, has been confirmed in that call by peers, undergone training, passed rigorous tests, and is now equipped for the cure of souls and ready to serve the flock.

This is all well and good, if slightly overplayed. But why is there only resounding silence when a believer graduates in secular training or commences a new phase of work? Do not all aspire to a sense of call in their places of work? Do not all labour strenuously and prayerfully over what field it is in which they can best serve humanity? Do not all need the support and advice of peers as they make career decisions? Do not all desire the blessing of those they respect when embarking upon a new phase of employment?

It is crucial that we develop new rituals for workplace transitions. When a person trains for a vocation and graduates, her or his worshipping community would do well to recognise this important transition. This person has worked hard for years, may well have sacrificed much time and money and strained friendships and family in order to achieve this goal. The graduation is real cause for celebration. So too is the move from one place of employment or one form of employment to another.

Workplace transition may involve a great deal of pain and anguish. To be deprived of a job due to downsizing or restructuring means to suffer the loss of one's dream and experience the anguish of self-doubt. To find a new job is, for many, the end-point of much soul searching and sometimes many bitter disappointments. Likewise the period of adjustment to new employment can be stressful and challenging. At these times people need the support of their communities. Sensitively conceived rituals for marking workplace transitions can be affirming, encouraging, and healing. They present an opportunity to acknowledge that all vocations, as the word itself implies, should be our calling.

A Ritual For One or More Persons Embarking on a New Phase of Employment

ONE: _____ (name/s of person/s being commissioned), we are placing on your shoulders some scarves:

One or more long, flowing, colourful scarves are placed on each person's shoulders. Those members who place the scarves also rest their hands upon the person/s being commissioned. The colours are chosen to suit the occasion. As each scarf is arranged on the person's shoulder, it is explained what is signified by the colour of that particular scarf. Scarves can be, for example: red for compassion; white for transparency or honesty; green for creativity, fertility, or growth; blue for serenity; purple for confidence; yellow for clarity or letting your light shine; brown or black for earthiness and reliability.

ONE: Though you may presently remove these scarves, our prayer is that compassion, transparency, honesty, creativity, fertility, growth, serenity, confidence, reliability, and clarity will always be exhibited by you in your new place of work.

Different members step forward and, resting their hands upon the person/s being commissioned, offer spontaneous or prepared prayers for each individual as they face new employment.

ONE: _____ (name/s), will you seek to treat with respect and dignity all those in your work place? Will you work to the best of your ability with passion and diligence? With God's help will you always treat others in your workplace with compassion and understanding? Will you seek to empower those who have no power and serve those who are in need? Will you endeavour to be transparent, fair, and honest in your dealings?

_____ (name/s) respond: With God's help, I will.

ONE: All those gathered here today, will you continue an active interest in _____ (name/s) in their places of work? Will you rejoice in their successes and support them when they face difficulties?

ALL: We will engage them with our interest and encourage them with our support.

ONE: _____ (name/s), may God bless you in this new phase of employment. May Jesus' example guide all your decisions. May God's spirit of love, compassion, and freedom be yours, inspiring and empowering all that you do. May your friends gathered here today be ever ready to support and encourage you.

In the name of God our loving parent, Jesus who shared his life with us, and the Holy Spirit our healer and comforter. Amen.

—Digby Hannah, Australia

Part Four

OUR HANDS JOINED AROUND THE WORLD

Resources for Justice and Peace

17 ❀ GLOBAL ISSUES FOR A GLOBAL FAITH

Freedom and Peace   He Qi

LIVING, LOVING GOD

(Refugee Concerns)

Living, loving God,
we are told that Mary, Joseph,
and Jesus travelled
as refugees
to Egypt.
They were strangers
in a strange land
separated from
loved ones,
their community, and
familiar surroundings.

We are told that during his ministry
Jesus surrounded himself with
strangers,
marginalised people, and
the outcasts of society.

We remember now
women . . .
men . . .
children . . .
who are separated from their families
homes
communities
because of
selfishness
broken relationships
greed
hatred
famine
war.

Encourage us,
enable us
to move
out of our comfort,
our complacency, and
get alongside the sad,
the strangers
who cry out
for understanding
for help
for love.

Motivate us through compassion
to be the prime movers
to bring about
a change in attitudes
in our communities and
to open our homes,
to give shelter
and sanctuary
and no-strings-attached love
to people . . . who
need us to be
Christ-like.

—Geoffrey Duncan, England

LORD, NO ONE IS A STRANGER TO YOU (Refugee Concerns)

Lord, no one is a stranger to you
and no one is ever far from
your loving care.
In your kindness watch over refugees
and exiles,
those separated from their loved ones,
young people who are lost,
and those who have left or run away
from home.
Bring them back safely to the place
where they long to be
and help us always to show your kindness
to strangers and to those in need.

—CAFOD (Catholic Agency for Overseas Development), England

CHILDREN IN THE STREET

Street children have become part of the global urban landscape. As many as 100 million children live and work on the streets; a quarter of them have no other home. Forty percent live in Latin America. Hostages of global economics, they are threatened daily—as in the example of Daniel—by hunger, violence, drugs, and disease.

A voice was heard in Ramah,
wailing and loud lamentation,
Rachel weeping for her children;
She refused to be consoled
because they are no more.
(Jeremiah 31:15)

Prayer

Mothering God,
open me to the pleading of this lamentation
     from Sao Paulo.
Open me—imagination, heart, and prayer—
     to the children of our world.
Help me in today's quiet to enter Daniel's pain
     and to join him in his hope:

Daniel's Song

If this street, if this street were mine
I would order Mrs. Hunger to go for a walk
And put in each post an inscription:
It is forbidden for a child not to have bread.

If this street, if this street were mine
I would order the exploiter to another place, and
On each corner only one voice would be heard:
Violence no longer lives among us!

If this street, if this street were mine
I would tear down the Forest of Loneliness
And shout in the new meadow:
Children are safe here!

Prayer

God of Daniel, let us meet him in the meadow,
life-filled and welcoming.
I unite my learnings and activities this day with Daniel's struggle.
We ask your Presence.
We trust its hovering.
We know its promise in Jesus Christ. Amen.

Daniel, author of "Daniel's Song," is part of the Community Alternatives Project, founded and directed by Rev. Zeni de Lima Soares, first woman Methodist pastor in Brazil.

—Church World Service

A RESPONSIVE READING FOR WOMEN OF THE DEMOCRATIC REPUBLIC OF CONGO

ONE: Spirit of Compassion, who hears the cries of all those who suffer from war, famine, and violence,

ALL: Be with the women of the Congo whose bodies, lives, and families are torn apart by sexual violence.

ONE: Spirit of Love, who sees the brutality and mutilation that have become daily realities for the Congolese women,

ALL: Bring healing to their bodies, their minds, and their spirits.

ONE: Spirit of Justice, who calls us to see, hear, and respond to the injustice and suffering caused by sexual violence,

ALL: Embolden us to speak out against those who use rape as a weapon of war.

ONE: Spirit of Oneness, who seeks to reconcile all that is broken in this world,

ALL: Unify us as we work to bring an end to violence against women and girls around the globe. Amen.

This prayer was originally written for use in the Religious Institute's online advocacy and educational Congo Sabbath Initiative 2008.

—Katey Zeh, USA, Democratic Republic of Congo

HER VOICE

I was a stranger and she welcomed me
We sat and talked that afternoon
As we shared each other's language
We spoke beyond the words

As I listened to her voice, I heard . . .

If you have come here to help me,
I don't need help.
I do need you to understand me,
To walk with me,
to be with me . . .

So, if you have come
Because you know
That your freedom is linked to mine,

Then come
And we'll work together
Walk together
Be together

And you will see
That justice for me

Is justice for you.

This song was written to share the vision of mission that recognizes that we are all human, one with the other, sharing our gifts of listening and learning as we share in the Spirit of Christ. This goes way beyond "doing a mission" for the less fortunate.

—Barbara Van Ausdall, USA

THE SORROW OF UNEMPLOYMENT

The pulp mill is closed, God.
No more steam blasting from pipes.
No more transports driving through town.
No more saws buzzing in the bush.
No more KA-TONK, Ka-Tonk, katonk of wet logs,
rolling down the woodpile.
We thought it would go on forever—
       the economic "lifeblood" of our town.
    But it's stopped. Silent.
    We aren't quite sure what to do, God.
    We aren't quite sure where to turn.
    We aren't able to answer, "What's next?"
    Help us, we pray!
       To not be afraid.
       To believe in our children.
       To support one another.
       To trust that, no matter what, you are with us—
          today, tomorrow, in all days to come.
    In Christ's name, let it be so. Amen.

—Richard Bott, Canada

LIVING WATERS FOR THE WORLD

God of the oceans
We bring before you those who make their living from your marine bounty. Be with those
who venture out in frail craft seeking food to feed their families.
We bring before you those who have suffered from tsunamis in the Pacific and elsewhere.
Comfort them and grant them willing helpers in the rebuilding process.
We bring before you those countries whose large factory ships plunder the ocean's bounty
without thought for the future. Give us the courage to oppose this and enable us to
win others to the cause.
We bring before you those who flee from oppressive regimes by taking to the sea. Help us
to make them feel welcome and supported and give them the fortitude to begin again.

God of the rivers, streams, and lakes
We bring before you those who are without water because their rivers have dried up. Help
those responsible for damming rivers in China and elsewhere to realise the long-term
consequences of their actions.

We bring before you those whose rivers have flooded, destroying their homes and livelihoods. We ask that they will receive the help they need.

We bring before you those who pollute your waterways. Help us to stand up to them and demand greater accountability.

God of the rain

We bring before you those who have too much rain. We think of the people of Afghanistan who have recently experienced flooding due to heavy rain and ask that sufficient aid may be given to alleviate their suffering.

We bring before you those who have no rain. We remember the farmers in Australia who have had no rain for several years and face the prospect of walking off their farms. Be with them as they seek new ways of living.

We bring before you those who suffer from the effects of acid rain, the people of Appalachia who no longer have trout in their streams and those in the Czech Republic whose forests are dead. Help us to convince those in power to see the necessity of legislating against the pollution that causes this.

God of the wells, tanks, pumps, and taps

We bring before you those who have to walk long distance to access safe water. Thank you for those groups who work to ensure all have access to safe drinking water. Be with them as they work and keep them safe and well.

We bring before you those who suffer from water-borne diseases. May their suffering may be alleviated and their water supply made safe.

We bring before you those in the Western world who use more water than they need. Prick our consciences and stir us to action to conserve water.

God of the living water

Like the beating of our hearts, water is so much a part of our surroundings and our bodies that we tend to take it for granted. But without water there is no life as we know it.

We thank you for your abundant gift of water and ask that you help us become responsible guardians of it and generous in sharing your gift with others. Amen.

—Penny Guy, Aotearoa/NewZealand

BRING THE WATER

Bring the Water—Senegal

LEADER: Keur Momar Sarr
O you are so far
Far away from me right here
Yet here within my heart

CHORUS: Bring the water now
Bring the water near
Bring the water to the soil
And feed a hungry world (repeat)

LEADER: You're a village of hope
You're a village of dreams
You're a village that shows
We can succeed

Jesus gives the command
Love others as ourselves
What better way to show that love
Than to help to build a well to . . . (Chorus, twice)

LEADER: Together we can win
If we work hand in hand
Leaning on each other so
This earth will not be sand

Refilling God's good earth
With water, plants and trees
Putting back all that we take—
Just taking what we need . . . (Chorus, twice)

LEADER: Each of us must reach
Deep within our soul
Find the love that God put there
To make another whole . . . (Chorus, twice)

Bring the Water—Eduador

CHORUS: Bring the water now
Bring the water near
Bring the water, clean and pure
To quench a thirsty world (repeat)

LEADER: Rainforest children who live
In villages that we know
Need clean water to keep them strong
And help them all to grow

We can help to provide
ways to make water clean

helping people to learn and share
this resource we all need . . . *(Chorus, twice)*

LEADER: *Minga**—a Quichua word—
that brings us together to care
working with each other
as God's gifts we learn to share

Responding to our God's call
To walk with others in love
While working here to better here
Blessed by God above . . . *(Chorus, twice)*

*Minga = "a good work together" in Quichua, the language of one of the largest indigenous groups in the rainforest. This song was written originally in 1986 after visiting with people in Senegal, West Africa—they were working with Church World Service to provide wells for villages in the Sahel (south of the Sahara and in danger of becoming a part of the desert). The song was revised in 2006 to raise awareness of the work in Ecuadorian rainforest providing water filters for over 1500 villages.

—Barbara Van Ausdall, USA, Senegal, Ecuador

MISSION HAS BECKONED: LIVING WATERS FOR THE WORLD

Mission has beckoned
From earth's four corners;
Water as God's force
No longer gives
Life and health freely.
How can we share what
We're given so that
Everyone lives?

Show us the web, Lord,
Of our connection;
Teach us to value
Gifts that all bring.
Covenant people
Bringing together
Resources garnered
Makes Your heart sing.

Give us the courage,
Give us the wisdom,
To be your hands and
To be your feet.
Give us compassion,
Give us the love to
See Christ reflect in
Each face we meet.

People are waiting
Wond'ring and watching:
Who will remember?
Who'll be our grace?
We are an answer,
We've felt the calling.
With God's empow'ring,
We're mission's face.

Sung to "Bunessan," Gaelic melody known as "Morning Has Broken." A soloist may sing the first verse and the congregation respond with the following three verses.

—Todd Jenkins, USA

HEALTH CARE AND GLOBAL WARMING CONCERNS IN BORNEO

Willfirmus Uwil

As I left on Monday the village in Indonesian Borneo where I live, the smoke haze made visibility only about a hundred meters and left people hacking and coughing. This is life on the frontier of ecological disaster. The smoke comes from forest fires burning the logged forest. Some are intentional to clear land for palm oil, some are slash and burn agriculture, and some are wildfires gone out of control. What you need to understand is that loss of rainforest is not like losing forests in the northern hemisphere; there are over a thousand species of trees per hectare, the animal life is diverse and amazing, and the trees may be up to 1000 years old—but, most importantly, it won't grow back on its own; the loss is forever.

The tropical rainforests cover 5 percent of the surface of the planet and contain 50 percent of the species, yet in Borneo 70 percent has been lost over the last ten years.

Only fifteen years ago life was wildly different in Borneo—pun intended. Some of the most diverse and beautiful forest in the world stretched to the horizon. I was privileged to live for one year in the deep forest. I followed orangutans all day and was alone in nature. For me, this was a deeply spiritual experience: "Be still and know that I am God." It is when the distractions of humans fall away that we can see God. We see that we are not all of creation. We are precious in God's eyes, but so is so much else.

The planet faces ecological collapse. When I was born there were a little more than three billion people on the planet; now there are six. But it is not evenly distributed. One of the towns where I work went from three thousand to twenty-three thousand people in fifteen years. Many of my friends had ten children in that time period. In Indonesia, for many, life has gone from hard to very hard. And at the same time, the vast expanses of rainforest have shrunk to a fragment. I find it hard to know how to convey to you what a planet in crisis feels like as I look around me here and see the beauty. Do you realize that the northeast is the only place on the planet where forest is increasing? In Indonesia we are daily confronted with extreme poverty, lack of choices and hope in the people, and the pain of watching God's creation be destroyed in front of our eyes. We have a front row seat to what is likely going to happen to the whole planet. The rate of global warming is so far proceeding faster than the worst models predicted. This will likely have horrible consequences for all of us—even in a place like Vermont that feels so immune.

So how we do find hope?

I am a doctor. I believe in healing. But I also see health as something greater than being physically free of illness. I fight for health care. I care for extremely poor people and try to provide them with the highest quality care possible. But I also see the big picture. I recognize that all of our health is threatened if we do not curb our excesses and honor the planet that gives us life.

The first world is rich in money, education, and technology. Many parts of the developing world are rich in biodiversity. Despite all the burning and illegal logging, the national park where I live, called Gunung Palung, is still one of the most beautiful places you could ever see and home to 10 percent of the world's remaining orangutans. We also have sun-bears, clouded leopards, argus pheasants, eight species of hornbills, and untold and uncounted other biodiversity. This forest also powerfully helps mitigate global warming. We believe that the first world and the developing world have much to offer each other and that by working together, we can improve all of our health.

My husband (who is an ecologist) and I started a project, Health in Harmony, that will hopefully become a model. We have a little clinic on the border of Ganung Palung National Park in Borneo. This clinic provides high quality health care to a population of sixty thousand people. We never deny health care to anyone, but we also offer extra incentives to villages that do not participate in illegal logging or have any burning within the national park that borders on their village. These extra community-chosen incentives are: ambulance service, mobile clinics, discounts in the fixed clinic, and organic farm training. We say to the communities that these incentives are a gift of thanks to them for protecting a resource that is valuable to the whole planet. We also allow people to pay with ecologically friendly noncash payment options. These include working in our organic garden, watering the seedlings we will use to reforest land in November, doing laundry in clinic, and exchanging goods such as seedlings, chickens, beautiful hand-woven mats or manure for the garden. These methods allow people to pay even if they have no money and at the same time maintain their dignity.

I am extremely honored to receive the Tikkun Olam* award, but it feels strange as well, because I don't feel that I can take credit. This project was not my idea, it was God's. God has opened each opportunity, guided us, sometimes shoved us, and always rescued us when we feel we just can't go on. And when I say we, I don't just mean my husband and I, I mean our whole team. There are now more than forty Indonesians and twenty Americans who spend large portions of their time on this project. I particularly want to honor Hotlin Ompussungu, without whom this whole project never would have happened. She is just another example of God's guiding, and sometimes pushing, hand. When I first started, a friend called me and told me to hire Hotlin. I said, "Well, I'm not sure a dentist is the first person I should hire," but she kept at me until I finally gave in and called Hotlin. Thank goodness I did, because her passion for service, wisdom, creativity, and strong faith have made our work flourish. We have had to step off the cliff many times—no job, the large medical school debt, not enough donations, no permit, no visa—just trusting that God will find a way, and each time, a step materializes out of the mist and we don't fall off the cliff. I imagine we will always have to keep stepping off the cliff, but I also trust that there will always be a step there. It has been terrifying at times and often we have thought the whole program might fall apart (and it still may), but we are encouraged daily that we are where God wants us to be, and my reward is in the smiles and the gratefulness of the people we are able to help and in the encouraging signs that we are helping to save rainforest.

I ask you to step off the cliff with me: radically trust God, honor creation—all of it—and together we may yet find a way to heal our planet and heal the people who call it home.

*tikkun olam—Hebrew for "repairing the world."

(Sermon, September 6, 2009, Randolph, Vermont, by Webb, founder of Health in Harmony in Borneo, an organization that combines health care with reducing earth's carbon footprint.)

—Kinari Webb, Borneo

MAKING CHOICES FOR JUSTICE AND PEACE

Words and not bullets
Hands for working and fewer words
Books and not TV
Fresh air and not smog
Smiles and not tears

Proactive and not reactive
Fresh water and not drought
Flowers and not thorns

Hugs instead of fights
Friendship instead of indifference
Mutual respect instead of solitary pride
Forgiveness instead of revenge

Health from within and not prescriptions
Community where there has been sadness
Warmth beyond cold hands
Light to see in shadows

Responsibility instead of forgetfulness
Punctuality instead of excuses
Music in the place of silence
Silence in the place of uproar and racket
Landscapes of creation more than malls
Parent time more than daycare hours
Letters that touch more than cell calls
Freedom beyond all slavery

Color and not shades of gray
Sports and not games
Progress and not waiting
Walking and not stagnation
Growth and not regulation
Love and not grievances
Living and not killing
Creativity and not draining routine
Believing and not becoming lost

In the light of our Creator and Savior, we understand that there is so much to offer each other and yet much that we should not give. Indeed, there is much we should unlearn. Everything we do affects the growth and enrichment of our neighbors. If we truly learn to live we will realize that giving results in receiving—all is mutual. Scripture says there is no greater love than to give life for one's friends. Jesus is our friend and gave his life for me and for you. How can we give thanks? What can we give? What hidden treasures do we not show to others? Let us begin. We choose some things on this list and begin to give them without counting the cost. God guides us to decide what and how to give without offending others or asserting ourselves. There are many things among our treasures. This we can do—Christ is still looking for our hands to work.

—Mario Dekker, Qatar

PRAYER OF INTERCESSION FOR PARTNERSHIPS

God, we belong to your beautiful, but fragile creation. Give us compassion, that we may nurse it and be nursed. Give us knowledge, that we may protect it and be protected. Give us love, that we may love it and be loved. Give us desire for reconciliation with all your creation.

God, You have brought us together in partnerships, You have caused us to depend on each other. We thank You for this. May we use this opportunity to discover each other. Open our hearts to see the problems and needs of our partners in Afrika, Asia, Europe, and in our own church. Strengthen us as we give and receive, sharing material and spiritual gifts.

Strengthen those who are serving in the partner churches as full time or as voluntary workers, that they may not lose heart as they face the many challenges in their congregations.

God, we belong to one another; help us to see one another as you see us. Help us to build fair structures and follow just practices that bring us closer to one another. Help us to be followers of your true image, Jesus Christ, your Son, appreciating our differences, not as dividing facts, but as gifts of being and belonging in your divine multitude, so that peace in the world can grow. Amen!

—Detlev Knoche, Germany

A LITURGY FOR UNITY AND SOLIDARITY

A large candle is lighted at the moment the celebration begins. There are small candles on a small side table (one for each participant), strips of cloth of various colors rolled by color, and ingredients for the celebration of the Holy Meal.

Reading of the Psalm 133

Prayer of Invocation

Include expression of thanksgiving and prayers of intercession.

Those present are invited to create a tablecloth that covers the table where we will celebrate the Holy Meal with the strips of clothes interlaced, in silence, while we listen to the following verses.

Let's renew life—
wherever hands intertwine,
wherever bread is broken and broken again;

wherever life is celebrated by an embrace,
by an attentive look.
Your love, oh God,
is like the perfume of spring,
the air of September,*
that announces the awakening of life,
coloring our dreams and our hopes.
Let's renew life
throw away the old hue,
let's paint with new and bright colors
such that we can be your collaborators
in the space where we build
and reconstruct our life. Amen.

(Maria Dirlane y Edson Ponick)

(Indicating the colorful strips of cloth on the table, forming a tablecloth, relate the following story)

The History of the Harlequin's Clothes

There was in a distant time, a group of children who have left us a beautiful lesson of friendship and solidarity. The story goes like this—there was a group of children who played together winter and summer. They loved the daytime games and watching their grandparents play bocce in the evening. It came the time for a costume party and mothers sewed the costumes of a dancer, a firefighter, a medieval knight, a butterfly, an astronaut, and a lion, but in one of the more humble cottages, a child had nothing to wear and his mother cried. The children, when they learned that one of their playmates didn't have a costume to wear to a grand party, came together to help create one. Each child cut a piece of cloth from his own homemade costume and took it to the friend's house. The mother used the individual pieces to create a costume for her son. Although each child had a piece missing from his or her special costume, they were proud of their beautiful and creative costumes. The king of the party was the boy who was helped by his friends, for his mother had taken every bit of material and, with great thoroughness and care, put them together and gave them form. His costume had the most beautiful colors that exist: the colors of friendship and love. *(Adapted by Claudia Ursini)*

This table, formed by all the colors, assembled by the work of all, represents to each one of us, with our color, with our shade, yet in unity—the table of God's love.

Scripture: Ephesians 4:1–6

Confessional Moment *(in silence)*

A Declaration of God's Love: *Read 1 John 4: 9–10.*

Affirmation of Faith

(Read together):
I believe in the human being
Who each day renews his/her commitment
To justice and truth.
And in God who supports us.
I believe in the powerful force of the almighty and in diversity,
Because it opens us to new horizons.
And in God who sustains us.
I believe in this world so maltreated.
We can be twinklings of light in a new kingdom
I believe in God, who sends us
To cry with the weeping,
To share a smile,
To hug the sad,
And who allows us to embrace,
To be a cradle of a new world
Where everyone has space and air,
And where, free of oppression and bonds,
We find Peace. *(Claudia Ursini)*

Communion: *(Participants are invited to surround the table of celebration.)*

Prayer of Our Savior

Light, necessary for Life, to see, to not stray from the path, to see everyone and everything, and to be seen. We light these candles and upon leaving we share this light with others and ask them to pass it on *(Invite those present to take a small candle and light it from the large one, while we read together):*

Spirit of Jesus
An inspiration in our communities, a support of our endeavors,
Quicken our steps toward the Kingdom
Give us audacity and courage
To plant in the world the seeds of justice and peace
That are born of the Gospel. So it may be.
(Marcelo A. Murúa-Periódico Dialogo)

Benediction

*September is the beginning of spring in the Southern Hemisphere.

—Claudia Ursini, Argentina

ORDER FOR A RETREAT ON THE PRINCIPLES OF STEWARDSHIP AND SHARING

If possible arrange the chairs in a circle and in the center set an altar with a candle (any color or the liturgical season color), flowers, and two small baskets with hard candies of all different sizes, shapes, flavors, and colors. Another, larger empty basket should is prepared to receive offerings.

Further create the mood with pictures that allude to the theme (giving with joy and open hands), such as someone offering a gift or preparing communion. These can be paintings or drawings, projected or placed in a strategic location to create atmosphere for the meeting.

Welcome to the Community

As an act of welcome, hand out to everyone a candy from those that are in the baskets. Explain that this represents a present from God, who always has good things for those he loves. Ask the participants to keep the candies in their hands until the time comes to use them.

Entrance Song

"Va Dios mismo en nuestro mismo caminar" ("God himself walks on our own path") If you prefer, use a favorite hymn that is appropriate for the occasion.

Symbolic Gesture

Ask that all take in their hands the candy that they have received and tightly squeeze the hand closed around it. Each participant should try to pry open the hand of his or her neighbor, but nobody should get the candy out.

Several minutes pass with all participants still holding their candy in their hands.

Explain that now comes part two of the symbolic gesture. Now all must open their hands and hand to their neighbor, with no reservations whatsoever, the piece of candy each is holding. All together everyone gives and everyone receives a candy from another person. All end up with a piece of candy and may eat and enjoy it.

The third part of the symbolic gesture is to share impressions and testimonies of how participants felt in each of the two dynamic moments of the activity. What emotions, ideas, feelings arose in people while sharing in this symbolic action?

Bible Reading: 2 Corinthians 8:1–15

Reflection

Emphasize verses 8:2 and 12–14 (Dios Habla Hoy version). How do we understand this Word in the light of the fact that people live affected by the realities of poverty and misery? How does this Word speak to our lives of deaconry today?

Song

The one who gives for God will shine like the sun. Give and it will be given to you with joy, with joy that which is given for God, with joy that which is for God.

Closing

Use the empty basket. Ask that people place in it various offerings. They can be symbolic offerings representing a commitment to those who suffer. It can be something one could offer for the enlargement of the Kingdom of God and to reach economic equality in the world and in our own context. Some people can express the meaning of their offering. If some only want to offer money, they should do it with the sense or symbolism that they are making a commitment to giving always with generosity and with open hands for the work of God in the world.

Once the type of offering has been explained sufficiently so it may be accomplished by all present, you can sing another brief song, preparatory to the offering. In the Union Evangélica Pentecostal Venezolana (UEPV) we have an offertory song:

Open the window of the heavens, Lord,

And send your blessing.

Bless my brother and my sister, Lord,

Send your blessing.

After the song, leave time for people to bring forward their offerings. If time and mood permit, sing the offertory again during the act of bringing forth the offerings.

Prayer:

At the completion of this act a minister elevates the basket with the offerings and offers them to God, blessing the hands that have been opened to give with generosity.

I propose this prayer: Receive, Lord God, these offerings. They represent all that is in our hands to give. They are the fruit of our work, or our love for your reign and of our desire that nothing be lacking, above all in those places where scarcity and hopelessness abound. Bring from all corners of the world more and more open hands for giving, and bless these hands in your grace and loving kindness. Amen.

Depart with a hug of peace.

—Elida Quevedo, Venezuela

GIVING—HARAMBEE

Throughout our time serving as missionaries in Kenya we were awed by the concept of "Harambee." The word literally means "unity," but it was lived out as fund-raisers, which united communities around specific purposes, like building schools; or causes, such as paying exorbitant medical bills.

The most powerful example of the "Harambee" spirit we experienced was centered around the plight of two young boys: Munene and Mutembi. During our time living in Kenya, much of the country was plagued by drought. The drought-strained resources made it difficult for students at the college to come up with their tuition fees and for the college to meet payroll.

A group of students approached my husband and me for advice. Two young boys had been discovered sleeping under the eaves of the dining hall after begging for food earlier in the day. The students did not want to send these young boys away, but they did not know what they could do with their own meager resources. As Munene and Mutembi's story unfolded, there was no doubt that the only Christian response was to help them. Their father had died, and their mother had become mentally unstable. They had been living with an uncle and his family until the drought had forced him to make the unthinkable decision, to kick these two boys out in order to be able to feed his own family. After some discussion, our students decided to hold an impromptu "Harambee" the following Sunday, which just happened to be Easter. The students, as financially strapped as they were, raised enough money to support the two boys for several weeks. But their unity and generosity did not end there. They agreed to tithe their weekly offering indefinitely to support the boys. The boys went to live with the deputy principal of the college on her farm, and the money the students raised paid for their food, clothing, and school fees.

About a year later our students realized, after a severe and expensive illness one of the boys suffered, that this arrangement could not be maintained. A local church was approached to help share the burden. The only reservation this church had about helping the boys was whether or not they were members of a church. I was blessed to be asked to baptize Munene and Mutembi on the day that this church held a "Harambee" of its own. In a community where, if people were employed they tended to earn less than $1 a day, they raised roughly $2000. From that day to this one, I cannot help but remember the story of the widow's mite whenever I remember the concept of "Harambee," or unity.

Prayer: God, open us to Harambee so that we may be united in giving and receiving. Amen.

—Janice L. Burns-Watson, USA, Kenya

DEDICATION PRAYER

Universal God, accept the offerings of your people. May these gifts be used to spread the good news concerning Jesus Christ throughout the world. We especially pray for and send our gifts to the exploding churches of Kinshasa, Democratic Republic of the Congo; Buenos Aires, Argentina; Addis Ababa, Ethiopia; and Manila, Philippines, in the Southern Hemisphere, where extraordinary spiritual and social vitality abounds. As we send these gifts abroad may we be willing equally to receive the witness of the global church to our own land in a reciprocal partnership. We offer these petitions and intercessions in the name of Jesus, who prayed that we all might be one. Amen.

—Richard A. Hasler

IF THERE IS
A DIVINE SPARK
THAT IS IN ME,
LET IT FLAME;
THAT I MIGHT BE
CONSUMED
FOR PEACE.

—Erice Fairbrother
Aotearoa/New Zealand

18 PEACE AMONG NATIONS

Dearest Friend, gentle Spirit, breath of life, source of our being, from the peacefulness of silence, the silence that preceded creation, your Word entered the void and said, "Let there be light." This afternoon we sit mindful that we are kin and covenanted to that Word and to your light. We are grateful to you, source of our being.

Yet we are bold to come before you with our prayers of petition for peace. We pray for peace among the nations. Help us to cease our warring madness. May we no longer send our young men and young women to foreign lands to fight for what, we are not sure. We are told, or we tell ourselves, that it is for national security. How feeble our faith must be in you if in our need for security we must send our youth armed, off to other lands to kill other people that we might be secure.

Our lives are more than just a handful of years, three score years and ten. Strengthen our resolve to put our trust in you. We pray for peace in conflicted countries around the world. We pray for Iraq, Afghanistan, Palestine, Israel, Sudan, Sri Lanka, Northern Ireland, and North Korea to name but a few. May we work for the health, wealth, and justice for the peoples of these lands and for justice for all the peoples of the world, for all your children, our sisters and brothers.

In the silence of this moment, hear our individual prayers for peace.

Lord in your mercy,

ALL: Hear our prayers.

ONE: Finally, we pray for peace in ourselves. We know people afflicted with physical conflict, or we ourselves suffer from the conflict of illness and aging. Perhaps the outcomes of these conflicts will not be what we desire. Sometimes disability or even death follows illness and not our longed-for healing and recovery. Help us to remember that nothing can separate us from your love, not death nor life, nor angels, nor rulers, nor things present, nor things to come, nor power, nor height nor depth, nor anything else in all creation will be able to separate us from your love. Bear with us, as we wrap our minds around your constant, steadfast love, which surrounds us no matter what our conflict. Lord, in your mercy,

ALL: Hear our prayer.

ONE: And grant us your peace as we pray as Jesus taught us to pray saying,

ALL: (*Pray the Prayer of our Savior.*)

—Theodore Gobledale, Prayer for the Order of St. Luke, Dandenong, Victoria, Australia

In the midst of the rivalries that cause us to fall out
you call us, Lord, to unity and love.
Give us open eyes for our unity in you
And let us see the picture of your new humanity,
so that we may meet one another in love. Amen.

—The Evangelical Church of Kurhesses-Waldeck, Kassel, Germany

SHALOM, SALAAM, LA PAZ, HER-PING, PEACE

ONE: My peace I give to you.

ALL: Pieces of my heart—

ONE: Shattered on the barbed wire of the West Bank,
Blasted into bits in Iraq,
Broken in the barrios,
Sentenced to hard labor for telling the truth,
Dying of frostbite in the streets.

ALL: Pieces of my mind—

ONE: Despairing in the death camps,
Despairing in the refugee camps,
Despairing with the campesinos,
Struggling to stay alive in the work brigades,
Hopeless at the welfare office.

ALL: Pieces of my soul—

ONE: Scattered by a suicide bomber,
Hungering for a land to call our own,
Working to death so that others can buy cheap clothes,
Worshiping in fear,
Waiting on death row.

ALL: This is my body broken with you.

ONE: Shalom, Salaam, La Paz, Her-ping, Peace.
Will you help me mend the shattered world?
Heal my broken body?
Treat the wounds and stop the violence?
Share the bread of life from your plate so that all may live?
In a world gone mad,
will you choose to be a peacemaker
even if it leads to death on a cross?

ALL: Shalom, Salaam, La Paz, Her-ping, Peace.

This is a prayer for peace that I wrote for the Just Peace Players. It reflects my experience of Christ in my life and in the lives of many people I have been privileged to meet around the world. The title contains the words for peace in Hebrew, Arabic, Spanish, Chinese, and English. It can be read as a litany by several people or as a meditation by one person.

—Frances A. Bogle, USA

ONE: Let us pray to God in peace:
For an alert conscience, for forgiveness of our debts
and an open, quiet heart,
Let us pray: God, have mercy upon us.

ALL: God, have mercy on us.

ONE: For an understanding of our fellow human beings,
for a readiness and courage
to speak the truth, let us pray:

ALL: God, have mercy on us.

ONE: For the ability so to behave to all people
that they also through us
might experience the love of God, let us pray:

ALL: God, have mercy on us.

ONE: For our church and for all Christians,
that they beyond all past divisions might be one
in faith and in deed, let us pray:

ALL: God, have mercy on us.

ONE: For our nation and for all nations of the world,
that, where there is war, justice and peace might prevail, let us pray:

ALL: God, have mercy on us.

ONE: For those who are in need and distress,
that they may find help, let us pray:

ALL: God, have mercy on us.

ONE: Stay with us, God,
with your Word and the gift of your goodness.
May your Kingdom come.
And so we pray in the faith of Jesus Christ, our Lord. Amen.

—Evangelisches Gottesdienstbuch, Berlin, Germany, 2000

INTERCESSORY PRAYER FOR PEACE, IN SHONA AND ENGLISH, FROM ZIMBABWE

Mwari wedu unotida tose,musiki wegore nenyika: Mwakatiunza munyika kuti timude
nekumunamata tiri ndudzinendudzi dzavanhu asi tose tiri vana venyu. Imwi mwakavenga
kudeuka kweropa rezvipuka zvenyu, mukaripa neropa renyu pamuchinjiko. Onai ropa
iro ririkudeuka munyika zhinji kunyanya muAfrica nemuMiddle East. Hapana unesimba
rekukonywa kweropa iri kunze kwenyu imwimwi muvambi nemupedzisi weupenyu
hwedu. Onai majongonyi akushandisa sex sechombo chehondo kunevasina simba, pindirai. Vanhu kadzi vabviswa chimiro chavo cheunhu vafananidzwa nenhuka. Tipeiwo mweya
wekudanana kunyange tiri marudzi akasiyana-siyana. Vhurai masiso, pfungwa nemoyo
yedu kuti tisabvume kushandiswa kutungamirira kuita zvakaipa kuneumwe munhu
wakasikwa ndimwi Mwari. Mwari pindirai kuti upenyu hwevanhu huveneshanduko.
Raramai mumoyo mwevanhu venyu.

Our Father who loves us all and creator of the world: You brought us into the world
so that we love and worship you from different cultures and languages but bearing in
our minds that we are all your creation. You hate the shedding of human blood so that
you send us your son Jesus Christ to shed His blood on the cross. Hear our prayers as
we look at what is happening in Africa and the Middle East. There is nobody with
power to stop this bloodshed but only yourself. Sex is used as a weapon tool of war in

different African countries as a punishment against the opponent but targeting women. Women have lost their human dignity in many war-torn African countries and they are like animals. Give us the spirit of loving one another as children of one Mighty Creator even though we are of different nationalities. Open our eyes, minds, and hearts so that we will not be used by power-hungry leaders to do inhuman activities. Come in our lives that we can change the way we see and understand issues affecting other people's lives.

—Fugayo Mutsumbei, Zimbabwe

PRAYER FOR BURUNDI

Prayed by a Burundian man, a politician and a Catholic in a Danish Baptist church, at a memorial service in 1998 in memory of the start of genocide on Burundi's Hutus, which was on April 29, 1972.

Lord! At this occasion of the 26th anniversary of the genocide on Hutus in Burundi we have come together in this Baptist Church to pray for the 500,000 persons who were massacred so dreadfully and without any sympathy. That was in 1972.

Lord! First of all I pray for the 500,000 victims. Receive them in your eternal paradise, where they hopefully may find eternity and comfort.

Until this day we do not know where their dead bodies were buried, that we might lay flowers, even though they were our parents, our uncles, our brothers, our sisters, our cousins, our friends . . .

But we shall never forget them.

Lord! Many families of the victims are still alive. They need your comfort and your support. May these families be able to find medicine, food, clothes, schools, and houses for shelter . . .

Lord! Allow me to commemorate especially Omer Kirahagazwe, Minani Henri, and Stanislas Kasa. They were my teachers, and they taught me. May their souls rest in peace, and may they have a share in the eternal life, in your heavenly paradise.

Through this prayer I also want to mention Boniface Nkundwanabake, my classmate in fifth modern class at the College of the Holy Spirit in Bujumbura. He was torn away from the class room on that evening, Friday, the 5th of May, 1972. He was my friend. He was killed, because he had similarities with an ethnic Hutu. Do receive him in your heavenly realm.

And finally, Lord, our country Burundi needs peace, that these killings, these daily murderings, may stop once and for all, so that all Burundians without ethnic difference may live in mutual respect as humane persons.

That is possible as we know that you are almighty. You are the creator of heaven and earth, your son died on the cross, and after being buried he arose from the dead and ascended to heaven to your paradise. He will return to earth in order to judge the living and the dead. Amen.

—submitted by Hanna Kristensen, Denmark *("I have many Burundian refugee friends living in Denmark, and Baptists in Denmark are about the few ones who know about the conflicts in Central Africa and their traumas. So we have a special responsibility for pastoral caring.")*

REFLECTION ON STRUGGLE IN THE PHILIPPINES

The church in the Philippines has developed a theology of struggle. Much of it is expressed in action: involvement in demonstrations, teach-ins, community organizing, and human rights activities. All these involve risks and dangers, and some of our pastors have been assassinated, and continue to be endangered. My reflections on "struggle" have to do with the very basic theological concepts and how they can reinforce and deepen our commitment. Traditional theology portrays God as acting in history, and our people say, "Why is it that we can hardly see or even perceive God as involved in our struggles?" Or, "Why is it that there has been a very, very long silence on the part of God?" And, of course, there are the usual questions on why does God allow evil to happen, horrendous evil, though we say that God is both omnipotent and absolutely loving. Our theology of struggle is in response to these questions.

—Levi Oracion, Philippines

EN SOLIDARIDAD CON EL PUEBLO HAITIANO/
IN SOLIDARITY WITH THE PEOPLE OF HAITI

"... pero Dios tampoco estaba en el terremoto." (1 Reyes 19:11)

La tierra se sacudió como animal furioso,
temblaron los montes y el mar desató su enojo,
los suelos se abrieron y lo construido fue destruido,
y un pueblo cansado de sufrir vuelve a sufrir.
Vimos sus rostros y oímos sus llantos,
las imágenes estremecían y golpeaban,
personas deambulando, cuerpos aplastados,
destrucción y muerte, dolor y angustia,
tras el terremoto cruel y devastador.

Pero Dios no estaba en el terremoto . . .

Hijos sin madres, madres sin hijos,
hermanos sin hermanos, amigos sin amigos,
miles y miles de vidas aplastadas en segundos,
historias, esperanzas, sueños, ilusiones
qué desaparecieron en un abrir y cerrar de ojos.
El horror dejó su marca indeleble
en las miradas perdidas, en las caras desoladas,
en los muertos, en los atrapados, en los mutilados,
en cada vida quebrada por lo no esperado.

Pero Dios no estaba en el terremoto . . .

Alguien gritó su espanto, otras voces se unieron.
alguien elevó una plegaria, otras siguieron,
alguien cantó y muchos cantaron,
alguien levantó una escombro
y otros más comenzaron a levantar las piedras,
alguien abrazó a un herido
y otros más los cargaron en brazos,
alguien tendió su mano
y miles de manos se unieron.

Y Dios estaba entre ellos.

"But God was not in the earthquake." (1 Kings 19:11)

The ground shook like a furious animal,
the mountains trembled and the ocean let loose its anger,
the ground opened and all that was built was destroyed,
and a village tired of suffering began to suffer anew.
We saw their faces and heard their cries,
the images shook and beat us,
people wandering about, crushed bodies,
destruction and death, pain and anguish
after the cruel and devastating earthquake.

But God was not in the earthquake . . .

Children without mothers, mothers without children,
siblings without siblings, friends without friends,
thousands and thousands of lives squashed in seconds,

histories, hopes, dreams, wishes
disappeared in the opening and closing of an eye.
The horror left its indelible mark
in the blank stares, in the desolate faces,
on the dead, on the trapped, on the mutilated,
in each life broken by what was not expected.

But God was not in the earthquake . . .

Someone shouted in shock, other voices joined in.
Someone offered up a prayer, others followed,
someone sang and many sang,
someone lifted a piece of rubble
and others began to lift the stones,
someone hugged one of the wounded,
and others carried the wounded
someone offered their hand
and thousands of hands were united.

And God was with them.

—Gerardo Oberman, Argentina, January 13, 2010

LAMENT FOR BRITISH COLUMBIA, CANADA

ONE: When we learn that the salmon have disappeared from the rivers, we cry:

ALL: Oh, God, what have we done?

ONE: When we see the First Peoples—
    the Haida, the Nisga'a, the Secwepemc (She-whwp-m) and their cousins—
    burdened by *our* presence and *our* ways, we cry:

ALL: Oh, Christ, what have we done?

ONE: When we look to East Hastings, and touch broken lives
that seek to be deadened by needle,
    by bottle,
        by smoke, we cry:

ALL: Oh, Spirit, what have we done?

ONE: God, what have we done?
    God, what can we do?

ALL: What can we do that shows your Hope?
What can we do that offers your Life?
What can we do that lives your Love?
God, what can we do?

ONE: We repent of our—

ALL: greed.

ONE: We repent of our—

ALL: fear.

ONE: We repent of our—

ALL: apathy and willful inaction.

ONE: Forgive us, God.

ALL: Forgive us, God.
Open our ears, our hearts, our hands, and our lives.
That we might seek healing,
    even as we seek to help heal.
(*A time for silent reflection and prayer.*)

ONE: Amen.

ALL: Amen.

—Richard Bott, Canada

Dayak's Sape' Motif
Willfirmus Uwil

PRAYER FOR INDONESIA AND GERMANY

Lord, we thank you for your support in our lives,
for both the beautiful and the dark sides of life.
You promise more than just bare survival. We ask
you to give strength to all those in the Churches
of the Minahasa and Hesse and Naussau who are
committed to fellowship, peace, justice, and
dignified living conditions for people. Let all those
who make economic and political decisions develop
new visions and strategies so that people all over
the world may share in the fullness of life.

—Detlev Knoche, Germany

PRAYERS TO EMBRACE THE HOLY LAND

1

Loving God

We pray for children living with the conflict in Israel and Palestine.

For children living with destroyed homes and broken family life.

For children living without the opportunity of education.

For children living with minds and bodies damaged by the terror and violence.

We remember especially the work of the YMCA and the YWCA in the occupied
Palestinian territories, and the many children they embrace with love and
compassion. We ask that workers and helpers may find within themselves the
resources to bring care, help, and hope in difficult circumstances. Give to medical
staff special skill and understanding, enabling them to work effectively despite the
restrictions they face. As shattered lives are slowly rebuilt, we pray for the gift of
new beginnings, that those who could see only a desperate future may find
themselves living a vision of peace.

Amen.

2

God of us all:

You called Sarah and Abraham to risk everything in the journey of faith,

To leave familiarity behind in the search for a new country,

And so to be a channel of blessing for generations to come.

We remember the many who find in their story the inspiration for their own faith today.

For Jews, Christians, and Muslims.

May the trust shown by Sarah and Abraham enable us to trust one another,

Discovering new depths of respect and understanding.

May the courage shown by Sarah and Abraham mark our own pilgrimage,

Reaching out hands to one another across all that threatens to divide and alienate.

May the blessing that was known by Sarah and Abraham be poured out on us,

In seeking your peace and living your peace within the world we share.

Amen.

3

As we remember Hebron and all places where barriers divide . . .

ONE: To those who are denied the opportunity to travel freely:

ALL: Lord, bring the hope of freedom.

One: To those who cannot move from one place to another without the indignity of
being stopped and searched:

ALL: Lord, bring the hope of freedom.

ONE: To those who have lost their livelihoods because of barriers and closures and checkpoints:

ALL: Lord, bring the hope of freedom.

ONE: To those who are separated from family and friends, and who are unable to delight in a shared meal:

ALL: Lord, bring the hope of freedom.

ONE: To those who cannot see through the divides and recognise the human in the other:

ALL: Lord, bring the hope of freedom.

ONE: To those whose minds and hearts have been closed by hatred and enmity:

ALL: Lord, bring the hope of freedom.

ONE: To those who are imprisoned by the past and afraid of the future:

ALL: Lord, bring the hope of freedom. Amen

4

ONE: Compassionate God
In the silence, we listen to the cries that are carried to us.
The cries of a child whose sleep is broken by rocket fire and the shouts of soldiers.
The cries of soldiers who know they are brutalised by what they have to do.
The cries of a family whose hearts are broken remembering those no longer with them.
The cries of all broken and scarred communities who long for peace.

ALL: Compassionate God, in the silence, we cry out to you.

ONE: For our acceptance of violence as normal and everyday.
For our failure to seek peace and to make peace.
For our participation in powers and systems that oppress.
For our failure to speak for justice and live for justice.
Hear our cries of pain and lament—the cries in our hearts.
Come and heal us with mercy and grace.

ALL: Compassionate God, Hear the cries of the world. Amen.

5

As we remember Gaza . . .
We pray in solidarity with the lives of women who have yearned for peace as they have
    nurtured their lovers and their children.
We pray in solidarity with the lives of women who have wept for peace as they have re-
    ceived the torn bodies of those they love.
We pray in solidarity with the lives of women who have held the keys and remembered
    in their hearts a place that is home.

We pray in solidarity with the lives of women who have worked to teach and heal and
lead as their communities are violated.
Vulnerable God, we join our prayers with those of many others.
May peace and justice come. Amen.

In the taste of milk and honey, tender lamb and salt water, bitter herbs and lemons,
olives and lentils, we experience sensations of the land many call "holy."
We taste and see. We seek to understand.
Disturbing God, challenge our assumptions and prejudices that we may learn to seek
your peace. Amen.

*These prayers were written for Christian Aid, a church relief and development organisation in the
United Kingdom, and formed part of a Lenten pilgrimage*

—Graham Sparkes, Anthea Sully, England

ECUMENICAL SERVICE FOR PEACE IN THE HOLY LAND

Welcome (German, Arabic, English)

Hymn: "So Much Wrong"

[1]Ayyu hal Mass lubu zulman / ya munaa Qalbi elkaiib
Kabidi Harraa Waqualbi / aaliqon fauq asaliib

Congregational Refrain after each verse:

Wa habibi, wa habibi, ay-yu haalin anta fi,
zuqta kasal mauti keima, yah-ya shabon taftadi.
(*Translation: My beloved, tell me, where can I find you? You who drank the cup of suffering that
your people might have life*)

[2]Schagaru—z-Zeituuni yahnu / baakian Rabbal Galaal
Watanuuhu-l-Quddsu huzznan /watulabbiihal Gibaal. *Refrain*
[3]Ya Habbibi ayyu lahnin / min Schaga-l-Qalbi-l-hazin
Yamnahu aruuha ʿazaaʾan wayusalli-l- Muʾminin. *Refrain*
[4]Ya Habiibi kullu Qaulin / faaden min ghaali-l-kalaam
La yafiika-d-Dahru Schukran/laka ya Faadi-l-Anaam. *Refrain*

Multinational Peace Liturgy

Call to Worship (English)

ONE: The world belongs to God,

ALL: the earth and all those who dwell in it.

ONE: How good and pleasant it is

ALL: to live together in harmony.

ONE: Love and Faith come together,

ALL: Justice and Peace meet each other.

ONE: If the disciples of Jesus remain silent,

ALL: these stones would cry aloud.

ONE: God, open my lips,

ALL: so that my mouth shall proclaim your glory.

Glory be to the Father and to the Son and to the Holy Spirit. As it was in the beginning is now and ever shall be, world without end. Amen, amen.

A Reading of Mary's Magnificat (Arabic, German): Luke 1:46b–55

Call for Blessing

ALL SING: Someone's crying Lord, Kumba yah
    Someone's crying Lord, Kumba yah
    Someone's crying Lord, Kumba yah
    Oh, Lord, Kumba yah.

ONE (German):
Someone's crying, Lord, somewhere.
Some is a million
Somewhere is many places.
There are tears of suffering.
There are tears of weakness and disappointment
There are tears of strength and resistance.
There are the tears of the rich, and the tears of the poor.
Someone's crying. Lord, heal the times.
Someone's dying, Lord . . .

ALL SING: Someone's dying, Lord, Kumba yah . . .

ONE (English):
Some are dying of hunger and thirst.
Someone is dying
because someone else is enjoying
too many unnecessary and superfluous things.
Someone is dying
because people go on exploiting one another.
Someone is dying
because there are structures and systems
that crush the poor and alienate the rich.

Someone's dying, Lord,
because we are still not prepared
    to take sides,
        to make a choice,
        to be a witness.
Someone's dying. Lord, heal the times.
Someone's shouting, Lord . . .

ALL SING: Someone's shouting, Lord, Kumba yah . . .

ONE (Arabic):
Someone's shouting out loudly and clearly.
Someone has made a choice.
Someone is ready to stand up against the times.
Someone is shouting out,
offering her very existence in love and anger
to fight death surrounding us,
to wrestle with the evils with which we
crucify each other.
Someone's shouting, Lord, heal the times.
Someone's praying, Lord . . .

ALL SING: Someone's praying, Lord, Kumba yah . . .

ONE (Swedish):
Someone's praying, Lord.
We are praying in tears and anger,
in frustration and weakness,
in strength and endurance.
We are shouting and wrestling,
as Jacob wrestled with the angel,
and was touched,
and was marked,
and became a blessing.
We are praying, Lord.
Spur our imagination,
sharpen our political will.
Through Jesus Christ you have let us know
where you want us to be.
help us to be there now,
be with us, touch us, mark us,
let us be a blessing,

let your power be present in our weakness.
Someone's praying, Lord, heal the times.
Someone's praying, Lord.

ALL SING: Someone's praying, Lord, Kumba yah . . .

Old Testament Readings: Micah 6:6–8, Micah 4:1–5

The Holy Gospel: Matthew 5:43–48

Nicene Creed

Hymn: "The Peace of the Believers" (Arabic)

[1]Birrun salamun ma' surur
ausafu mulkil bari
Tabka ila dar riduhur
lilmu'minil mukhtari.
(*Translation: Righteousness, peace with joy, are the attributes given from the Creator. They remain with the elected believer unto eternity.*)

(*Refrain*) Hada salamul mu'miniin
min rabbihem hulwun thamin.
Salamun, salamun, salamun,
kula hiin.
(*Translation: This is the peace of the believers, which is from their God—sweet and precious. Peace, peace, peace all the time.*)

[2]Hada salamun li sharah
rabbul fida bissaulbi
Kannahri yashri fi safa'
yurwi 'idashal kalbi.
(*Translation: This peace is bought for me by the Lord of redemption on the cross. It flows like a clear river that quenches the hearts of the thirsty.*)
(*Refrain*)

[3]Inn tattmu hauli na'ibaat
kallushi wastal bahri
yadom salaami fi thabat
asasuhu fi sakhri.
(*Translation: If problems and crises surround me like a wave in the midst of the ocean, my peace remains steady, for its foundation is built on a rock.*)
(*Refrain*)

Responsive Prayer of Intercession

ONE: Heavenly Father, we praise and glorify you. You are our only refuge in a troubled world.

ALL: We praise and glorify you, Lord.

ONE: We thank you for the birth of your Son, Jesus Christ, in Bethlehem, his refuge in Egypt, his childhood in Nazareth, and his ministry in this land.

ALL: Father, we thank you.

ONE: We thank you for his death on the cross here in Jerusalem, where he carried our sin and suffering, and for his glorious resurrection in which he gave us new life with him.

ALL: Father, we thank you.

ONE: So, Lord, we come before you with all our troubles and pains.

ALL: Lord, have mercy on us.

ONE: We pray for all victims of bloodshed and violence as well as for the perpetrators of these evils.

ALL: Lord, have mercy on us.

ONE: We pray for the children and young people that you may give them hope for the future.

ALL: Lord, have mercy on us.

ONE: We pray for all bereaved families, the unemployed, the elderly, and all who seek to help them.

ALL: Lord, have mercy on us.

ONE: We ask the guidance of your Holy Spirit for all the leaders of this land; that they may be inspired to work for your peace with your justice.

ALL: Lord, have mercy on us.

ONE: So we pray together:

ALL: Gracious God, your love knows no limits. Fill our hearts with your compassion; open our eyes to your presence in the world; enlarge our minds to understand your will. Take our hands and minister through them. Speak through our words and direct our feet in the path of peace, that Christ may be revealed in us and the world may believe. Amen

The Lord's Prayer (each in his or her own language)

The Prayer of St. Francis

Lord, make me an instrument of your peace;
where there is hatred, let me sow love; where there is injury, pardon;
where there is doubt, faith; where there is despair, hope;
where there is darkness, light; and where there is sadness, joy.

The Sharing of the Peace and Blessing

Song (sung as a canon): "Dona Nobis Pacem"

—Middle East Council of Churches, contributed by Munib A. Younan, bishop,
   Evangelical Lutheran Church in Jordan and the Holy Land (*from an occasion at the
   Lutheran Church of the Redeemer, Jerusalem, August 26, 2008*)

Rini Templeton

LITANY FOR EL SALVADOR

ONE: O God who knows no borders or boundaries, who created the universe and all its inhabitants, and whose image is borne in the Salvadoran people, today we remember our sisters and brothers who have been subjected to tyranny and oppression. In solidarity we pray for the families of those massacred and other victims of violence in El Salvador and throughout the world, that their deaths may be a call for peace and reconciliation.

ALL: Lord, have mercy. Hear our prayer.
Señor, ten piedad. Escucha nuestra oración.

ONE: Today we remember that the whole of your creation—land and water—is holy because it was created by you. Your intention, O God, was that we care for these resources with respect and reverence. In solidarity we pray for those who do not have access to clean water, and we vow to work for justice until all receive this basic need.

ALL: Lord, have mercy. Hear our prayer.
Señor, ten piedad. Escucha nuestra oración.

ONE: Today we remember your son, Jesus Christ, who brought good news to the poor, proclaimed release to the captives and recovery of sight to the blind, and who let the oppressed go free. In solidarity we plead for those who are impoverished and those bound by oppressive social and political systems, and we pray that your reign may soon be realized.

ALL: Lord, have mercy. Hear our prayer.

Señor, ten piedad. Escucha nuestra oración.

ONE: Today we remember the stories of the people of El Salvador—the stories of anguish and lament and the stories of hope and healing. In solidarity we carry those stories with us and pray that we never forget to rely on your transforming power to create hope and new life.

ALL: Lord, have mercy. Hear our prayer.

Señor, ten piedad. Escucha nuestra oración.

—Robin D. Dillon, USA *(written for a chapel service after cross-cultural trip to El Salvador, January 2009)*

REFLECTION ON THE STRUGGLE IN CHINA FOR RELIGIOUS FREEDOM

Five years ago, the religious policy was not completely implemented in my hometown yet; there were only three meeting points registered by the government, but over one hundred thousand Christians. Nearly all meeting points were not registered, and so their activities were unlawful.

There is a meeting point far away from my church, about forty kilometers. This meeting point was not registered as well four years ago. One day, when they were gathering together, three main lay workers were seized by policemen. These policemen took all the Bibles and all the hymn books and all the benches, etc. The three lay workers were interrogated for three hours and then were fined fifty yuan each in the local police station. As soon as I got the bad news, I immediately called the City Religious Affairs Bureau (RAB) and the City Police Station, and hoped for the best. Later, I submitted a formal report to the Provincial RAB. I asked my congregations to pray for this event on Sunday services and prayer meetings. God is a true God who hears his children's prayer; he wipes away the tears from his children's eyes, he loves his own church so much. After two months, the Provincial Police Station sent out a notice to the local police station that they must return all the Bibles and all the hymn books and all the benches and all the fines. After this, when I went to this meeting point to preach, all the members cried. I gave them advice in my sermon, "Keep alert, stand firm in your faith, have courage, be strong" (1 Cor. 16:13).

In spring 2003, this meeting point was registered by the government and set up as a church. They had a great ceremony for the new church, and about three hundred members joined in this meeting; some leaders of the local government were invited to attend also.

Now I still remember what the head of the local police station said to the congregations: "Here I apologize to you. Because you suffered persecution for your beliefs before, I will protect you by law from now. We can be good friends, please believe me!" He was applauded for a full three minutes after his speech.

In these days, I feel that God gives me strength and courage to stand up for my belief, and protect his sheep. At the same time, I was deeply moved by Jesus' words also. Jesus said, "Do not fear those who kill the body but cannot kill the soul; rather fear him who can destroy both soul and body in hell" (Matt. 11:28), and Paul told us, "for rulers are not a terror to good conduct, but to bad" (Rom. 13:3). We believe in God. We never break the law, so we don't have fear in our heart.

As of this summer, forty-two meeting points were registered in my hometown. I often give thanks to God in my prayers. I can do nothing without his power, mercy, guidance, and peace.

—Zheng Yuoguo (Timothy), China

REFLECTION ON BICULTURAL UNDERSTANDING IN AOTEAROA/NEW ZEALAND
"Happenings"

There was a "bicultural happening," a beginning.
Important visitors came, speeches were made,
And there were welcomes and songs.
And I sat and was a spectator—alone, in a crowd.

There was a "bicultural happening."
We talked about words, about land, the way we remembered our ancestors,
But we forgot to feel about words, about land, and to remember our ancestors.

There was a "bicultural happening," but I did not go.

There was "bicultural travelling" and I heard
Of all the wrong that was perpetuated by my ancestors.

There was a "bicultural happening,"
And there was action, movement, and response,
Eloquent guides who shared the history of their treasures, their taonga,*
With intensity and passion,
Sometimes tongue in cheek, always eloquence,
Not knowing all the answers, but sharing feelings,
Tracing the history of their tribes as etched in carvings
In wood and greenstone, pumice and bone,

Sharing their understanding of the world—their mana,* their mauri*—
Art presented from the inside.
And I stood tall as I shared in the heritage of this land, our home.

There was a "cultural happening," and we were there,
And we learnt more about our roots of Methodism.
We travelled back in time to early days last century
When missionaries came to share their faith, enthused to spread good tidings,
To bring words of peace and freedom to people of the South Pacific—
    the islands of the sea . . .
They brought their words, they brought their creeds tied up with cultural trappings.
They brought their human frailty too.
Life was strange and unfamiliar, and they worked hard and long
Trying to dispel the darkness that they saw,
And in that darkness they were not able to perceive
The dawn light of another culture;
And soon those whom they had come to free were tied up stronger,
    bound by ways and feelings, thoughts, ideas
Not fully comprehended, not understood.
      But now, the wrappings once so tight
         were being loosened, shed, and cast aside.
As we listened to each other together we began to glimpse a freedom,
A new way, a new beginning, a rainbow covenant.
There was another "bicultural happening."
We were welcomed, made to feel at home.
The spoken words I could not always understand
But I felt the warmth and the humour too.
I gazed at the meeting house—resplendent with its carving
    telling the story of the people.
I was surrounded by the spirits of those ancestors who had lived and loved,
Worked and been part of this land, this Aotearoa.
And I looked at the trees—totara* and cabbage, willow and kauri,
And I thought of my ancestors . . .

I have stood in the places in the lands from whence my people came.
I wonder—why did they, too, cross the oceans wide and settle in this far distant land?
A sense of adventure? a pioneering spirit?
Were they ever homesick, longing for familiar faces?
Were they scared and frightened, lonely and alone?
How did they cope with living as strangers in a strange land?

What were their attitudes, what their understanding?
Did they soon find friends and learn new ways? I do not know.
Like mists along the river, time hides the answers we would seek . . .

After speeches at this happening we shared together in a meal,
Fruit of the land and harvest of the sea, set before us amidst the beauty
    of modern architecture, sculpture, art.
Beside me, dressed in black, an old lady, a kuia,* did not understand the words I spoke
    but we smiled, in shyness.
And then came time for us to leave.
We spoke to friends. One who offered caring greetings briefly spoke to us
And I was reminded that in the reality of life
There is always power and thoughtlessness, indifference and pain,
And I cried.

I am part of this land, Aotearoa, New Zealand,
Rooted in a far-off land, planted and cultured, transplanted and nurtured,
And I long for the day when there shall be understanding
Between people and people,
    and people and their God.
For where there is understanding, there is sharing,
Where there is sharing there is love,
 and where there is love
HAPPENINGS will be for real.

*Maori words: taonga—tangible or intangible treasured thing; totara—tall conifer, prized for height and durability of wood; Kuia—a social group of the southern island of Aotearoa. Mana and mauri are hard to squeeze into a definition. Loosely, mana is honor or character, and mauri is life force.

—Marcia Baker, Aotearoa/New Zealand

LITANY FROM A PRAYER FOR PEACE IN THE TIME OF CONFLICT AND BLOODSHED

(during the Russian-Georgian War in September 2008)

ONE: Come and be with us as a comforting Mother as we mourn the death of soldiers, children, men, women, and elderly from both sides, because for you there is only one side—broken humanity.

ALL: Lord have mercy, Christ have mercy, Lord have mercy.

ONE: Come and be with us as the protecting Father as we experience destruction, humiliation, powerlessness, and feelings of abandonment.

ALL: Father have mercy, Son have mercy, Spirit have mercy.

ONE: Come and be with us as the Lord of love as we feel hatred and fear.

ALL: Lord have mercy, Christ have mercy, Lord have mercy.

ONE: Come and be with us as the Lord of repentance as we struggle to change our minds and seek renewal.

ALL: Father have mercy, Son have mercy, Spirit have mercy.

ONE: Come and be with us as the Lord of justice as we see justice being sidelined by the fear and favour.

ALL: Lord have mercy, Christ have mercy, Lord have mercy.

ONE: Come and be with us as the Lord of reconciliation as we make great efforts to find the ways for reconciliation.

ALL: Father have mercy, Son have mercy, Spirit have mercy.

ONE: Come and be with us as the Lord of freedom as we suffer under political, emotional, and spiritual captivity.

ALL: Lord have mercy, Christ have mercy, Lord have mercy.

ONE: Come and be with us as the Prince of Peace as we long for wholeness and integrity.

ALL: Father have mercy, Son have mercy, Spirit have mercy. Amen.

—Malkhaz Songulashvili, Evangelical Baptist Church of Georgia (country)

O GOD, LOVER OF THE WORLD, WE PRAY FOR OUR WOUNDED WORLD, TORN APART BY WARRING AND GREEDY FACTIONS. MAY WE BE MAKERS AND MENDERS.

—Barbara Peddie
Aotearoa/New Zealand

Part Five

OUR HANDS OFFER

New and Old Treasure for the Householder of God

19   ❀   TREASURES — POETRY

MORNING PRAISES

If I was asked to praise something I would
praise the morning, first light of day,
and even the fog when ships horns do their
best and rouse me. Praise the dark rain
song of December, prowling winter gales
that howl at my window like childhood
monsters. I would praise morning whatever
the weather; tomorrow is promised
to no one. Praise the rising from my bed,
whether groggy or perky, the first
shock of water as I splash my face, praise
the soap, the razor blade, the mirror
as I take stock. Praise my blue striped bathrobe,
hung in my closet these twenty-two years,
praise the corridor path to my kitchen.

Praise spaces between spaces.

And each cracked egg scrambled in my blue
pottery bowl, the communion of omelettes,
toast, a cup of orange juice, raised to my lips.

—Ray McGinnis, Canada

THE CRAB SHELL

Molting of the shell—ecdysis—is a distinctive feature of all Crustacea—crabs, lobsters, prawns, and even barnacles. These animals wear their skeletons on the outside, in the form of an armour. As the crab grows, its shell becomes too small and must be discarded. This process, known as ecdysis, is a fraught one. Pulling limbs from the shell is a bit like pulling fingers from a glove—except that a crab's fingers are delicate and its claws wider than the basal joints of the limb. If all limbs survive ecdysis, the crab finds itself for a time soft, vulnerable, and quite delicious to several enemies. Apparently transition was not meant to be easy!

Ecdysis
A fading crustacean on the sand
seems as white as death.
Rather it speaks of growth and change
Transition is indeed painful.
Much worse to hide within one's shell
Safe from new ways of thinking, feeling
and living—the soul imprisoned,
ever tighter.
With each new spurt of growth
the crab must cast off its old armour:
this ecdysis leaving it soft and
fragile for a time.
So too the ecdysis of our soul—
the breaking out all sensitive and exposed
to find the strength of a new and bigger
wisdom

—Digby Hannah, Australia

YOU'LL SLEEP HERE

(A conversation in Zimbabwe)
"Let not your heart be troubled. You believe in God . . ." (John 14:1)

"You'll sleep here tonight," she said,
as rain drummed on the iron roof
and wind shook the loose-set panes.
Water spilled from the rusted eaves
and overflowed the drum beneath.
The village slopes turned slick with mud,

paths became creeks, lanes were streams,
and the only road to town
was two feet under water:
I knew, from wading in it.

"You'll sleep here," my hostess smiled.
"I'd rather not," said I.
"The storm seems localized;
in the city it may be dry.
My wife will worry if I don't come home."
"Worry? Why? She's a Christian.
She believes in God, who cares for you."
Humbled, I was still.

—Allen Myrick, USA, Zimbabwe

PRAYER FOR VOCATION

Gracious Lord
I finally let it all out.
The tears came running out.
I have finally given up the fight.
Maybe this time I will let you get it right.
My heart hurts so badly and I keep having to move on.
There is no need to hang on any longer.
I give my life to thee, Lord.
I am here.
I exist as is.
A vessel for you.
The children are my teachers.
You have so much to show me, Lord.
A language of the heart I can't ignore.
I have to let it flow from me like the raging sea.
Prayer keeps me where I need to be.
God's timing is not mine to own.
I have to leave this one alone.
You know what I speak of, Lord.
Thank You, Lord, for giving me the grace I need.

—Valerie Ann Miller, Honduras

CREATION SPEAKS

Creation speaks, surpassing understanding
Light in the darkness, time and space entwine
We who inherit vistas of true glory
Sense growing wonder for the works divine

Fill now our minds with wakening comprehension
Fill too our hearts, with all that love might bring
Grant that our senses tune to hidden beauty
Causing real music in the hymns we sing

Heeding the call to follow in Christ's footsteps
Offering commitment for the things we pray
Taking the challenge to be true disciples
Taking the cross to follow come what may

Teach us the way to show due care and reverence
For all we hold in trust for those to come
Planning ahead as we build for the future
Holding a vision for a world begun

Tune: "O Perfect Love"

—Bill Peddie, Aotearoa, New Zealand

ROYAL SEED

From you a royal seed sprouted
marching gallantly to her Queenly womb
Her womb opened perfectly
To the drumming beats
on rawhide skin.
With melodious ululating sounds
from the village women.
celebrating the birth of a royal son.
A Rozvi Prince.

I was born in a village hut.
Without the assistance of a medical doctor
But with the wisdom of a wise grandmother.
The best midwife for the royal family.

in a sub-Saharan African village.
My Queen mother was given every gift from the village folks.
In celebration of my new arrival.
Goats, reed mats, winnowing baskets, millet, bows and arrows.

Later, as I swam in the river of life.
I realized that I needed an anchor.
I wanted a cornerstone,
As powerful as that of the Great Zimbabwe monuments.
I had everything in our village.
Tribal power, livestock, servants, and children.
I possessed all the greatest gifts of our village.

However I lacked love and life
Hope and power
Liberty and knowledge.
For years I had searched but in vain.
Eventually I met the author of life—God—
Who was there before the genesis of humankind.
He gave me the gift of life
In open hands through his royal prince—Jesus Christ.
Today early in the morning I am using my hands in praise
Playing the mbira, marimba, and rawhide skin drums.
In the sunny afternoon I am using my mouth
To sing and play the African flute from the psalmist.
To create rhythms of praise and worship.

Deep in the silence of the village night
All human legs in the royal house
are busy dancing in celebration
Of the birth of new life.

—Lancelot Muteyo, Zimbabwe

Lancelot Muteyo (born 1982) is the author of African Prophecies, *a poetic compilation of African stories of survival. He is an HIV and AIDS activist and is responsible for a programme that takes care of three hundred HIV and AIDS orphans in Zimbabwe.*

The life becomes beautiful because of this,
   —we know you, Christ Jesus.
Our silent souls.
   invoke your love on the cross
Even though they are full of hurts,
Your love heals them with peace.
Even though my wandering steps lost the targets,
   Your loves call us back to your house.
Even though we neglect you,
   You increase love and grace.
So many times we seek the true love
   Your palms with the print of nails show me.
So many times in hopelessness I almost forsake myself
   You show me the path in the desert.
To love is to give,
   Life becomes beautiful because of this.

—huang yan jie, China

QUIET IS THIS NIGHT

Quiet is this night.
Sitting in the light of nothing.
The willows dance in my spirit.
You are silent with space unknown.
Cradle me, Holy Spirit, in the shadows of self.
It is the whispers that are so loud in my soul.
The time alone is solemn in its newness.
A language known yet foreign tosses me about.
My head longs to take in each word like honey from a pot.
My roots keep me strong with a new people a new land.
My ancestors reach out to me calling me home again.
Celtic roots are my trunk as I branch out to the quietness of silent space.
No material things are ever needed for the feeling is real.
The feelings are real as each breath I breathe in a place of healing.
The quietness kills the demons with the help of my Lord God.

Lord God who never leaves this woman ... this woman once more.

The evolution has started ... this is my life ... the evolution of lovers that have
come and gone.

The evolution of the quiet once a scared woman in her cocoon.

I am always a larva ... a butterfly I am in the quiet ... with God. Amen

—Valerie A. Miller, Honduras

BELONGING

What privileges have been ours!
We have seen tall green casuarinas* trees,
Misted mountains losing themselves in the sky,
Rain splashing relentlessly on an ever devouring earth
and flashes of lightning brightening up the thundering heavens.

We have seen little brown babies lying securely amongst the leaves
in their mother's bags,
Children uneducated by western standards, unable to read and write,
Happy in their play,
Men and women, still young by our reckoning,
Grown old by the rigours and hard work of their survival,
and yet able to laugh and find happiness.

And we have seen pink blossoms on a peach tree
a spider web sparkling with the jewels of dawn,
a tui* singing in the yellow flowers of a kowhai* tree,
the laughing carelessness of breakers in the surf,
the mellowness of coloured leaves which is Autumn
and icy cold snow-covered mountains.

We have seen the marvels of modern technology,
showing us diversity and unity,
and lifting us up as part of a global village.
We have heard an orchestra playing,
each instrument with its own part in the master score,
bringing harmony and enjoyment.
We have seen a sculptor take a lump of clay in her hands,

and with skill and patience
mould it into a Wise Man who, with love and devotion,
offers his gift to an Infant Christ.

And still the stars of the Southern Cross shine down upon us
as we look up and see them there.
And many times when darkness comes,
Calling from the bush, we hear again
The song of the owl that means we're home again . . . Morepork . . . Morepork,

*Casuarinas—commonly known as she-oak or ironwood, is a tree tolerant of windswept locations;
kowhai—a legume tree, famous for its beautiful yellow or golden flowers that blossom in early spring,
is the national flower of New Zealand; tui—Maori name for honeyeater bird with two voiceboxes,
which can (like a parrot) imitate human speech.*

—Marcia Baker, New Zealand, Papau New Guinea, land of seven hundred languages

In the dawn
You walk toward me
When I am confused
You shower me in Love

In the darkness
You bestow light
When I am hesitant
You show me Your Words

In my days
You grant a mission
When I am weak
You lend me Your Power

In sickness
You are by my side
When I am suffering
You offer me the Cure

In conflicts
You increase my strength
When I am in pain
You grace me with Peace

In all my life
You leave your footprints
When I am empty
You give me Your All

—Dongxia Shi, China

SKYE SPIRIT

Refrain: Spirit Divine, so like a fair breeze,
come to us like a dove;
bring me refreshment, wisdom, and peace,
fill me with Jesus' love!

Wisdom you spoke through folk below,
glows through the Gospel Word:
Help me to let its message flow,
so your own voice is heard. *Refrain*

Help us to cease our stumbling on,
turn us back to the Way;
help us to help each other on,
with Jesus' Word each day. *Refrain*

(Tune: "Skye Boat Song": in F)

—Gordon Piesse, Aotearoa/New Zealand

ONLY WHEN I COME TO KNOW YOU

Only when I come to know the Lord of Love,
do I see the ultimate affection exists in the universe.
When I lie in the arms of my Lord,
My soul is nurtured and surrounded by the love of my Lord.

Only when I come to know the Lord of Truth,
do I discover that He is what my heart has long desired.
Sin can not lay hold of me,
because the light of my Lord shines upon me.

Only when I come to know the Lord of Almighty,
do I realize how powerless I am.
Without my Lord on my side,
I can accomplish nothing.

Only when I come to know the Lord of Eternity,
do I cease to sigh for the short span of my life.
Full of faith in joyful living,
is what my Lord enjoys to see always.

God bless you! God is with you!

—Zhang Yanhua, China

TAKING LEAVE

When the trees are shaken and bending
And my head is pressed to the wind;
When the sun falls and my heart is in shadow
And the earth is hard under my feet;
I leave for the track through the foothills
For the bush that is silent and still,
Where totara* lie ancient and fallen,
At peace with their scars and their death;
Where the ferns have no fear of unfolding,
Nor the sky, of the kauri* and beech;
I find in this bush that is wordless,
Where light is at ease with the dark,
A greening on paths that are endless
And earth that gives speech to the heart.

*totara—a conifer prized by the Maori for its timber's durability and length
*kauri—also an evergreen, the world's oldest wood

—Erice Fairbrother, Aotearoa/New Zealand

20 ❀ TREASURES—SCRIPTURE ILLUMINATIONS

Praying at Gethsemane   He Qi

THE REHABILITATION OF THOMAS John 20:24–29

Part of the task of Pacific Rim theology is redefining who we are, and what we believe, as opposed to what was handed down to us from afar.

It need not be the paparazzi,
    but a trusted colleague,
    or a well-intentioned cousin.
Then "click!" etched in a nano second:
    an unbecoming portrait—
    dutifully framed, wondrously displayed:
    "Doubting Thomas"
               —yes, that was me.
Would you like to be a snapshot stilled in time,
    sepia-ed in dullest, darkest doubts?
    Developed in a dark room of anxiety—
    and, dare I say, agony?
               —for that was me.

Am I to be held in memorial
    for doubting,
    and daring to proclaim questions
    which lay buried,
    burdening my brothers' hearts—
    too charged with fear and shame
    to be exposed to light?
                —it would appear so.
But—
    why me?
Why not Doubting Martha, or Peter, or Judas?
    for they too were carved with troublesome headstones.
    But I alone bear the epitaph.
May I ask,
    are you courageous enough to challenge and change?
May I request,
    that with new century lenses
    you recapture me,
    redigitalise my image.
For I am—
    the one who was unafraid to question,
    the one who exposed his fears
                —and through them knew redemption.
May the blessing of "Honest Tom"
    be your camera.

—Janet Marsh, Kiwi, Aoreatoa/New Zealand

THE BODY OF CHRIST IN HONDURAS 1 Corinthians 12:12–31

Following a military coup in Honduras in June of 2009, the de facto government declared a state of siege that temporarily required churches to get permission from the government to congregate. As well, there is ongoing extreme tension among "church and state," as some church bodies have declared support of the de facto government, while others beg to remain neutral.

A leg alone could not walk, nor could a hand alone clap. An ear alone would only *hear* one side of the story, while an eye alone would only *see* one side. One lip alone could not speak but would be bound to indefinite silence.

The *body* of Christ is not one, but many, working together through the challenges of taking the first steps in a new direction, celebrating change, and setting aside differences to care for its overall well-being.

May the people, all fingers united, be the hands that rise up and reach for justice.

May the people also be the legs that support one another in walking a new path, moving in a new direction.

May our ears hear the proclamation of the grace of God.

May our eyes see the work of the body of Christ in motion.

May our lips speak comfort to one another.

Dios le bendiga, God bless you; AMEN

—Chelsea E. Bicknell, USA, Honduras

FRAGMENTS OF A PSALM Psalm 102

Turn your ear to me; when I call, listen to me.
My days are like smoke.
My bones are like burning coals and searing heat.
My heart is weak. I am withered, like grass;
I forget to eat my bread.
I am like a vulture in the wilderness;
Like an owl among the ruins.
I lie awake;
I have become like a bird alone on a rooftop.

I tell myself all is well,
And yet you have searched my heart
as I lie awake

So in this moment,
while I am free from distractions' grip
listen to me

I recall past days—my old friend
Worshiping—not you but his ego
And fearful, let words fly at me and others
like burning coals and searing heat.
All day long I toss it over

and late into the night
I forget to eat my bread

Old games of childhood storm past the dyke,
grown men speak like a child, put on childish things
Harm is buttoned up with the coat of denial
And I am like an owl among the ruins.
I am like grass withered.

May your justice flow like a mighty river.
Heal what is broken. Help me return to myself
that my joy may be full.
Do not let me remain here like a vulture in the wilderness.

—Ray McGinnis, Canada

THE SYRO-PHONECIAN WOMAN AND THE EXPERIENCE OF EXCLUSION Mark 7:24–30

ONE: God of surprise and awe, whose creation is wondrous and diverse, we rejoice in the diversity of our world, the richness of life, and the many cultures of humanity.

ALL: You are the Living God, and all life is your witness.

ONE: You have shown us your own self in the life of Jesus,
one man who shows your promise to all people.

ALL: We have chosen to follow Jesus as part of your new and diverse people.

ONE: You call people from every race and nation, from a multitude of experiences, from diverse lives. For everyone born there is a place offered at your table. We confess that we struggle with the inclusiveness of your love, for your disregard of the things that carefully keep us from them. We imagine that grace and mercy are for people like us alone.

ALL: Forgive us our lack of vision; help us live with the truth that everyone is welcome to come as they are, not as we would like them to be.

ONE: Hear then the good news: God's love is enough for everyone. Even for us.

ALL: Thanks be to God. Amen.

—David Poultney, Aotearoa/New Zealand

JESÚS Y LA MUJER EXTRANJERA/JESUS AND THE FOREIGN WOMAN
Mark 7:24–30, Matthew 15:21–28

Jesus, Son of David, have mercy on me,
heal my daughter, who is so very ill.
This illness has consumed
everything we had to live.

Attend to my prayers,
They say a devil haunts her forever.
I kneel before you, Messiah of foreign people.

Do not ignore me.
Look into my eyes and see,
Feel with me the pain of a mother.
I'm desperate, and so I watch your eyes, your soul,
I know you are a sensitive man.

My daughter has a distorted face,
from a pain which has no relief.
People's words are cruel—crazy they say.
We are all each other has.
Nothing else is left.

I am a woman growing old,
and when I die, my daughter will be homeless,
Have mercy on me.

"God has sent me only the sheep from Israel.
It is not right to give the children's food to the dogs,"
you said, as if searching for my response
accurate and adequate.

Hearing those words from your lips,
is hard and disconcerting.
You call us bitches,
What kind of holy man are you?
Why do you insult us?

I seek you as a last resort,
I come before you, Prophet of Nazareth, with only my faith.
Doctors and medicines have failed.
You say, "Let the kids eat first."

I do not understand your words,
I look at your eyes, Master of Galilee,
I do not find that they hate me
even though I am a foreign woman.

Why do I hear those words from your lips?
They sound harsh to my ears,
and my mother's heart is in despair.

Yet you look at me with your eyes full of love,
looking inside me
at my pain but also my abundant faith.

I see in your eyes reflected
my spirit in anguish—a desperate mother.

Sir,
I say, even the dogs eat the crumbs
that children drop under the table.
Your eyes smile,
look me at me forcefully with love.

I feel my faith grow in me,
my confidence, my self-esteem.

You did not want me to come to you
as a foreigner begging the crumb of your infinite love.
You wanted me to come as a friend,
as a brother, as God.

Did I discover in myself a woman
who rescues her lost dignity,
lost to the prejudices of this society
that rejects women, the elderly, especially the sick,
foreigners and refugees,
all those who have nothing?

You wanted me to stand tall with dignity,
I will not feel small in your presence,
being female, foreign, or poor.
When I realized that I could hear your words,
for the healing of my daughter:
"¡Grande es tu fe!"—"Great is your faith!"

Because I dared to speak as you did,
when you forbade religious conventionalism
with its macho and patriarchal prejudice.

"Go, you have been healed,
The evil gone out of your daughter for your faith."

I went home,
I returned to my reality,
I regained my faith and dignity.
I felt liberated from the prejudices of society,
and all my complexes.

—Obed Juan Vizcaíno Nájera. Venezuela

BLESSING THE PRODIGAL Luke 15:11–32

Then he laid his hands upon me
 and with grief he let me go.

There was no turning back to spurn
 the twins of envy and hatred
 clenched in my brother's fists.

What freedom! To live and love
 with generosity of golden hands.

I freely gave and gave and gave,
 until my purse was emptied
 and my hands laid bare.

From parties to pigs—
 my hands grasped husks
 a sorry saga best left untold . . .
Till all that was left in my palms
 was the DNA of love.

It was a long walk home.

Then he laid his hands upon me
 and he would not let me go.

—Janet Marsh, Kiwi, Aotearoa/New Zealand

WE PLAYED THE FLUTE BUT YOU DID NOT DANCE; SANG SAD SONGS BUT YOU DID NOT CRY (LUKE 7:32)
Luke 7:24-35

Today I made the sun, as every morning,
to advertise the warmth of my presence,
to caress your window on waking,
to accompany the way of your work.
But, you said the sun was very strong.
Then I sent the rain to water your hopes
and to renew your strength
and give you the joy of a day without sunshine.
But you complain about the inconvenience
because your clothes are wet
and you might be late for your commitments.
I stopped the downpour,
peeked through the clouds and the rainbow
for what happened in "our agreement"
Do you remember?

Now when your kids have asked you to look at the sky,
you say you have no time for these things.
You know? Sometimes I do not understand . . .
I wish, sometimes,
you'd quit complaining about everything
and realize that life has wonderful things
that call out for your thanks.
And to live is much more
than what you are calling a life.
I came that they might life,
to be able to live abundantly.
Look, I'm playing the flute,
I'd be enchanted if you'd dance with me.

—Gerardo Oberman, Argentina

The Dream of Jacob   He Qi

JACOB WRESTLES WITH GOD Genesis 32:22–32

The dark night drew its sombre cloak around
A man whose look conveyed an equal dark,
That filled him to the depths with seething dread.
He thought of flight; but still he stood his ground.

And then he could not flee, for someone strong
Had caught him in a grip and he fought back.
They wrestled there, those two, but who was this?
His hidden past, the dark side of himself?

And back and forth and down and up all night,
For Jacob would not slack until he came
Right through to resolution and was blessed.

A new day saw a new man stand up tall.
Injured, but whole, ready to face what came,
For Israel had won, but so had God.

—Isobel de Gruchy, South Africa

CHRISTIAN UNITY, AFTER PSALM 100

God of compassion,
we thank you
that with all our diverse traditions
we belong to your people.
We are glad
that you have led us from defensive separation
to a reconciled community.
We rejoice over the diversity of churches in Europe
and we discover in one another
the richness of our diverse religious histories
which testify to the kaleidoscope of your grace.
We pray, let our reconciliation
in the world-wide Church
be a sign of hope
that unity in diversity is possible,
despite all opposition.
Strengthen above all the confidence in your goodness
which crosses our frontiers
and is already binding what is still separate.

—Sylvia Bukowski, Germany

THE BENT-OVER WOMAN IN HONDURAS Luke 13:10–17

Bare, gnarled feet came into view, testifying that the owner must have spent most of her long life without shoes. However, I barely noticed this woman in my rush to enter. I had never had the opportunity to visit a cathedral before. I was not disappointed—the gilt and gold literally made the room glow. My eyes could not help but be drawn to the magnificent crucifix of Jesus above the altar. I paused at the back of the sanctuary full of awe and reverence. Sitting down in a pew I bowed my head in prayer, not because a service was being conducted, but as a natural response to what was before me.

After a brief period of meditation, I stood up and walked out of the cathedral. There were those feet again. Only this time I noticed the whole woman. She was nearly doubled over in agony. Due to her deformity, she could not stand up straight. Her hands were cupped together asking for alms. She was not alone; many others were begging, but none touched me as did the plight of this woman. Her situation was the epitome of being bent by the struggles of life. She was unable to look up the sky or even to see the beauty of the church building. She could not even look others in the eye to plead with them to give her a few coins.

Christ had pity on such a woman, saying: "Woman, you are set free." Today, how are we called to minister to those bent over and weighed down by life? How can we offer the hope to enable them to stand up straight and praise the Lord?

Prayer: God, open us to your stories, which cannot be trapped by the Bible's covers but are alive all around us. Amen

—Janice L. Burns-Watson, USA, Honduras

"I WILL BLESS YOU THAT YOU BE A BLESSING" Genesis 12:1–3

The Lord had said to Abram, "leave your country, your people and your father's household and go to the land I will show you. I will make you into a great nation and I will bless you; I will make your name great, and you will be a blessing. I will bless those who bless you, and whoever curses you I will curse; and all peoples on earth will be blessed through you." (Gen. 12:1–3)

Wherever God sends me, I will go! Though I may feel homesick if I leave my hometown, which I love very much, I will go.

I will be a blessing., The people who are living wherever I go will be blessed through me. I will bring the good news, the benefits, the wonderful gifts, and the words of God to them; and if they need me, I would try my best to help them, for God loves them, and I love them as well.

I believe that God is speaking to me all the time with the little voice, sometimes in the events, sometimes in the Bible, sometimes from the people around me. I never know the way God will use me. I must pay more attention to God, and so I might not neglect the valuable words.

God is speaking and I am listening.

—Wang Xi Cheng (Luke), China

FIVE EARTHEN CUPS Psalm 116

What shall I render to the Lord for all his bounty to me?
I will lift up the cup of salvation and call on the name of the Lord. (Psa. 116:12–13)

So you lift up your gift of thanks,
Zimbabwe mother, five earthen cups
molded of soil from your plot,
your meager ground of sustenance:

maize for your children,
grass for your beasts,
blooms for your soul's joy.

Offer your gift of thanks
with all who come to church today
bearing their harvest fruits—
grain from their fields,
eggs from their birds,
handmade bowls and mats—
bearing too their seeking hearts,
their weariness and steadfast hope.
They lift all up in thanks,
and call on the name of God.

Five red-brown cups from the earth
at risk from flood and drought,
tilled by hoe and aching arms
to feed the ones you love.

Hands hardened by earth's toil,
heart gladdened by earth's gifts
in concert offer up a thankful life
and call on the name of the Lord,
the One whose hands and heart
reach out in joy to take the one
who offers five earthen cups.

—Allen Myrick, USA, Zimbabwe

SORROW TURNED INTO JOY 1 Samuel 1:4–20; 2:1–10

[1]Hear me, Lord, in my distress;
turn this tide of barrenness;
cause my dark despair to cease;
bless me with your gift of peace.

[2]As did Hannah in her prayer,
all my anguish I lay bare.
Help me, then, with her, to know:
Out of sorrow, joy may flow.

³When you granted her request,
 your intentions were expressed,
for, through her, though once forlorn,
Israel's hope would be reborn.

⁴Fashion, then, this life of mine,
 molding it to your design,
and enable me to see
your good purpose grow through me.

⁵How the fortunes are reversed!
Sad ones blest, the proud dispersed!
Praise for works of grace begun!
Praise to you, the holy One.

Can be sung to any tune with 7.7.7.7. meter

—Norman J Goreham, Aotearoa/New Zealand

"HERE AM I, SEND ME!" Isaiah 6:8

GOD: And the Lord said, "GO!"

ME: And I said, "Who, me?!"

GOD: And God said, "Yes, YOU!"

ME: And I said, "But I'm not ready yet.
    And there is company coming,
    And I can't leave my kids;
    You know there's no one to take my place."

GOD: And God said, "You're stalling."

GOD: And the Lord said, "GO!"

ME: And I said, "But I don't want to,"

GOD: And God said, "I didn't ask if you wanted to."

ME: And I said, "Listen,
    I'm not the kind of person to get involved in controversy.
    Besides, my family won't like it,
    And what will the neighbors think!"

GOD: And God said, "Baloney!"

GOD: And yet a third time the Lord said, "GO!"

ME: And I said, "Do I have to?"

GOD: And God said, "Do you love me?"

ME: And I said, "Look, I'm scared . . .
People are going to hate me . . .
And cut me up in little pieces . . .
I can't take it all by myself."

GOD: And God said, "Where do you think I will be?"

GOD: And the Lord said, "GO!"

ME: And I sighed, "Here am I, send me!"

—Lois Hodrick, USA, Democratic Republic of the Congo (Zaire)

PRAISING GOD IN THANKSGIVING Psalm 103

Dear sisters and brothers, let's praise God with our heart and with our mind and with our spirit. The psalmist said: "praise the Lord, O my soul; all my inmost being, praise his holy name. And forget not all his benefits."

Then what kind of praising is God's pleasure? C. S. Lewis said, "In commanding us to glorify him, God is inviting us to enjoy him." This means God wants us to praise him by motivated love, thanksgiving, and delight, not duty. Praising is a lifestyle of enjoying God, loving God, and giving ourselves to be used for God's purpose. When you use your life for God's glory, everything you do can become an act of worship. This is our life purpose, to praise God always.

Dear sisters and brothers, let's praise God in thanksgiving and delight every day.

—Lin Yu Jie (Caleb), China

VOCATION AS A TEACHER: GOD IS STILL SPEAKING 2 Timothy 2:15; 4:2

"The light shines in the darkness, and the darkness didn't overcome it" (John 1:5). Jesus Christ is the true light. But why does the world refuse him? According to Ephesians 2:1–10, we were dead through the trespasses and sins in which we once lived. We lived in passions of our flesh, following the desires of flesh and senses, God made us alive together with Christ; this is not our own doing, it is a gift of God.

In the beginning, I didn't want other people to know I was Christian. I thought maybe they would laugh at me. Now, I realize that it is an honor to be a Christian. This change is not my own doing. This change is God's doing. God is changing my mind gradually over a long period.

"Go therefore and make disciples of all nations, baptizing them in the name of the Father and of the Son and of the Holy Spirit, and teaching them to obey everything that I have commanded you, and remember, I am with you always, to the end of the age" (Matt. 28:19–20).

So God is still speaking through the Holy Bible in a different time; proclaiming the Good News to the world is the responsibility of all of us. I have worked as teacher in a seminary for years. God is still speaking to me; God wants me to help my students understand the Holy Bible correctly. Every day, I pray for my class; God always energizes me to share the Holy Bible with my students. Also, I always preach in the church on Sunday morning. Which scriptures should I preach to the congregation? I need prayer. I believe God will help me if I depend on him. "Do your best to present yourself to God as one approved by him, a worker who has no need to be ashamed, rightly explaining the word of truth" (2 Tim. 2:15).

"Proclaim the message, be persistent whether the time is favorable or unfavorable; convince, rebuke, and encourage, with the utmost patience in teaching" (2 Tim. 4:2). These are scriptures God is still speaking to me. They tell me that I should not forget the responsibility of God's worker, proclaim the Good News in different circumstances.

—Chen Yi (Kevin), China

SING TO GOD A NEW SONG—WORSHIP FROM HONDURAS Psalm 33:3

The Evangelical and Reformed (E&R) Church in Honduras, partner church for the Maine Conference of the United Church of Christ, is essentially a neo-Pentecostal movement. There is no written liturgy that is part of their worship. Most unique in their worship is the minimalist role of their clergy. Essentially the clergy preach the sermon (which averages forty minutes in duration). That is the ONLY part of the service in which the pastor provides leadership. Often the rest of the service is lead by young adults. There is always a band with electric guitar, drums, and keyboard. The service usually begins with twenty minutes of praise music, followed by a common ritual of shaking each person's hand. There is often a *corito* sung during this time.

Prayer is always spontaneous. What is unique about Honduran E&R prayer time is that while one person leads, most of the congregation is praying aloud at the same time in charismatic fashion, and the leader's words are among many. It usually appears that the only "listener" is God.

The worship service contains much singing, often forty to fifty minutes during the service (this does not include the pre-service praise music). Everyone seems to know the words of the songs and rarely are they projected on a screen. There are no hymnals. After the sermon there is a prayer given by a lay leader that leads to an altar call. During the altar call every person prays their own spirit-led words aloud. There isn't classic benediction, but the service ends in prayer.

Because E&R Honduran worship is SO spontaneous, there is very little written liturgy.

—David R. Gaewski, USA

GROUNDBREAKING Psalm 127

Unless the Lord builds the house,
those who build it labor in vain. (Psa. 127:1)

Women stand in the searing sun
and watch the spade scrape loose stones,
then break the dried-up ground.
"Here we'll build the church," they say.
So they stand upon the site
and sing, and offer prayers
that soil which grows so little food
may grow a church and harvest faith.

So much labor lies ahead.
So many backs must bend to mold
blocks of cement to raise the wall.
So many feet must bear the weight
of water borne from distant stream.
So many hands must pay out cash
required for so many needs.

But such "so manys" do not daunt
these few. They will begin,
in trust they labor not in vain,
for God surely toils along with them,
using their backs and feet and hands
to manifest God's glory.
Empowered by a fervent faith,

they will work through months and years,
and raise the house which tells the world
they labor not in vain,
for on this barren plain God lives.

—Allen Myrick, USA, South Africa, Zimbabwe

Rini Templeton

PRAYER FOR UNITY Psalm 67

Dear Father in Heaven,
we come from the peoples
whom you have created in their multitude and variety
and who live before you in your present.
You gather your community from the midst of them.
With their many voices, insights, and hopes.
In it we search for the place,
where we can offer you
our prayers of praise and thanksgiving,
of supplication and intercession.
We pray: help us to stay loyal to our faith,
to what we have understood from you.
We come to you from many different churches
and congregations,
so that you may gather us into one great congregation.
Help us to testify together

That you are Lord over heaven and earth,
over death and life,
over what we do and what we do not do.
Grant that your Word may find room in our hearts,
Sow in compassion and righteousness.
For that we wait in confidence in your Holy Spirit.

—Achim Reinstadtler, Germany

THE MYSTERIES OF GOD'S CREATION 1 Corinthians 4:2–5

Stargazing . . . the morning after a lunar eclipse

The sermon starts with the singing of a song from Zimbabwe and concludes with time for reflection and prayer by all. The words of reflection are interspersed with scripture, read by different voices in the gathered congregation. There was a hand-out including photographs from the Hubble Telescope, but other similar photographs can be substituted.

Song

What a mighty God we have! What a mighty God we have! What a mighty God, what a mighty God, what a mighty God we have! Let us sing and praise the Lord! Let us sing and praise the Lord! Let us sing and praise, let us sing and praise, let us sing and praise the Lord!

Reflection—Part 1

Aren't these photos from the Hubble Telescope amazing?! The Sombrero Galaxy with 800 billion suns! And the two merging galaxies 114 million light years away! Wow!
Did any of you gaze at the moon last night, hoping, even through the clouds, to witness the lunar eclipse? I was out in the courtyard with Merrill's class gazing "in awe and wonder" at God's good creation.

Read Genesis 1:1–19.

Reflection—Part 2

One time in Zimbabwe, Tod bundled me and our two kids into our ute [pickup truck] and mysteriously drove us out the Dombodema Road, away from our little town, away from the few lights, away even from the cooking fires. About five kilometers out, where the baboons and warthogs begin to reside, he stopped the truck, right in the middle of the road—not lots of traffic! Then he switched off the headlights, plunging us into blackness—the kind where you can not see your hand in front of your face. The children squealed. Tod opened the door and led us, holding hands. to the flatbed of the ute where we lay down and peered up. The heavens opened up above us, bursting into a shimmering canopy of light. Then he passed the binoculars around, and the moon's craters and mountains jumped into focus, and the distant stars appeared that much closer. We gazed in awe at God's amazing dome of creation.

God, like Tod on that starry night in Zimbabwe, invites us on a journey into unknowing, into mystery. God invites us into a risky activity, stepping beyond the brightly lit solid ground on which we stand into a world of complete trust and faith in that which is invisible to the eye. The wise fox in *The Little Prince* aptly states, "It is only with the heart that one can see rightly. What is essential is invisible to the eye." God invites us to dream of possibilities beyond our personal galaxy, beyond our familiar world of church, family, and community. To envision a realm in which no one is hungry, no one is cold, no one is alone, no one is marginalized or hated, a universe in which stars expand into Red Giants and collapse into "black holes." To employ a new lens, like the Hubble telescope, in our seeing and understanding.

Read Psalm 145:3–5.

Reflection—Part 3

Christ invites us to meditate on these things, to look both inward and outward, into the mystery of our ground of being and outward into the mystery of the ever-expanding universe, always being open to the possibility of transformation—of ourselves and of our "universe." Paul writes to the Corinthians:

Think of us in this way, as servants of Christ and stewards of God's mysteries. Moreover, it is required of stewards that they be found trustworthy. . . . Therefore do not pronounce judgment before the time, before the Lord comes, who will bring to light the things now hidden in darkness and will disclose the purposes of the heart.

Read 1 Corinthians 4:1–2, 5.

We can be grateful to those stewards of God's mysteries who have guided us, who found us where we were and offered us new lenses, new perspectives—a new telescope or pair of binoculars. Grateful to those who have seemingly plunged us into darkness only to bring to light the things once hidden in the darkness, sometimes with a vivid new brilliance. Grateful to those who, like the scientists using the Hubble Telescope, invite us to look into the mystery and unknown expanses of God and our universe

Read Psalm 105:1–4.

Prayer

I invite you during this time of prayer to speak from your heart as we meditate upon the mysteries of God's creation.

God, we praise and glorify your name, for you are the creator of all that has been, all that is, and all that shall be. Open our minds and hearts as we strive to be worthy servants of Christ and stewards of your mysteries. Amen.

Read Psalm 113:1–9.

Let all the people say together, "Praise God!"

ALL: Praise God!

Amen.

ALL: Amen.

—Ana K. Gobledale, USA, Zimbabwe, Worship Message at Churches of Christ Theological College, Mulgrave, Victoria, Australia

21 ❦ Treasures—Personal Reflections

GOD'S GRACE

Our oldest child was born while we were at the Presbyterian Teachers College at Rubate, Kenya. We struggled during the pregnancy to chose a middle name for her. We wanted her to remember the place she was born by giving her a Swahili name. The name had to meet three criteria. It had to be a real name, used by the community. It had to have a sound comfortable for American ears. Most important, we had to like the meaning of the name. Working with the Swahili instructor at the college we ministered with we finally settled on the name "Naima," which means God's Grace.

Her birth certainly was a means of grace for my husband and me, blessing and enriching our relationship. An unexpected benefit was how her birth allowed our ministry to blossom and grow. As parents we were granted more esteem and respect as ministers. Because we were willing to risk having and raising a child in their community, we were accepted in a way that cannot be easily explained.

This fact was brought home to us at our good-bye ceremony, with the most meaningful words being directed towards our twenty-month-old daughter. We were told to make sure that, even if she forgot all the other Swahili she knew, we were to make sure she remembered the phrase: "Naima cia Rubate" or "God's Grace from Rubate." We were to teach her that she was God's Grace from Rubate, and that she was called to share that grace with all those she came into contact with. And that God's Grace would always come to her from Rubate as well, with all of her Christian brothers and sisters praying for her constantly. What a powerful concept to consider in our transient society, that God's Grace comes both from within and from all our brothers and sisters who are part of our lives no matter how near or far.

Prayer: God, open us to the way you name each of us through the voices of all your children. Amen.

—Janice L. Burns-Watson, USA, Kenya

Favored One   He Qi

REFLECTION—EMMANUEL—GOD WITH US

I open my eyes. Barely. Undefined movement of light and dark objects fills the world. I close my eyes again; the doctor has instructed me to do so until he calls for me again. I listen. People come from all over India for medical treatment here at the Christian Medical College Hospital in Vellore, Tamil Nadu, so the waiting room resounds with many languages. I lean back against the straight wooden bench-back and think about the last time I went to get my eyes checked for contact lenses—a cushy seat in the Montclare Mall in southern California. No lines, no people coming in and out. It is a different experience here where many people move through a labyrinth of offices, waiting areas, and testing rooms. I arrived over an hour and a half ago, and I probably have over an hour before my eye examination ends.

My ear hones in on two voices behind me, a mother and son perhaps, speaking Tamil.

"Hello Sister," the woman, clearly addressing me, lowers her voice, having captured my attention.

"Vannakam akka, greetings sister," I reply in Tamil. I hear the smile in the woman's voice as she responds, "You speak Tamil?" "Only a little," I say, rapidly depleting my limited vocabulary. We exchange names; hers is Vatsala, and her son is Sanjay. I tell her that I come from the United States and live and work at a school and orphanage in a small village near Vellore. I smile and nod, as she speaks to me, my eyes still awkwardly closed.

Vatsala says something to her son in Tamil. I squint my eyes open and see Sanjay's outline slide from the bench. I hear footsteps patter across the concrete floor towards me. They stop beside me, and I can hear Sanjay's soft breath near my face. Again, I slit open my eyes, light rushing into the dark pools of my dilated pupils. Sanjay stands beside me, his head reaching my shoulder. Judging by his size, I guess that he is about three years old.

"Akka. Sister." Sanjay's hand casts a shadow over my face as he reaches toward my forehead. I close my eyes as he touches the space between my eyebrows. The shadow falls from my face as Sanjay lowers his arm. I reach up and feel a fuzzy circle where he has touched my brow. I smile. He has given me a stick-on tikka that many of the women here in Tamil Nadu wear. "Ungulukke, akka. It's for you, sister," he tells me.

Sanjay returns to sit with his mum. I smile at Vatsala, trying to express my recognition and gratitude for the barriers her son has crossed to present me with this gift. Across language, culture, class, age, race, and religion, Sanjay has reached out to me and blessed my brow with this symbol of his country and culture.

Immersed in my thoughts, it takes a moment to realize that the nurse at the front desk is calling my name. I open my eyes enough to make my way to the doctor I met with earlier. I sit down across from him and feel his eyes upon my face. "You weren't wearing that before." After a meaningful pause, I understand that the doctor refers to the tikka on my forehead.

Smiling, I explain, "A little boy in the waiting room gave it to me."

"Oh? Christians do not wear tikkas. Hindus wear them. They symbolize idolatry," the doctor informs me.

I try to revive my faded smile. "He was a very little boy," I explain to the doctor, unable to find words to adequately express the tenderness of the boy's gesture. "Maybe only three or four years old. I could not say no."

"That was a perfect opportunity for you to share the gospel, the good news of Jesus' love. You could have shared the true way with this little boy."

I miss a breath and open my eyes trying to focus for a moment on the doctor's expression as he talks to me. My vision, like my thoughts, blurs, and I cannot get either clear. With no response for the doctor, I close my eyes again and set my teeth together.

In the stillness of my room back at the orphanage where I live and work, I contemplate this exchange. I formulate in my mind what I was unable to express to the doctor earlier as my eyes focus on the texture of the tamarind tree trunk outside my window. He was right, I did miss an opportunity to share the good news. He would have been surprised, however, to learn that he was the one in need of the gospel—the good news of God's love and grace, the news of Jesus' presence among us in the least of these. I had missed the opportunity to share with the doctor the truth of God's love expressed in the gesture of a Hindu boy. For Sanjay—reaching out to me, a foreigner and strange in his home, placing a blessing of welcome and inclusion upon my brow—Sanjay WAS Jesus. Emmanuel. God with us.

—Thandiwe Gobledale, USA, India

PERSONAL REFLECTIONS FROM CHINESE SEMINARY STUDENTS

This notebook was created by pastors, seminary instructors, and staff members working in local CC/TSPM offices who participated in the Huangshan Summer English Teaching Program taught by Debra Pallato-Fontaine. These entries were written by students in the Level Three Christian Materials class. Students wrote two ministry stories based on personal experiences and one essay sharing how they believed God was still speaking in their lives or their ministries. There are currently around seventeen million Protestants in China with approximately fifty thousand churches and meeting points, most built in the last twenty years. There are eighteen seminaries and Bible schools in China and sound theological training is a priority. Pastors are taught to be "good shepherds" to their congregations as well as effective church leaders. Chinese Christians are extremely faithful and devout. Christianity is growing rapidly in China with high attendance in the churches.

Two months ago, I read a psychological examination in a book. I found it to be very interesting. I wanted my husband to do the examination, so I brought out a big white paper, and drew a small black dot on it. After that I lifted up the paper and asked my husband, "what do you see?" I waited for his answer and then I would analyze it according to what the book told me: If he only sees a white paper, he will be a positive person. But sometimes he can't find the problems. If he only sees a black dot, he will be a negative person. He only realizes the problem, but ignores others in his life. If he can see a white paper with a small black dot, he is an objective person.

While I was waiting for my husband's answer, my son, who is four years old, came to me and said loudly: "Mum, I see an eye, a bird eye," Then he drew a bird on the paper quickly.

I was surprised at my son's answer and the book didn't tell me how to judge his answer, but I know it was excellent. He can change the shortcoming to be a useful and beautiful thing. I meditate how can I use this in my life.

—Liu ling wei (Ann), China

"You crown the year with your bounty; your wagon tracks overflow with richness" (Psa. 65:11). I was born in Hunan province. I had never heard of Christianity before I graduated from high school. I didn't know what I was living for; I was unhappy and there was no peace in my heart.

God had mercy on me and brought me to Suoga Middle School as an English teacher. There I met my wife. God was speaking to me by her. Maybe she was not pretty, but she was beautiful. She was warm-hearted and was always ready to help others. She was full of love and joy. I just wondered why she was like that, and she brought me to the church, where I found the answer. The first time I stepped into the church, I felt the peace I had never felt before.

After studying the Bible and praying with brothers and sisters for about half a year, I came to know the grace of salvation and I was baptized in 1997. The more I knew God, the more I wanted to know. In 1999, I went to Nanjing Seminary. There I got my bachelor degree of theology.

Now I am a teacher at Guizhou Bible School. There are more than three hundred thousand Christians but a lack of ministers. God let me know that the students in the Bible School are the future of Guizhou churches. So I try my best to lead them according to God's way. I pray with them, read the Bible with them, improve their knowledge, and play with them.

No matter what I do, I keep an aim in my mind that I'll try my best to make them hear the words from the still-speaking God. The still-speaking God not only asks me to do that but also cares about the difficulties of the churches. Many elders in the rural churches ask me to pray for them and their churches. What I am now praying for is the moving of the Church on Rock in Suoga. This church has about four hundred church members. They are so poor that the government decided to move them to a better place. Surely this is a good thing for these people. But the trouble is the government didn't move the church. The church members have to build a new church by themselves in the new place, for it is too far to go to the old church. They don't wish to have a splendid church building but only a shelter to worship God. But they are too poor to build that shelter; even the ground they can't afford. I am sure the still-speaking God will speak through the poor church and to the poor church.

For myself, I am looking forward to an opportunity to improve my education and do more for my Lord. I surely believe the still-speaking God will prepare the way for me.

Because of my belief in God, I have a new life different from before. Before I knew God, I thought life was meaningless. There was no hope, no love, no peace, no joy in my heart. I even thought of suicide. But after I came to God, I was transformed by the renewing of my mind. Now my life is full of joy, happiness, peace, hope, and love. How good it is to be alive!

—Ning Zuoqun (Paul), China

God is still speaking in my life. One Sunday worship in my church, when I graduated from high school (eighteen years ago), I saw so many church members sitting in the benches, looking like they needed more and more feeding by spiritual bread. Just at that moment, I was greatly moved. I don't know how to describe the feeling (but I know it's my real experience; it's God's calling). I just knew I was moved, and a voice seemed to say, "As a young man, what shall you do for them?" After that, I was pressed to go to seminary, then church . . . till now, I will never forget the calling from God.

—Rev. Li Bei Zhan (Wolf), China

Yes, the Lord, our God, is still speaking. He knows what we face, what we suffer and what we need. He always speaks to us through the Bible.

In 2003, I had an amazing experience of the still-speaking God. At that time, we worshiped God in a rented room. It was so cramped that half of the congregation had to sit outside. (After the Cultural Revolution, there was almost nothing left for us.) What we desired was to get land to rebuild our church. We did many, many things, but no way. What would we do? On July 24, 2003, we gathered, fasted, and prayed for a whole day. Finally a four-year-old girl opened the Bible. It was Judges 18:9–10: "Do not be slow to go, and enter in and possess the land. When you go, you will come to an unsuspecting people. The land is broad; yea, God has given it into your hands, a place where there is no lack of anything that is in the earth." This verse fit our situation exactly. Although it is hard to explain, we believed that it was God who spoke to us.

The next day we went to the Religious Affairs Bureau. After we read the Bible and asked for land two thousand meters square without paying, the office said, "It sounds fine in theory, but in fact, it's impossible!" We just kept praying. At last in October 2004, God answered our prayers. We got the land, it was free, not two thousand meters square, but thirty-three hundred meters square. Hallelujah!

Before I believed in God in 1995, I was a sad person, and always had a negative attitude. It's God who changed me. He gave me a new life, and in Him everything is new. Now I am happy and full of optimism for the future. I have many visions and dreams.

Yes, God is wonderful. He answers our prayer. He helps us and gives us a new life. I believe He always speaks to us through the Bible, "The prayer of a righteous person has great power in its effects" (James 5:16). And I think He would speak to others as well.

In my ministry, sometimes I face difficulty. I really didn't know how to solve it. What I did was just to pray and wait. God always answered my prayers, He encouraged me by His words, and helped me through certain persons. So I know God is still speaking to me in my ministry.

—Zhong Lin (Timothy), China

When your mother shouts at you,
Please don't be angry
Because she is very tired.
When your teacher criticizes you,
Please don't be angry.
You may have made some mistake.
When your boyfriend doesn't love you,
Please don't hate him.
Maybe love goes away.
If you can do that,
You will be happy.
Please enjoy your life.

—Qiang Wei (Alice), China

How is God shaping you?

God loves me, and guides me in my life. When I was eight years old, in 1986, I followed my mother to church. Then I found the church needed me to do something, even as a young girl. Some old man needed me to handwrite and copy the Christian songs for them, so I became a very diligent Christian. When Sundays came, I went with my mother very early in my small village church. Later, I found some preacher to come to my church to preach on Sunday; we were so happy to welcome them to come. In that time, the church in my village had about fifty Christians.

One Sunday morning, we sang the song again and again, we waited and waited, but the preachers did not come. During that time, there was no telephone in my village. We did not know why, so we prayed for that, then one church volunteer read the Tianfeng magazine to us, and we were dismissed. I was so disappointed when the preacher would not come. If it was raining, the road is so bad to come, and, if there is no bus, it is also difficult to come. Few people can preach the message if no preacher came in the church. I thought if I could preach, that would be a wonderful thing.

God shapes me in my life, even though I have several times had to give up my study. God has amazing grace with me. Now I can see God's imprint in my life. I found God used me to serve, and God has his beautiful will for me.

—Fu (Lily), China

Diane Wendorf

The Christian practice of hospitality is the practice of providing space to take in a stranger. It also encompasses the skills of welcoming friends and family to our tables, to claim the joy of welcoming.

In the Bible, offering hospitality is a moral imperative. God asks us to share our belonging with people in charity not only in Leviticus 19:33–34, but also in Romans 12:13. Stranger, guest, and host are the same Greek word *Xenos*, and hospitality in the New Testament comes from *Xenos*. The need for shelter is a fundamental human need. God orders us to open our hearts to others. A Christian's love must be completely sincere.

Being a hospitable people is a hard work that may make us live under risky conditions. The story of the wedding feast at Cana and the service of Martha are good lessons for us to reflect on our practice of hospitality. They tell us we need to share with others not only the material things, but also the enjoyment of hospitality. In the practice of sharing, guests may become hosts and hosts may become guests. Hosts and guests all can learn many things out of the richness of experience different from their own. We can overcome our fear and live in God's love. We can really understand that we are all human beings made in God's image. So we should treat other people as having equal worth with ours. When we are hospitable to others, we also receive the hospitality of them at the same time.

—Yuzhen Tan (Tammy), China

Putting God First

What is the most important thing in our life? Is the answer family or career? It is very important for everyone to have a loving family. Family is like a harbor. Career is also extremely important . . .

Yet I believe putting God first is the eternal subject of our life. Let us play the theme of our life, and write new chapters of our life. I hope everyone will let God have the first place in everything. May our lifetime be blessed before God because of such decisions.

—Xu (Grace), China

PRAISING GOD IN THE DISCIPLES OF CHRIST IN CONGO-BRAZZAVILLE

The principal element in the fellowship at the Disciples of Christ in Congo-Brazzaville, as in any Protestant church in black Africa, is the singing and dancing. This is to say dancing and singing occupies about 50 percent of time spent during worshiping. Therefore this event makes the worship lively, paving the way to the period of offerings, as the offering moment is an ideal in community participation. The whole assembly will raise up in two queues, men and women separated on each side. They will move forward in the same rhythm. The women and the youth are most active participants in this exercise.

Before this happens, motivating the believer to offer with joy, the moderator of the day will read some Bible verses, in particular: "God loves one who gives with joy" (2 Cor. 9:7). Sometime the parish pastor, feeling that this effect has been well conducted, all of a sudden interrupts and exhorts the believer to sing and dance well, for God takes pleasure in this utility.

As an example to others sometimes the pastor will descend from the pulpit to demonstrate to the rest of the church. This gives more motivation to the whole assembly, seeing their leader involved wholly in this activity. Despite the overwhelming joy, the amount of offering does not always correspond to this pleasure manifested.

It is this manner of praising, this pleasure, that denotes the authenticity of worship that is purely African. The rhythm and movement in this form of praising in our community is not all that different from what we observe outside the church. Sometimes our songs of praises are refrains of popular songs. The contrary is also true. Some popular songs, sung in the stadium while a team plays to motivate the players, have been adapted from Christian. In that measure the songs gather the same people in the entire arena.

The difference between Christian and non-Christian is not clear at this moment. Since the beginning of Christianity in the black African world, the first missionaries were more concerned about the issue of statistics. The numbers of baptized and believers was more important than repentance. As a result the Gospel was not deeply apprehended. That is why people have become Christians in church, but pagans outside. As God spoke to the Israelites: "My people worship me by lips but their heart is far always from me" (Isa. 29:13).

One principal factor that made people become Christian was education in Christian schools created by the missionaries. Then the songs too: so many youth become members in the church in hopes of being registered in choir groups. That's why many will leave the church before the preaching and after their choir has sung. Some others will not even come to church if their choir group is not scheduled. Concerning the rhythms of songs, there is saying that the "dance originated from heaven," making a comparison to the service the angels render in heaven.

For us, whoever doesn't sing or dance is not of God. The children of God must be happy all the time during worship, as the great musician David said: "My heart is filled with joy when they told me go to the house of the Lord" (Psa. 16:9).

A question we must ask is: What characterizes a true child of God? Is it singing and dancing, or his/her conduct in society? I recall the early days of our community, in the year 1994 after a worship during which I sang and danced well, almost above every body in the church, one evangelist congratulated me that he saw that I was filled with the Holy Spirit. I asked him how did he recognize this? He responded that he observed me how I was praising with courage. Does this imply that those who don't praise God in singing and dancing are not part of the life of the Africans, especially the Congolese who are always happy all the time?

In all circumstances of life here in Congo, people are always happy, in dancing and singing, for example at new birth (especially twins), birthdays, marriage, success in academic examinations, journeys taken, victory in sports games, elections, promotions in working places. However, even sad situations like mourning include singing and dancing and these rituals occur at funerals. The Congolese, who are used to manifesting emotions through dancing and singing, find no reason not to manifest their joy through the same when worshipping God in their communities. In the traditional religions they used to do the same when invoking the spirits of ancestors.

A major concern of the Disciples of Christ in Congo is to find how we can adapt ourselves to the Gospel to allow the Gospel to transform totally this culture, in order to restore the Congolese to Christ according to the plans of God. The Disciples of Christ in Congo is called to reform and adapt the church life to the African culture considering the Gospel. We have a young church. Our church should be capable of convincing the Congolese society to the Christian faith. We must then give a deep message to ameliorate the quality of believers. We need to fight the deep hypocrisy which each Christian carries in him/her self by the announcing of God's message, which needs to be the focus of the worship service.

We spend time in singing and dancing with numerous choir groups; this brings about the length of services, sometime taking the whole day. These are the things we talk about in the Disciples of Christ Church in Congo-Brazzaville as a Protestant African church in this third millennium.

—Lucien Kobele, General Secretary, Disciples of Christ in Congo-Brazzaville

St Andrew's By the Sea Community Church in Whitianga, Coromandel Peninsula, New Zealand, is a simple timber structure built in 1898 by the bushmen who worked in the great kauri timber forests. They were plain, devout Christians, mostly settlers from Britain and Europe, who worshipped alongside the Maori Chiefs and people of the bay. In 2002, by a series of financial miracles, we were able to add a much needed community hall onto the old church, providing a welcoming home to the whole community. I wrote this hymn with a full heart, and we first sang it on the occasion of the opening of the new hall. It is sung to the tune "Londonderry Air."

Eternal God, the Architect of ages,
O Saviour Jesus, Carpenter of old,
And Holy Spirit, Teacher and Interpreter,
We stand in awe, to see Your plans unfold.
For we are here, as witness to Your faithfulness,
And we have built this place to honour You,
For we have seen your hand in all our labouring,
And so we come, to praise You who makes all things new.

The prayers and praise of countless faithful people,
Here in the past claimed kinship in Your grace,
And we can feel a crowd of silent witnesses
Assembled here within this sacred place.
And this we know, that we can trust Your promises,
Who blesses us so mightily today,
And Who has giv'n this place to meet as family,
A place to witness, and a place to teach Your way.

O may this building ever be a citadel
Of light and love, a haven of your peace,
And may we bear true witness to Your purposes,
Enabling troubled souls to find release.
O may Your people be forever faithful
To Christ, Who welcomes all who choose to come,
O may His voice be heard in this community,
And we, in generous service, ever bring them home!

—Dorothy Preece, Aotearoa/New Zealand

22 ❀ TREASURES—BY AND FOR YOUNG PEOPLE

Teach Me About God   Elena Huegel

The first part of this chapter includes offerings written by children and youth, although other writings by young people appear throughout this book.

PRAYERS FROM CASA SAN JOSÉ DE LOS HUÉRFANOS (ORPHANS), COLIMA, MÉXICO

Señor yo te quiero pedir por todos los pobres del mundo. Ayúdales a todas las familias de todos los niños de que no les pase nasa malo y por todas y todos los trabajadores de aquí y por todos los holandeses y americanos que nos han visitado.

Lord, I want to pray for all the poor of the world. Help all the families of all the children so that nothing bad happens to them. I pray for all the men and women workers from here, and for the Dutch and the American [volunteers] who have visited us.

—Edgar

Diosito te quiero pedir que mi mama se alivie por esta enferma y mi papa porque ya se salió del batallón. Diosito cuida a mi hermano por favor Diosito y a mí porque tengo ampollas en los dedos.

Gracias señor por lo que me has hecho.

Diosito [a diminutive of God; that is, sweet little God], I want to ask you to heal my mama from this sickness, and my daddy because he is going off to war. Little God, take care of my brother please, God, and me too because I have blisters on my fingers.

Thank you Lord for what you have done for me.

—Maria

Diosito hoy te quiero pedir en esta noche que me cuides muy bien y también que me cuides en el día también. Y que cuides a mi familia y señor yo te pido que ayudes a los que no tienen zapatos ni que vestir y también a todos los pobres y a los que no tienen ropa. Ayúdanos toda la vida siempre y toda la vida.

Little God, today I want to ask you to take care of me in the night, very well, and also to take care of me in the daytime. And that you take care of my family and, Lord, I ask you to help those who have no shoes nor anything to wear, and also all the poor and those who have no clothes. Help us for our whole lives, always, our whole lives.

—Estefania (Stephanie)

Gracias por darnos lo que nos das cada día. Muchas gracias por darnos alimento apoyo que no has dado también por la vida que nos has dado tan siquiera no puedo verte. Algún día quiero que nos quite poquita comida para que se las des a las pobres que no tienen comida y a los que están en la calle tirados pidiendo dinero, a toda la gente gracias por entenderme y escucharme por esos mereces un descanso espero que con lo que le dieron a los pobres les ajuste para todos los meses y días espero que la comida a los pobres y a los que están en la calle por favor quítanos poquita comida.

Thank you for giving us what you give us each day. Thank you for giving us food, the support you have given us, also for the life you have given us even though I can't see you. Someday I want you to take a little food away from us so that you can give it to the poor who have no food, and to those who are flat out in the street asking for money, to all those people. Thank you for hearing me and listening to me, for those who deserve a rest. I hope that with what they gave to the poor it fills them every month and day. I hope that the food to the poor and to those who are in the street—please take away from us a little food.

—Damary

———

Lo que pido señor Jesús, Señor Jesús yo te quiero pedir que ayudes a los enfermos a los discapacitados y a todos los de África por que les hace falta comida u otra casa para que se les des o las medicinas y a todos los que fallecieron o a los que están vivo pero que cures a los que tienen la influenza o cáncer o pulmonía otra caso pero cúralos por lo que más quieras porque sin ti no podemos hacer nada. Te queremos mucho y tú lo sabes por eso quiero que tu estés con todos nosotros en nuestro corazón o en las partes que vayamos.

What I'm asking Jesus, Lord Jesus, I want to ask you to help the sick, those who are incapacitated and all those in Africa because they lack food and other things, medicine; and [help] all those who have died, or those who are alive but heal them, those who have flu or cancer or pneumonia; heal them, because without you we can do nothing. We love you very much and you know for that reason I want you to be with us all in our hearts or everywhere we go.

—Isabel Valencia

———

Mamita María yo quiero pedirte por las siguiente personas yo se que tu siempre me escuchas y yo se que nunca nos dejaras de escuchar porque tu mamita María nos envuelves y nos guardas en tu manto y te pido por los violadores, marginados, rateros, cholos, secuestradores, señor toca los corazones y renuévalos y que tengan un buen corazón y sea amables con sus semejantes.

Little Mother Mary, I want to ask you for the following people: I know that you always listen to me and I know that you will never stop listening to us because you, Mother Mary, surround us and protect us in your robe/mantle; and I pray to you for the rapists, the outcasts, the thieves, the mixed-race/half-breeds, the kidnappers. Lord, touch their hearts and renew them and may they have good hearts and may they be kind to their fellow human beings.

—Anonymous

———

Mi virgencita te doy gracias por todo lo que me has dado como clases de inglés, coro, computación también doy gracias porque me has dejado vivir un día mas y por todo lo me has dado y porque en un tiempo tenemos voz y tranquilidad en algunas personas que habitamos en este planeta, también te doy gracias por dejarme vivir un día mas a mi madre pero has tu voluntad déjala o llévala según como veas si está sufriendo aunque me duela llévatela según tu voluntad. Amen

My little virgin, I give you thanks for everything you have given me: English classes, choir, computer classes. Also I give thanks because you have given me one day more to live, and for everything you have given me and because we have a voice and tranquility [affecting] some people who live on this planet. Also I give thanks for letting my mother live one more day, but let your will be done. Leave her or take her according to how you see. If she is suffering, although it hurts me, take her according to your will. Amen.

—Vanessa

Señor yo te pido que me ayudes a poder hacer mis tareas bien, que me vaya muy bien en la escuela y controlar mi carácter. También te pido señor por todos los niños pobres los que no tienen un hogar y comida y también por los que están muriendo y naciendo. Amén.

Lord, I ask you to help me be able to do my homework well, that it go well for me in school, and to control my behavior. Also I pray to you Lord for all the poor children who have no home nor food, and also for those who are dying and being born. Amen.

—Luis Angel

Gracias Dios por este día tan bonito te pido por mi hermana que está en Celaya, también te pido por mi familia y por mi papá que no sé donde vive. Gracias Dios por escuchar a todos los que rezan.

Thank you, Lord, for this day, so beautiful; I pray to you for my sister who is in Celaya, also for my family and for my papa, who is living I don't know where. Thank you God for listening to all those who pray.

—Sara

Dios te pedimos con todo nuestro corazón que nos ayudes a fortalecer nuestra conducta a que nos ayude a hacer trabajadores, honestos y respetuoso. A que todos los Americanos que vengan la casa hogar que fortalezcas sus familias y a todas las familias de todos los niños de aquí y que ayudes a nuestra madres y que sostenga nuestra casa hogar. Y que mis hermanos se superen en todo.

God, we pray to you with our whole heart that you help us to strengthen our conduct, that you help us to work hard, be honest and respectful. May you strengthen the Americans who come to the Casa Hogar (the orphanage), strengthen their families and all the families of the children who are here; and help our mothers, and support our orphanage. And may my brothers and sisters overcome everything.

—Josue

Papa Dios te amo porque tu cuidas a todas las personas buenas del mundo te pido por mi mamá te doy gracias por el gran corazón que tienes por cuidarme en casa.

Papa God, I love you because you take care of all the good people of the world; I pray for my mama, I give thanks for the big heart that you have for taking care of me at this Casa Hogar/orphanage.

—Monica

Five loaves and Two Fish later
there's plenty of Good News for the Poor.

June 22, 2008

Diane Wendorf

Virgencita yo te pido por las siguientes personas mi familia mis compañeras, ladrones drogadictos vagabundos y por cada persona que se encomienda a Dios también por cada ser vivo, plantas, animales etc. Virgencita te doy gracias por cada día que nos dejas vivir, comer, dormir e incluso reír y por este planeta maravilloso y las sorpresas que tiene y también por mi familia que las has mantenido unida en las malas y en las buenas, estoy feliz de mi familia por mi que no me a pasa nada y también que ha nadie no pase nada,

Querido Papá Dios te queremos todos los de la Casa Hogar y gracias por todo el apoyo que nos das todos los días felices que he tenido.

Little Virgin, I pray for the following people: my family, my close friends, thieves, drug addicts, the homeless, and for each person that they be entrusted to God, also for each living thing, plants, animals, etc. Little Virgin, I give you thanks for each day that you let us live, eat, sleep, and also laugh; and for this marvellous planet and the surprises that it has, and also for my family that they stay united through the evil and the good. I am happy about my family because nothing has happened to me or to anybody.

Dear Papa God, we all love you, here at Casa Hogar, and thank you for all the support that you give every happy day that I have had.

—Leslie

<hr>

Señor yo te quiero dar gracias por ser cariñosa, bondadosa, afortunada porque puedo sentir, soñar, comer, reír, querer, escribir, dormir, hablar, escuchar, comprender, entender, pensar, estudiar, participar, jugar, correr, bañarme, vestirme, ponerme mi ropa, pararme, caminar porque puedo ir al baño, tender mi ropa, hacer aseos, tareas, caminar, porque puedo crear enseñar, aprender, compartir, también por todos los valores que tenemos como la amistad, el trabajo la confianza, la honestidad, el respeto, la familia, el patriotismo a mi

Lord, I want to give you thanks for being caring, kind, happy because I can feel, dream, eat, laugh, desire, write, sleep, speak, listen, understand, hear, think, study, participate, play, run, bathe myself, dress myself, put on my own clothes, stand up, walk; because I can go to the bathroom, take care of my clothes, do my chores, my homework, walk; because I can create, teach, learn, share; also for all those values that we have like friendship, work, confidence, honesty, respect, family, patriotism, and my flag, and goodness. [Thanks be] to God for all that I lack, and for that which I have more than enough of.

—Rocio

Señor yo te doy gracias por escuchar, correr, gritar, reír, comer, bailar, saltar, nadar, amar, por mi papa y mama y por poder beber agua, por poder jugar con mis amigos y también por sonreír a mis hermanos.

Lord, I give you thanks [because I can] listen, run, shout, laugh, eat, dance, jump, swim, love; for my papa and mama; for being able to drink water, for being able to play with my friends, and also for smiling at my brothers and sisters.

—Ana Maria

⸺•⧫•⸺

Introducción de Oración que Lupita Muñiz practica semanalmente con los niños/ Introduction to the prayer that Lupita Muniz practices weekly with the children:

Dios Todopoderoso en el nombre de Jesús
Hijo de la Virgen María
Bajo tu gracia plena
En Armonía con los demás
De manera perfecta
Yo te suplico Señor . . .
Yo te ruego Señor . . .
Yo te imploro Señor . . .
Yo te pido Señor . . . este milagro etc.

All Powerful God, in the name of Jesus
Son of the Virgin Mary
Beneath the fullness of your grace
In harmony with others
In a perfect way
I beg you, Lord, for . . .
I pray to you, Lord, for . . .
I implore you, Lord, for . . .
And I ask you, Lord, for . . . this miracle, etc.

—Maria Guadalupe Muniz Cortez, Mexico

REFLECTIONS FROM SOUTH AFRICAN HIGH SCHOOL STUDENTS

Life in My Country

Walking down the street of my country
I observed so much
Lovers, friends, children having fun
I could see they were happy

As I turned around the corner
My grin faded
I took a giant step back
I felt traumatised

He was raping a five-year-old child
She screamed for help but no one helped
I turned around
Only to turn to a gun pointed at me
He commanded all I had or see no tomorrow

I gave him all
My cell was gone,
I couldn't call 911
I felt helpless

Crime is our everyday meal
People have no respect for others
Most are miserable and in pain
What has South Africa become

Self-discipline is gone
Violence is a way to make money
We are no longer safe
We don't recognize those in pain

We care only about me, myself, and I
No one is trustworthy
Unity and peace is no more
We do the opposite of what we are supposed to do

But my goal is to change South Africa
Slowly over time
And bring life back into my country.

—Naledi Luthuli, Inanda Seminary (High School), Durban, South Africa

—◦—

Are We a Rainbow Nation?

Rainbow nation is a popular term which holds a very significant meaning. This word was introduced into this country after the liberation as a sign of hope. There was hope for a new way of living and expectations that all South Africans could unite and work hand in hand to build a new happier and united South Africa.

The government has been planting the images of a rainbow nation in people's minds through the mass media and political publications. By comparing this country to a rainbow, the government was trying to emphasize a point: that if a variety of colours can come together to form something so beautiful as a rainbow, then people can also reunite to form one whole nation despite their differences. The colour yellow represents the prosperity or the wealth of this country obtained through mining. Green symbolises one of the greatest environments found in the world. Orange stands for projects and organizations which grow food and also encourage communities to start vegetable gardens in order to fight poverty and promote employment.

Red symbolises love that flows throughout the nation. People have learnt to appreciate one another despite their skin colour. There is no black or white population, but a rainbow nation, where everyone is seen as equal. Blue creates a very calm and peaceful effect in a rainbow; one can never fail to notice the peacefulness of the beautiful ocean in this country. The three levels of the government work together to ensure that everyone who lives in this country is happy and satisfied. As violet gives life to indigo the same thing happens in this country. Compassionate people recognise a problem, but they don't sit down and complain; instead, they stand up and try to make a difference. This is what they call the spirit of "ubuntu." By doing so, they are promoting a happy country where people do not wait for the government but work together to fulfil all their needs.

Although this rainbow nation has worked for many people, some still feel they have been left out. Their promises have not yet been fulfilled such as employment, housing, health centres, and proper nutrition. The colours of the rainbow have been up-held, but have also been violated. Yellow represents the wealth of the country through mining but that money is not distributed fairly. The rich remain rich while the poor get poorer. Green represents the environment which is slowly being destroyed because of human ignorance. As already mentioned, there are many food projects, but there are still a great number of people suffering from starvation.

Red is meant to symbolise love, but today it symbolises the blood of many people who are murdered daily in our country. There is no love for one another; people are ruled by hatred. After Apartheid, the government had hoped to destroy the terms "white population" and "black population" and promote a rainbow nation. If you take a look around and observe how people live, one will find that different races are still living very separate lives. People of different races are polarized, and they are still finding it hard to mix. Blue is for the mood of the people, they are unhappy because there is no peace in this country. There is violence and crime committed against women and children. Some people are sitting and expecting the government to make a difference. The colours violet and indigo are being violated because instead of showing compassion, people care only for themselves and not those around them.

I think that people look at the phrase "rainbow nation" as belonging to the recent past and to the politicians. They are failing to understand that this is not just a name for our country but a name that describes and evaluates us and how we live together as one. My hope is that the churches will wake up and realise that they also have a significant role to play in reviving this country. We might not be a rainbow nation yet, but I strongly believe that if we unite and work together, we will one day succeed.

—Khululiwe Khanyile, Inanda Seminary (High School), Durban, South Africa

---

Prayer for a Rainbow Nation*

ONE: God, we give you thanks for this rainbow nation of South Africa and all the rainbow nations in the world.
We give thanks for the yellow of wealth and prosperity through mining . . .

ALL: . . . and pray that money be distributed fairly.

ONE: We give thanks for the green of our amazing South African environment . . .

ALL: . . . and pray that it not be destroyed through ignorance.

ONE: We give thanks for the orange hue standing for organizations which grow food, empower communities, fight poverty, and promote employment . . .

ALL: . . . and pray for those who suffer from poverty and starvation.

ONE: We give thanks for the blue peacefulness of the ocean and the calm of spirits . . .

ALL: . . . and pray for those who lack peace, who suffer depression, who experience the violence against women and children which brings an ocean of tears.

ONE: We give thanks for the red of love that flows through this nation and all the ways in which black and white inequality of the past has changed . . .

ALL: . . . and pray for those whose blood is shed each day in our country,

and pray that all racial polarization and hatred end.

ONE: We give thanks for the violet and indigo of compassion, of "ubuntu," of self-reliance . . .

ALL: . . . and pray for all the places where self-interest drains our very sky of light.

ONE: God, we give you thanks for this rainbow nation and all rainbow nations . . .

ALL: . . . and pray that churches unite to make a difference in your beautiful world.

Amen

Written to follow a reading of Khululiwe Khanyile's essay in a liturgical setting

—M.C. Tirabassi

A LITANY FOR GIVING THANKS

From student voices in the rainforest of Ecuador, sharing excitement about being able to go to school beyond the sixth grade because of the Yachana Colegio Technico high school founded in 2006 by the Yachana Foundation

ONE: Come gather as the people of God and let us thank our God together in this holy place.

ALL: We gather to pray together, conscious that we gather with others around the world to be with our common God, united through the Holy Spirit and our love for Jesus Christ.

ONE: O God, help us to hear the voices of others around the world who pray and praise and move us closer together in your name.

ALL: Hear our prayer, O God.

VOICE 1: Thank you, Dios, for our school where we can learn for our families and our communities. Bless our teachers and help us to share what we learn with others about caring for your earth and all its creatures when we are home.

(Christian, second year student, age fifteen)

VOICE 2: Thank you for the work I have here at the school. I learn so much that I can share with my family. Thank you that my brother has graduated and will learn English in the United States, then share his experiences with all of us.

(Lizbeth, volunteer from Mondaña who works in the school office, age nineteen)

ALL: Thank you, loving God.

VOICE 3: Thank you for music and my love of singing. Help me to share my songs with others. Thank you for our work here at the school—learning to grow our own food, making jewelry, and learning about animals and birds and how to care for all of your creation. Thank you for our teachers who give us helpful advice.

(Jessica, second year student, age fifteen)

VOICE 4: Thank you for helping us to find ways to have a practical sustainable life, using the resources you provided.

(Byron, third year student, age sixteen)

ALL: Thank you, loving God.

VOICE 5: Thank you, O God, for my time here in Ecuador where I am learning with people so different from me. Help me to know the full extent of your love beyond our boundaries of race, ethnicity, education, social status, economic privilege, and perception. I came to teach, yet I have learned far more than I have taught, and I thank you.

(Eric, volunteer ESL teacher from the United Kingdom)

ALL: Thank you, loving God, for helping us to hear other voices in our prayer to you. Grant us ears to hear daily, as we walk in your way, serving you and serving others in your name. Amen.

—Barbara W. VanAusdell, USA, Ecuador

The remainding selections are written by adult authors for children and youth.

CHILDREN AT WORSHIP AROUND THE WORLD Children's Sermon

Do you remember the verse: "Here is the church, and here is the steeple. Open the door and see all the people"?

Today we are going to visit some other lands. These are countries that most of us have never seen. You will see that there are places of worship, but they may not look like where we go to worship. They may not have a steeple, and some don't even have a door! But everyone loves to gather together to pray and to sing there.

This church has four walls, made of poles and mud. There is a gaping hole in the roof, where the thatch grass has worn out.

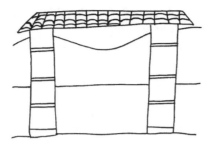

This church is a classroom inside a schoolhouse made of cement blocks. There are no windows—just open spaces to look through.

This church has cement columns holding up a roof, but no walls. The breeze can pass right through on a hot day.

This church is a shady spot under a big tree in the middle of the village.

Illustrations: Anne C. Brink

This church looks like someone's home. It *is* someone's home, with the door wide open so you can walk right in.

These churches don't have steeples, do they? They don't have pews either. They have homemade benches, or the people bring grass mats to sit on.

They don't have organs. The people might bring a drum, or a guitar, or an mbira. The sound of their voices makes us all happy.

These churches don't have pulpits. They may use an old wooden table, or a teacher's desk.

Can you find the Sunday school rooms? No, there aren't any! The children learn and sing outside—under a tree, or next to a shady wall.

Who are the children who go to these places of worship? What do they do when they gather there?

They may speak a different language from you. They may look different from you, but . . .

Illustrations: Anne C. Brink

. . . they sing hymns and pray, just like you do.

. . . they listen to God's message and thank God for their blessings, just like you do.

. . . they tell each other stories, just like you do.

... they share what God has given them, just like you do.

What is a church? Is it a place? Is it a building? Is it the minister? Is it the grownups? Is it the children?

—Judith C. Myrick, USA, South Africa, Zimbabwe

GRACES FROM CASA SAN JOSÉ DE LOS HUÉRFANOS (ORPHANS) COLIMA, MÉXICO

Director—Maria Guadalupe Muñiz Cortez (Lupita Muñiz)

Bless Us and This Food, O God

V. Bendícenos, Señor, y bendice estos alimentos que por tu bondad vamos a tomar.

R. Amén.

V. El Rey de la gloria eterna nos haga partícipes de la mesa celestial.

R. Amén.

V. Te damos gracias por todos tus beneficios, omnipotente Dios, que vives y reinas por los siglos de los siglos.

R. Amén.

V. El Señor nos dé su paz.

R. Y la vida eterna. Amén.

ONE: Bless us, o Lord, and bless this food that because of your goodness we are about to eat.

ALL: Amen.

ONE: The King of Glory Eternal makes us guests at the celestial feast.

ALL: Amen.

ONE: We give you thanks for all your blessings, omnipotent God. May you live and reign for ever and ever (literally: for centuries and centuries!).

Bless, O God, This Food from Your Hands

Bendice señor estos alimentos que de tus manos vamos a tomar, bendice también a las manos que los prepararon y a todos quienes han hecho posible que llegaran a nosotros.

Bless, O Lord, this food that from your hands we are going to eat. Bless as well the hands that have prepared it and bless all those who have made it possible that it could come to us.

Hunger for God

Here's a prayer we used to pray at the Casa San Jose orphanage in Colima, México, where Peter and I worked, and to which we bring a mission team every two years. It touched me deeply coming from the mouths of kids who, in the lean months, would get only powdered milk and animal crackers for dinner. It goes like this:

Señor Poderoso,
Cuando no tenemos pan, danos pan.
Cuando tenemos pan, danos hambre de ti.

All Powerful Lord,
When we have no bread, give us bread.
When we have bread, give us hunger for you.

—Molly Phinney Baskette, USA, Mexico

23 ❀ TREASURES — MUSIC

Sal y luz / Salt and Light

Gerardo Oberman
Horacio Vivares

Us - te - des son la sal de'la tie - rra'us - te - des son la
You are the salt___ of the earth,___ you___ are the

sal. Us - te - des son la sal de'la tie - rra'us - te - des son la
salt. You are the salt___ of the earth,___ you___ are the

sal. La luz_____ del mun - do, a - sí di - jo Je -
salt. The light of___ the world,_____ for thus___ says___

sús. La luz_____ del mun - do, a - sí di - jo Je - sús.
Christ. The light of___ the world,_____ for thus___ says___ Christ.

Nuestra ayuda

Salmo 124:8/Gerardo Oberman

Nues - tra 'a - yu - da 'es en___ el nom - bre del Se -
Our_____ help is_ in___ the name___ of the

ñor que 'hi - zo los cie - los___ y la
Lord, Mak - er of heav - en___ and of

tie - rra.___ Nues-tra 'a - yu - da 'es en___ el nom - bre del Se -
earth._____ Our_____ help is_ in___ the name_ of the

ñor, en el nom - bre del Se - ñor.
Lord, in the name_____ of_ the Lord.

Credo

Gerardo Oberman
Campamento Jóvenes
IRA 2007 Claromecó

Cre - e - mos que to - dos jun - tos po -
To - geth - er we be - lieve____ that

de - mos dar vuel - ta la'his - to - ria. Cre -
we can break free from our his - t'ry. To -

e - mos que'a - sí se - rá, cre -
geth - er we be - lieve, be -

e - mos que'a - sí se - rá.
lieve____ that this will be!____

Que a nadie le falte/Let No One Miss Out

(Merengue Dominicano)

Gerardo Oberman
Horacio Vivares

No muy rápido
Estribillo/Refrain

Que'a na-die le fal-te la gra-cia de Dios y na-die que-de'a-
Let no one miss out on the bless-ing of God, and no one be ex-

fue - ra___ de su ben-di - ción. Que'a de su ben-di - ción.
clud - ed___ from the grace of God. Let from the grace of God.

1. Que na-die se que-de'a fue - ra de la ge-ne-ro-si-dad,
2. La fe se-rá siem-pre jo-ven y'el al-ma sa-brá co-rrer
1. No one left out - side the cir - cle of the love God shares with us,
2. Faith in God will keep us mov-ing, keep us young in heart and soul,

de la ma-no siem-pre'a-bier-ta que Dios en su'a-mor nos da.
por el rum-bo que la gra-cia di-bu-je hoy an-te sus pies.
with a hand that's al-ways o-pen in a___ wel-com-ing em-brace.
keep us walk-ing in the path of grace that___leads and draws us on.

Que'ha-ya paz en ca-da dí-a pues e-lla con-du-ce'a Dios
Ha-brá luz, un ho-ri-zon-te, y'un lla-ma-do'a ca-mi-nar,
Ev - 'ry day may peace go with us, peace that leads our hearts to God,
Look a-head to see the light and hear the call to car-ry on;

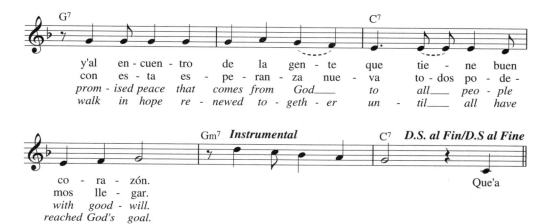

y'al en - cuen - tro de la gen - te que tie - ne buen
con es - ta es - pe - ran - za nue - va to - dos po - de -
prom - ised peace that comes from God___ to all___ peo - ple
walk in hope re - newed to - geth - er un - til___ all have

co - ra - zón.
mos lle - gar.
with good - will.
reached God's goal.

Que'a

Las puertas de tu casa

Gerardo Oberman
Horacio Vivares

Las puer - tas de tu ca - sa se'a-brie - ron pa - ra mi.
The doors__ of your house_____ are o - pen wide for me.

Oh Dios de cie - lo'y tie - rra ¡qué bue - no'es - tar a - quí!
Oh God of heav'n and earth_____ a bless - ing to be here!

Si'a bri - mos nues - tros bra - zos po - de - mos re - ci - bir
O - pen our arms, pre - pare__ us so that we may re - ceive

a quien te ne - ce - si - te y quie - ra com - par - tir tu Pa -
all those in need of your__ love, all those who want to share in your

la - bra y can - cio - nes,__ si - len - cio'y o - ra - ción,_____ un a -
Word and in your songs,_____ si - lence and times of prayer,_____ in a

bra - zo__ sin - ce - ro,__ la paz de tu__ per - dón._____ El pan que a - li -
heart - felt__ em - brace,_____ the peace of your good grace._____ The bread of life that

men - ta__ da fuer - za'y da va - lor_____ y'el fue - go de tu'Es -
feeds us,_____ gives strength and mean - ing, too;_____ the fire_____ of your

pí - ri - tu___ que'en - cien - de'el co - ra - zón, y'el
Spir - it lives,___ burns in our heart's de - sire, the

fue - go de tu'Es - pí - ri - tu___ que'en - cien - de'el co - ra - zón.
fire___ of your Spir - it lives,___ burns in our heart's de - sire.

Source of Our Call

Words: Neil Quintrell (1998)
Music: Norman Inglis (2005)

1. We asked for a home and you gave us a jour - ney. Faith, like a sin - gle
asked for a sign and your gave us a vis - ion. Hope, like a danc - er's
asked for a rest and you gave us a call - ing. Peace, like an ea - gle's
asked for_ love and you gave us com-mu - ni - ty. Trust, like a des - ert

flame, weav - ing_ light_ and shad - ow on an un-known way. 2. We
hands, form - ing_ shape and sub-stance from to - mor-row's
rise, lift - ing_ doubt and weak-ness in - to cer - tain - ty. 4. We
flow'r, bring - ing_ joy_ and beau - ty in its prom-ised

day. Source of our call, and source of our sus - tain - ing,_
spring. Source of our call, and source of our sus - tain - ing, re -

spin in - to_ our dance of_ time, faith - ful - ness in
new us by_ your Spir - it_ rain, that from the ston - y

days_ of_ doubt, that we may fol - low, fol - low bold - ly.
days_ or_ drought, our lives may rise_ up, rise_ up green - ing.

Interlude 1. G Am Bm Em D.S. 2. G Am Bm Em

3. We

Offering Song

Words: Neil Quintrell
Music: Norman Inglis

1. Move with-in our giv - ing, Spir - it of re - new - ing.
2. Touch us in our greet - ing, Spir - it of our heal - ing.
3. In the risk of giv - ing, hope and hurt and heal - ing

Breathe in - to our liv - ing strength e - nough to serve.___
Weave in - to our be - ing grace e - nough to love.___
are a - like re - ceived,___ ac - cept - ed as we give.___

As we bring our off'r - ings life and love and laugh - ter
Move with - in our giv - ing Spir - it of re - new - ing.
Lead us in our leav - ing Spir - it of our call - ing.

and our dai - ly tasks___ are___ off - ered with our gifts.
Breathe in - to our liv - ing___ strength e - nough to serve.
Pre - sent in our go - ing sur - prise us on our way.

Instrumental

After last verse

Minga

("Minga"—Quichua word for "a good work together")

Barbara VanAusdall
transcription: Marshall Jennings

Sing me a song a-bout Min - ga. Sing me a song a-bout Min - ga. Sing me a song a-bout Min - ga. Min-ga in God's world.

*Min - ga in the streets of Ec - ua - dor.___ Min-ga in the moun-tains of Ec - ua - dor.___ Min - ga in the rain - for - est of Ec - ua - dor.___ Min - ga in God's world.

Other lyrics may be substituted for "Minga in the streets . . ." to "Minga in the rainforest . . ."

Holy Spirit Be at Home in Me

Words and Music: Kathy Wonson Eddy

1. Ho - ly___ Spir - it, be at home___ in me.
2. Love be an o - cean, be an o - cean in me.
3. Peace make a ban - quet, make a ban - quet in me.

Ho - ly___ Spir - it, be at home___ in me, at
Love be an o - cean, be an o - cean in me, an
Peace make a ban - quet, make a ban - quet in me, a

home,_____ I wel - come_ Thee. Ho - ly___
o - - cean, to heal___ and_ free. Love be an
feast_____ for all to taste and see. Peace make a

Spir - it, be at home in me._____
o - cean in___
ban - quet in___ me._____
me._____

Júntenos, Espíritu/Unite Us, Spirit

Music and English text: Ryan H. Otto
Spanish text: Ryan H. Otto & Shantha K. Ready

Siem-pre te____ re-cor-da-re-mos. Siem-pre es-ta-rás'en
Al - ways in our minds you'll re-main. *Al - ways in our*

nues-tro co-ra-zón. Jún-te-nos, Es-pí-ri-tu. Mué-
hearts your soul will stay. *U - nite us, O Spir - it,* *to*

va-nos a ac-tuar. Cam-bia-nos, a-com-pá-ña-nos jun-to'a
ac - tion move us. *Re-cre-ate us in com-pa-ny* *with our*

nues-tros her-ma-nos y her-ma-nas.
bro-thers and sis-ters side by side.

God Has Made Laughter

Words and Music: Kathy Wonson Eddy
based on Genesis 21:6

1. God__ has made laugh-ter,_____ laugh-ter for me. God__ has made laugh-ter,_____ laugh-ter for me. Oh, God has made__ laugh-ter for me! Is an-y-thing im-pos-si-ble for God?_____

2. Ev-'ry-one who hears,_____ will laugh__ with me. Ev-'ry-one who hears,_____ will laugh__ with me. Oh, ev-'ry-one will laugh__ with me! Is an-y-thing im-pos-si-ble for God?_____

The Floor of My Heart

Lina Andronoviene

1. The floor of my heart— has been tiled with_ sad - ness, its
   wan - der through the cor - ri - dors, breath - ing_ win - ter once
   this be the cry—— of a glow - ing_ hope's birth here

walls have been pain-ted with gloom.—— Its win-dows cry-ing si - lent - ly
more stumb-ling o - ver my sin.——— Lord, how did I end up here a-
in the dark night of my soul?—— My self - ish-ness des-troyed and your

o - ver crum - bled_ life, for my heart is emp - ty,—— my
lone with - out your_ cross? Now my heart is emp - ty,—— my
grace e - nough to——change this heart that is emp - ty,—— this

heart is a - lone,—— for my heart is emp - ty,—— my
heart is a - lone,—— now my heart is emp - ty,—— my
heart that is a - lone, this heart that is emp - ty,—— this

heart is a - lone,_ a - lone,—— a - lone._ 1. & 2. I thirst for wa - ter,_ the
heart is a - lone,_ a - lone,—— a - lone._ 3. I thirst for wa - ter,_ the
heart that is a - lone, a - lone,—— a - lone._

MAMA MARIE BEYEKE AND MUSIC IN DEMOCRATIC REPUBLIC OF THE CONGO

Excerpt from "Regard Sur L'oeuvre de Maman Marie Beyeke, Un Pas Vers La Musique Des Sociétés Bantoues" by Philemon Ilumbe-Kayo

Introduction

African hymnology, as the product of the creative imagination of our ancestors, appears as a means of communication, a sacred symbolism, where the religious and social riches find their expression. Since it is a question of religious riches, we can definitely affirm that it gives real support to the work of evangelization.

In a church which preaches the principle of equality between men and women, the Community of the Disciples of Christ in Congo (CDCC) has lived through the work of Mama Marie Beyeke the prophecy of Joel 2:28–29: "Then, said the Lord, I shall pour out my spirit on every human being. Your sons and your daughters will prophesy, your old people will dream dreams, and your young people will see visions. Even upon your men and women servants I will pour out my spirit in those days." Formerly in our traditional societies, the work of the woman was limited only to family and housekeeping activities. Now, thanks to the liberating gospel of our Lord and Savior Jesus Christ, the situation has changed. The Gospel today allows women to leave behind this old logic and to offer them possibilities of exercising any kind of activity, so long as God gives them the gift, to have the power, the will, and the opportunity.

Named Marie Beyeke-Bofii, the famous singer of the Disciples of Christ 10th Community (CDCC) of the Church of Christ in the Congo (ECC) was born October 1, 1922, in Bonkende, a settlement of Djombo in the sector of Pendjwa in the territory of Kiri. She died in Mbandaka on December 9, 1996. This daughter of Nzaala-Bolole and of Bolekaya-Bobonga was married to Mr. Pierre Engomba Ifulunkoy, school director.

During that same year, it was found to be urgent that the young couple go to open a school of teacher training, of which the husband became director at Yoseki in the Cadelu. The unsuspected qualities of the singer drew the attention of the missionaries of that community, who did not hesitate to provide the gift of an accordion, an instrument she learned to play in three months. Nevertheless, the preponderant role that the song artist should play in the evangelization of our ancestral societies preoccupied the American missionaries of the CDCC. With regard to the good utilization of sacred hymnology in the classical traditional style, the group named "the Mama Beyeke Chorale" became the object of many invitations within and beyond the country.

The presidency of the Democratic Republic of Congo, at the time called Zaire, could not remain insensitive to the beautiful melodies of the Mama Beyeke Chorale. Its presentation in 1975 at Gemena on the death of Mama Yemo, mother of the late President Mobutu, is proof of that.

Confirmed head of the choir, [Marie Beyeke] expressed herself with her arms, her hands, also by her regard and her attitudes. Even as she directed with her whole body, she also sang with her body, and not only with her solid voice. But the gestures—those with the hands, the fists, the arms, the legs—were essential. It was thus that the singer commanded her choristers, gave the departures, designed the nuances, signified the stops, and translated the movement, without which the spectacular aspect of the group would not have been captivating.

Although essentially vocal, the singer realized that the voice alone is almost inconceivable in Africa without the company of instruments. In that respect, she chose a category of instrument which would underscore the rhythm. That means principally the single tones (*idiophones*) and the changing tones (*membranophones*).

In looking a little more closely at the chorale of Mama Marie Beyeke, one can easily see that all her songs have almost as a base the refrain. This is formed by short phrases to which the choir refers according to the rhythmic movement of the piece. The solo part, made up of changes in accent and tone, is reserved for the singer herself who, from time to time, develops the main theme of the song, executed for the most part in *ostinato*, that is, "the periodic movement which is made by the return of a same form or same melodic theme at regular intervals." The Hallelujah, O O, parts and Yendembe illustrate this phenomenon clearly. Thanks to this technique, the singer has enough freedom to enrich her discourse with biblical details, as well as showing her many talents: mime, broad smile, gesture of hands and legs.

On the thematic level, she told her peers, "I never developed a theme without having received its inspiration from God." In the Kinshasa-Righini congregation, during one of her last meetings for rehearsals on this earth, she affirmed: "It is especially at night when the Lord instructs me on the themes and sometimes even the melody which should accompany the theme. At the beginning, this practice of awaking at night to sing and write what I had received did not please my husband. But after he had realized that it came from God, he encouraged me and prayed for me. . . . Sometimes he joined me and wrote certain songs for me."

Illustrations: Maman Marie Beyeke

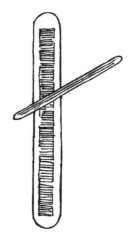

Bokwese (racle)
rhythm instrument

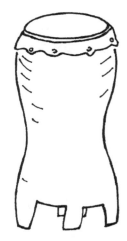

Ngomo (tambour à peau)
hand drum

Loalaka Bot'one Bon'owa Nzakomba

Voyez cet homme, L'enfant de Dieu

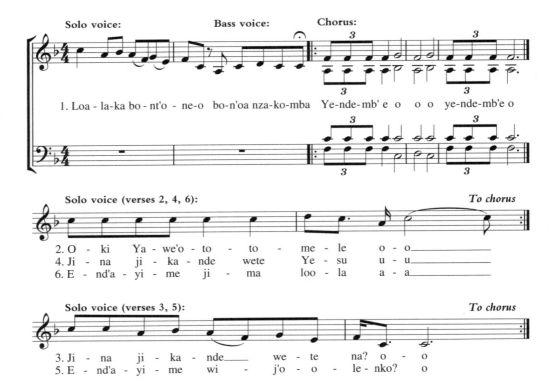

For verse 1: One person sings as a solo, a bass voice responds, followed by the chorus.
For additional verses: One person sings as a solo followed by the chorus.

Translation:
1. See this man
2. The one sent from God among us
3. What is his name?
4. His name is Jesus
5. Where does he come from?
6. He comes from heaven

French:
1. Voyez cet homme
2. L'envoyé de Dieu parmi nous
3. Quel est son nom?
4. Son nom c'est Jésus
5. D'ou vient-il?
6. Il vient du ciel

"Yendembe" to the Bantus of the Mongo tribe of the Ekonda, refers to the son born immediately after twins. For this reason, he is worthy of tenderness and good treatment. It is the term by which the singer refers to Jesus Christ, the Savior.

Yesu Nkolo Onkite

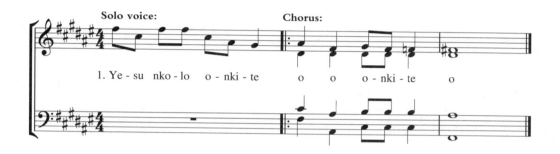

Verses:

1. Yesu nkolo onkite o o onkite o
2. Onkit'emi ndaloko
3. Emi ndangogindao
4. Baolotungya longondji'i
5. Baolotomb'eka pilato
6. Bakulaka baolosamboza

English paraphrase:

1. Uphold me by your arms, oh uphold me
2. I want to give in
3. I am taken by Satan
4. I want to give in
5. Seize me powerfully
6. Hear my prayer

❀ SOURCE NOTES FOR PERMISSIONS

Permission to copy any of these worship resources—both words and pictures—is freely granted for use in church bulletins, newsletters, special programs, and educational events, provided that the copyright notes and acknowledgements are included in the reproduction. Such free use does not extend to events (such as workshops and seminars) where admission is charged or registration fees collected or to reprints in books and other publications. These require the additional permission of the following copyright owners (listed below or with pictures throughout the book) or, if not listed, The Pilgrim Press, 700 Prospect Avenue, Cleveland, Ohio, 44115, www.thepilgrimpress.com.

We wish to thank those who have granted permission for the use of prayers and liturgical material, art and music in this book. We have made every effort to trace and identify them correctly and to secure the necessary permissions for those that have been reprinted. If we have erred in any way in the source notes or have unwittingly infringed any copyright, we apologize sincerely. We would be glad to make the necessary correction in subsequent editions of this book.

PART ONE

Page 3 Call to Worship from Africa (Psalm 104): Please contact Allen Myrick, 84 Edward Heights, Brattleboro, VT 05301.

Page 4 Disturbing Comforter: Please contact William Livingstone (Bill) Wallace, 215A Mt. Pleasant Road, Christchurch 8081, New Zealand.

Page 8 "You Asked for my hands . . .": Joe Seremane, South Africa, reprinted from *Prayers Encircling the World: An International Anthology*, Westminster John Knox Press, 1999.

Page 19 "God of kindliness . . . ,": Reformierte Liturgie, Wappertal, Germany, reprinted from "We Celebrate the Diversity of Churches . . . Prayers and Texts for commemoration services and celebrations of the Leuenberg Church Fellowship," Protestant Churches in Europe Community (CPCE), Peter Bukowski, Susanne Labsch, Helmut Schwier, English translations Rev. Fleur Houston; please contact f.herrman@leuenberg.eu.

Page 21 Prayer for Ecumenism for Two Voices and Congregation: adapted from Agenda I, edited by Church Office of the Evangelical Church of Kurhesses-Waldeck, Kassel, 1996, Germany, reprinted from "We Celebrate the Diversity of Churches . . . Prayers and Texts for commemoration services and celebrations of the Leuenberg Church Fellowship," Protestant Churches in Europe Community (CPCE), Peter Bukowski, Susanne Labsch, Helmut Schwier, English translations Rev. Fleur Houston; please contact f.herrman@leuenberg.eu.

Page 25 "Lord, we pray for your church to all the ends of the earth": adapted from Testi Liturgi Italy, reprinted from "We Celebrate the Diversity of Churches . . . Prayers and Texts for commemoration services and celebrations of the Leuenberg Church Fellowship," Protestant Churches in Europe Community (CPCE), Peter Bukowski, Susanne Labsch, Helmut Schwier, English translations Rev. Fleur Houston; please contact f.herrman@leuenberg.eu.

Page 28 Prayer of Thanksgiving and Intercession: Sylvia Bukowski, Germany, reprinted from "We Celebrate the Diversity of Churches . . . Prayers and Texts for commemoration services and celebrations of the Leuenberg Church Fellowship," Protestant Churches in Europe Community (CPCE), Peter Bukowski, Susanne Labsch, Helmut Schwier, English translations Rev. Fleur Houston; please contact f.herrman@ leuenberg.eu.

Page 35 A proposal for a service for churches, agencies, and institutions in Latin America, based on the Creed of Human Rights: Please contact Gerardo Oberman, gerkoberman@ gmail.com, Montes de Oca 2571, 1712 Castelar, Buenos Aires, Argentina xx 54 11 4629-2698.

Page 37 My Creed—My Beatitude: Geoffrey Duncan, reprinted from *Courage to Love: Liturgies for the Lesbian Gay, Bisexual, and Transgender Community* (Pilgrim, 2002). Please contact Geoffrey Duncan, Thames North Synod United Reformed Church, 32/34 Great Peter Street, London SW1P 2DB UK.

Page 37 "I believe, Lord . . .": A peasant woman, El Salvador, reprinted from *Prayers Encircling the World: An International Anthology* (Westminster John Knox Press, 1999).

Page 44 Bendición ternura de Madre/Benediction of a mother's tenderness: Please contact Gerardo Oberman, gerkoberman@gmail.com, Montes de Oca 2571, 1712 Castelar, Buenos Aires, Argentina xx 54 11 4629-2698.

Page 45 Benedicere: Kenneth L. Sehested, reprinted from *In the Land of the Living*. Please contact Kenneth L. Sehested, ken@circleofmercy.org.

Page 48 "We pray to you, living God . . .": Uwe Boch, Germany, reprinted from "We Celebrate the Diversity of Churches . . . Prayers and Texts for commemoration services and celebrations of the Leuenberg Church Fellowship," Protestant Churches in Europe Community (CPCE), Peter Bukowski, Susanne Labsch, Helmut Schwier, English translations Rev. Fleur Houston; please contact f.herrman@leuenberg.eu.

Page 51 "Lord God, we thank you for calling us into the company . . .": The Swanwick Declaration, England, reprinted from "We Celebrate the Diversity of Churches . . . Prayers and Texts for commemoration services and celebrations of the Leuenberg Church Fellowship," Protestant Churches in Europe Community (CPCE), Peter Bukowski, Susanne Labsch, Helmut Schwier, English translations Rev. Fleur Houston; please contact f.herrman@leuenberg.eu.

Page 53 A Prayer with Movement: Alyson Huntly, reprinted from *On Frequent Journeys: Worship Resources on Uprooted Peoples*, edited by Rebekah Chevalier (United Church Publishing, 1997). Please contact Alyson Huntly, ahuntly@gmail.com.

Page 62 "In the silence of the departing day . . .": Please contact Gerardo Oberman, gerkoberman@gmail.com, Montes de Oca 2571, 1712 Castelar, Buenos Aires, Argentina xx 54 11 4629-2698.

PART TWO

Page 66 An Advent Psalm: Please contact Ray McGinnis, #403-2095 Beach Avenue, Vancouver, BC V6G 1Z3 Canada.

Page 67 Come Emmanuel—An Advent Prayer for Africa: Please contact Allen Myrick, 84 Edward Heights, Brattleboro, VT 05301.

Page 68 Adviento de paz/Advent of Peace: Please contact Gerardo Oberman, gerkoberman@ gmail.com, Montes de Oca 2571, 1712 Castelar, Buenos Aires, Argentina xx 54 11 4629-2698.

Page 72 Bendición del Otro Mundo Posible/Blessing from Another Possible World: Joel Eli Padron Ibanez, Church of Peniel, Mexico. Please contact Gerardo Oberman, gerkoberman@gmail.com, Montes de Oca 2571, 1712 Castelar, Buenos Aires, Argentina xx 54 11 4629-2698.

Page 79 Reading for Palm Sunday: Please contact Gerardo Oberman, gerkoberman@ gmail.com, Montes de Oca 2571, 1712 Castelar, Buenos Aires, Argentina xx 54 11 4629-2698.

Page 80 Taste of Freedom and Power of the Towel Maundy Thursday Service: Please contact Archbishop Malkhaz Songulashvili, Regent's Park College, Pusey Street, Oxford OX1 2LB, UK, malkhaz.songulashvili@gmail.com.

Page 101 Yachana: Please contact Barbara Wass Van Ausdall, vanausdall@charter.net, or call 618-660-7061.

Page 102 Blessing the Gifts of Creation: Please contact Archbishop Malkhaz Songulashvili, Regent's Park College, Pusey Street, Oxford OX1 2LB, UK, malkhaz .songulashvili@gmail.com.

Page 120 A Prayer When Parched and Waiting: John Howell, reprinted from *Sighs Too Deep for Words: Prayers and Images from Taupo*. Please contact John Howell, http://www.stpaulstaupo.org.nz/.

Page 120 The Visitors: Please contact Ray McGinnis, #403-2095 Beach Avenue, Vancouver, BC V6G 1Z3 Canada.

PART THREE

Page 126 Selections from a Service of Adult Baptism: Please contact Archbishop Malkhaz Songulashvili, Regent's Park College, Pusey Street, Oxford OX1 2LB, UK, malkhaz.songulashvili@gmail.com.

Page 139 Post Communion Prayers: Adapted from Agenda I, edited by Church Office of the Evangelical Church of Kurhesses-Waldeck, Kassel, Germany, reprinted from "We Celebrate the Diversity of Churches ... Prayers and Texts for commemoration services and celebrations of the Leuenberg Church Fellowship," Protestant Churches in Europe Community (CPCE), Peter Bukowski, Susanne Labsch, Helmut Schwier, English translations Rev. Fleur Houston; please contact f.herrman@leuenberg.eu.

Page 139 "Dear Father in heaven,...": Achim Reinstadtler, Germany, reprinted from "We Celebrate the Diversity of Churches ... Prayers and Texts for commemoration services and celebrations of the Leuenberg Church Fellowship," Protestant Churches in Europe Community (CPCE), Peter Bukowski, Susanne Labsch, Helmut Schwier, English translations Rev. Fleur Houston; please contact f.herrman@leuenberg.eu.

Page 140 An Agape Liturgy: Please contact Graham Sparkes, grahamsparkes@yahoo.co.uk, 7 Elm Tree Walk, Shippon, Oxfordshire OX13 6LX, UK, or Anthea Sully, antheasully@gmail.com.

Page 145 A Litany of Hope and Connection for World Communion Sunday: Please contact Frances A. Bogle, 4 Nancy Lane, Framingham, MA 01701.

Page 148 Prayer Looking Back on a Marriage: Pamela Wilding, reprinted from *Prayers Encircling the World, An International Anthology* (Westminster John Knox Press, 1999).

Page 150 Selections for a Service of Love and Crowning—A Wedding Service: Please contact Archbishop Malkhaz Songulashvili, Regent's Park College, Pusey Street, Oxford OX1 2LB, UK, malkhaz.songulashvili@gmail.com.

Page 153 The Blessing (written for a same gender loving couple), reprinted from *Courage to Love: Liturgies for the Lesbian Gay, Bisexual, and Transgender Community* (Pilgrim, 2002). Please contact Geoffrey Duncan, Thames North Synod United Reformed Church, 32/34 Great Peter Street, London SW1P 2DB UK.

Page 154 Embracing Our Sexuality: Prayers of Passion and Pain: Please contact Graham Sparkes, grahamsparkes@yahoo.co.uk, 7 Elm Tree Walk, Shippon, Oxfordshire OX13 6LX, UK.

Page 155 Service of Tears and Hope—Memorial Service: Please contact Archbishop Malkhaz Songulashvili, Regent's Park College, Pusey Street, Oxford OX1 2LB, UK, malkhaz.songulashvili@gmail.com.

PART FOUR

Page 166 Living, Loving God: Geoffrey Duncan, reprinted from *Shine On, Star of Bethlehem: A Worship Resource for Advent, Christmas, and Epiphany* (Pilgrim Press, 2002). Please contact Geoffrey Duncan, Thames North Synod United Reformed Church, 32/34 Great Peter Street, London SW1P 2DB UK.

Page 168 Lord, No One Is a Stranger to You, reprinted from *On Frequent Journeys: Worship Resources on Uprooted Peoples*, edited by Rebekah Chevalier (United Church Publishing, 1997). Please contact Roland Unwin, CAFOD (Catholic Agency for Overseas Development), Romero Close, Stockwell Road, London, England, cafod.org.uk.

Page 168 Children in the Street, reprinted from *On Frequent Journeys*, edited by Rebekah Chevalier (United Church Publishing, 1997). Please contact Tom Hampson, Church World Service, 28606 Phillips Street, PO Box 968, Elkhart, IN 46515.

Page 170 Her Voice: Please contact Barbara Wass Van Ausdall, vanausdall@charter .net, or call 618-660-7061.

Page 182 Order for a Retreat on the Principles of Stewardship and Sharing: Please contact Elida Quevedo, Av. 49F Numero 175-36, El Canllao Maracaibo, Zulia, Venezuela, elidaquevedo@gmail.com.

Page 187 "In the midst of the rivalries that cause us to fall out . . .": The Evangelical Church of Kurhesses-Waldeck, Kassel, Germany, reprinted from "We Celebrate the Diversity of Churches . . . Prayers and Texts for commemoration services and celebrations of the Leuenberg Church Fellowship," Protestant Churches in Europe Community (CPCE), Peter Bukowski, Susanne Labsch, Helmut Schwier, English translations Rev. Fleur Houston; please contact f.herrman@leuenberg.eu.

Page 187 Shalom, Salaam, La Paz, Her-ping, Peace: Please contact Frances A. Bogle, 4 Nancy Lane, Framingham, MA 01701.

Page 188 "Let us pray to God in peace . . .", reprinted from "We Celebrate the Diversity of Churches . . . Prayers and Texts for commemoration services and celebrations of the Leuenberg Church Fellowship," Protestant Churches in Europe Community (CPCE), Peter Bukowski, Susanne Labsch, Helmut Schwier, English translations Rev. Fleur Houston; please contact f.herrman@leuenberg.eu.

Page 191 En solidaridad con el pueblo haitiano/In Solidarity with the People of Haiti: Please contact Gerardo Oberman, gerkoberman@gmail.com, Montes de Oca 2571, 1712 Castelar, Buenos Aires, Argentina xx 54 11 4629-2698.

Page 195 Prayers to Embrace the Holy Land: Please contact Graham Sparkes, grahamsparkes@yahoo.co.uk, 7 Elm Tree Walk, Shippon, Oxfordshire OX13 6LX, UK, or Anthea Sully, antheasully@gmail.com.

Page 204 Reflection on Bicultural Understanding in Aotearoa/New Zealand: Please contact Marcia Baker, 11 Merton Place, Christchurch 8053, New Zealand.

Page 206 Litany from a Prayer for Peace in the Time of Conflict and Bloodshed: Please contact Archbishop Malkhaz Songulashvili, Regent's Park College, Pusey Street, Oxford OX1 2LB, UK, malkhaz.songulashvili@gmail.com.

PART FIVE

Page 210 Morning Praises: Please contact Ray McGinnis, #403-2095 Beach Avenue, Vancouver, BC V6G 1Z3 Canada.

Page 211 You'll Sleep Here: Please contact Allen Myrick, 84 Edward Heights, Brattleboro, VT 05301.

Page 213 Royal Seed: Please contact Lancelot Muteyo, 69 9th Crescent, Warren Park, Harare, Zimbabwe, Africa, 263 4 222 808 or 263 774 633 336, lancemuteyo@yahoo.com.

Page 222 Fragments of a Psalm, Psalm 102: Please contact Ray McGinnis, #403-2095 Beach Avenue, Vancouver, BC V6G 1Z3 Canada.

Page 227 We Played the Flute but You Did Not Dance: Please contact Gerardo Oberman, gerkoberman @gmail.com, Montes de Oca 2571, 1712 Castelar, Buenos Aires, Argentina xx 54 11 4629-2698.

Page 229 Christian Unity, after Psalm 100: Sylvia Bukowski, reprinted from "We Celebrate the Diversity of Churches . . . Prayers and Texts for commemoration services and celebrations of the Leuenberg Church Fellowship," Protestant Churches in Europe Community (CPCE), Peter Bukowski, Susanne Labsch, Helmut Schwier, English translations Rev. Fleur Houston; please contact f.herrman@leuenberg.eu.

Page 230 Five Earthen Cups, Psalm 116: Please contact Allen Myrick, 84 Edward Heights, Brattleboro, VT 05301.

Page 235 Groundbreaking, Psalm 127: Please contact Allen Myrick, 84 Edward Heights, Brattleboro, VT 05301.

Page 236 Prayer for Unity, Psalm 67: Achim Reinstadtler, Germany, reprinted from "We Celebrate the Diversity of Churches . . . Prayers and Texts for commemoration services and celebrations of the Leuenberg Church Fellowship," Protestant Churches in Europe Community (CPCE), Peter Bukowski, Susanne Labsch, Helmut Schwier, English translations Rev. Fleur Houston; please contact f.herrman@leuenberg.eu.

Page 261 A Litany for Giving Thanks: Please contact Barbara Wass Van Ausdall, vanausdall@charter.net, or call 618-660-7061.

Page 262 Children at Worship around the World: Please contact Judith C. Myrick, 84 Edward Heights, Brattleboro, VT 05301.

MUSIC

Page 267 Sal y Luz/Salt and Light: Please contact Gerardo Oberman, gerkoberman@gmail.com, Montes de Oca 2571, 1712 Castelar, Buenos Aires Argentina xx 54 11 4629-2698

Page 268 Nuestra Ayuda /Our Help: Please contact Gerardo Oberman, gerkoberman@gmail.com, Montes de Oca 2571, 1712 Castelar, Buenos Aires, Argentina xx 54 11 4629-2698.

Page 269 Credo: Please contact Gerardo Oberman, gerkoberman@gmail.com, Montes de Oca 2571, 1712 Castelar, Buenos Aires, Argentina xx 54 11 4629-2698.

Page 270–71 Que a nadie le Falte/Let no one miss out: Please contact Gerardo Oberman, gerkoberman@gmail.com, Montes de Oca 2571, 1712 Castelar, Buenos Aires, Argentina xx 54 11 4629-2698.

Page 272–73 Las Puertas de tu Casa/The Doors of Your House: Please contact Gerardo Oberman, gerkoberman@gmail.com, Montes de Oca 2571, 1712 Castelar, Buenos Aires, Argentina xx 54 11 4629-2698.

Page 274 Source of our Call: Please contact Norman Inglis, norminglis@optusnet.com.au.

Page 275 Offering Song: Please contact Norman Inglis, norminglis@optusnet.com.au.

Page 276 Minga: Please contact Barbara Wass Van Ausdall, vanausdall@charter.net, or call 618-660-7061.

Page 277 Holy Spirit Be at Home in Me: reprinted from *Writing with Light*, Eddy and Eddy (United Church Press, 1997). Please contact Kathy Wonson Eddy, 802-728-5402

Page 278 Júntenos, Espíritu/Unite Us, Spirit: Please contact Ryan H. Otto, ryanottomusic@ yahoo.com, and Shantha K. Ready, shantha.ready@gmail.com.

Page 279 God Has Made Laughter: Kathy Wonson Eddy, reprinted from *Church Hymnary: 4th ed., Full Music*, Canterbury Press Norwich, St. Mary's Works, St. Mary's Plain, Norwich NR3 3BH, U.K.

Page 280–81 The Floor of My Heart: Please contact Lina Andronoviene, Zanavyku 3-1 92168, Klaipeda, Lithuania, or linaandr@yahoo.co.uk.

ARTWORK (alphabetically by artist)

He Qi: Please contact website http://www.heqigallery.com.
Baby Moses, p. 124; *The Dream of Jacob*, p. 228; *Favored One*, p. 241; *Freedom and Peace*, p. 166; *Jesus and the Samaritan Woman*, p. 56; *Knocking at the Door*, p. 3; *Praying at Gethsemane*, p. 220; *Sleeping Elijah*, p. 61; *Supper at Emmaus*, p. 77; *The Visitation*, p. 70; *Washing Disciples' Feet*, p. 81; *Wedding at Cana*, p. 149

Rini Templeton: Please contact Elizabeth Martinez for the Rini Templeton Memorial Fund, 3545 24th Street, San Francisco, CA 94110-3605.
Horizontal view of village, p. 44; Men working in the fields, p. 163; Picking coffee, p. 202; *¡Solidaridad p'siempre!* p. 38; Sower, p. 102; View of path and mountains, p. 1; Women and children walking, p. 236; Women at market, p. 140; Workers in the fields, p. 118

Diane Wendorf: Please contact Diane Elizabeth Lockwood Wendorf, nothingsinister@yahoo.com, 207-206-4942, 3 Park St., Sanford, ME 04073.
Be of Good Welcome, p. 247; *Five Loaves and Two Fish Later—There's Plenty of Good News for the Poor*, p. 255; Hands holding a village, p. 22; *Remember*, p. 157; *Shiprah and Puah*, p. 110; *Something Happens Here*, p. 131; *Weeds, Wheat Wonder*, p. 116

❀ INDEX OF WRITERS AND COMPOSERS

Note: We received the work of many contributors from China through facilitators and we depended upon them for the order of given names. These names were then adapted to a list for publication in the United States. With these names as well as several names originating in Spanish, we apologize if the index order is incorrect.

Young People from Casa San José de los Huérfanos (Colima, México)

❀ Index of Countries, Regions, Organizations

✿ INDEX OF LANGUAGES

✼ INDEX OF THEMES

This is a small listing of some themes in the book to assist worship planners. It is in no way exhaustive in scope and there are resources that touch on the topic listed below that are not listed because of space considerations. Please allow a wandering through the pages of this book to introduce you to its diversity.